AGINCOURT

GREAT BATTLES

AGINCOURT

ANNE CURRY

OXFORD
UNIVERSITY PRESS

OXFORD

UNIVERSITY PRESS

Great Clarendon Street, Oxford, OX2 6DP,
United Kingdom

Oxford University Press is a department of the University of Oxford.
It furthers the University's objective of excellence in research, scholarship,
and education by publishing worldwide. Oxford is a registered trade mark of
Oxford University Press in the UK and in certain other countries

Published in the United States of America by Oxford University Press
198 Madison Avenue, New York, NY 10016, United States of America

British Library Cataloguing in Publication Data

Data available

Library of Congress Control Number: 2014959909

ISBN 978–0–19–968101–3

Printed in Italy by L.E.G.O. S.p.A.

FOREWORD

For those who practise war in the twenty-first century the idea of a 'great battle' can seem no more than the echo of a remote past. The names on regimental colours or the events commemorated at mess dinners bear little relationship to patrolling in dusty villages or waging 'wars amongst the people'. Contemporary military doctrine down-plays the idea of victory, arguing that wars end by negotiation not by the smashing of an enemy army or navy. Indeed it erodes the very division between war and peace, and with it the aspiration to fight a culminating 'great battle'.

And yet to take battle out of war is to redefine war, possibly to the point where some would argue that it ceases to be war. Carl von Clausewitz, who experienced two 'great battles' at first hand—Jena in 1806 and Borodino in 1812—wrote in *On War* that major battle is 'concentrated war', and 'the centre of gravity of the entire campaign'. Clausewitz's remarks related to the theory of strategy. He recognized that in practice armies might avoid battles, but even then the efficacy of their actions relied on the latent threat of fighting. Winston Church-ill saw the importance of battles in different terms, not for their place within war but for their impact on historical and national narratives. His forebear, the Duke of Marlborough, commanded in four major battles and named his palace after the most famous of them, Blenheim, fought in 1704. Battles, Churchill wrote in his life of Marlborough, are 'the principal milestones in secular history'. For him, 'Great battles, won or lost, change the entire course of events, create new standards of values, new moods, new atmospheres, in armies and nations, to which all must conform'.

Clausewitz's experience of war was shaped by Napoleon. Like Marlborough, the French emperor sought to bring his enemies to battle. However, each lived within a century of the other, and they fought their wars in the same continent and even on occasion on adjacent ground. Winston Churchill's own experience of war, which spanned the late nineteenth-century colonial conflicts of the British Empire as well as two world wars, became increasingly distanced from the sorts of battle he and Clausewitz described. In 1898 Churchill rode in a cavalry charge in a battle which crushed the Madhist forces of the Sudan in a single day. Four years later the British commander at Omdurman, Lord Kitchener, brought the South African War to a conclusion after a two-year guerrilla conflict in which no climactic battle occurred. Both Churchill and Kitchener served as British Cabinet ministers in the First World War, a conflict in which battles lasted weeks, and even months, and which, despite their scale and duration, did not produce clear-cut outcomes. The 'Battle' of Verdun ran for all but one month of 1916 and that of the Somme for five months. The potentially decisive naval action at Jutland spanned a more traditional twenty-four-hour timetable but was not conclusive and was not replicated during the war. In the Second World War, the major struggle in waters adjacent to Europe, the 'Battle' of the Atlantic, was fought from 1940 to early 1944.

Clausewitz would have called these twentieth-century 'battles' campaigns, or even seen them as wars in their own right. The determination to seek battle and to venerate its effects may therefore be culturally determined, the product of time and place, rather than an inherent attribute of war. The ancient historian Victor Davis Hanson has argued that seeking battle is a 'western way of war' derived from classical Greece. Seemingly supportive of his argument are the writings of Sun Tzu, who flourished in warring states in China between two and five centuries before the birth of Christ, and who pointed out that the most effective way of waging war was to avoid the risks and dangers of actual fighting. Hanson has provoked strong criticism: those who argue that wars can be won without battles are not only to be found in Asia. Eighteenth-century European commanders, deploying armies in close-order formations in order to deliver concentrated fires, realized that the destructive consequences of battle for their own troops could be self-defeating. After the First World War, Basil Liddell Hart developed a theory of strategy which he called 'the indirect approach', and suggested that manoeuvre might substitute for hard fighting, even if its success still relied on the inherent threat of battle.

The winners of battles have been celebrated as heroes, and nations have used their triumphs to establish their founding myths. It is precisely for these reasons that their legacies have outlived their direct political consequences. Commemorated in painting, verse, and music, marked by monumental memorials, and used as the way points for the periodization of history, they have enjoyed cultural afterlives. These are evident in many capitals, in place names and statues, not least in Paris and London. The French tourist who finds himself in a London taxi travelling from Trafalgar Square to Waterloo Station should reflect on his or her own domestic peregrinations from the Rue de Rivoli to the Gare d'Austerlitz. Today's Mongolia venerates the memory of Genghis Khan while Greece and Macedonia scrap over the rights to Alexander the Great.

This series of books on 'great battles' tips its hat to both Clausewitz and Churchill. Each of its volumes situates the battle which it discusses in the context of the war in which it occurred, but each then goes on to discuss its legacy, its historical interpretation and reinterpretation, its place in national memory and commemoration, and its manifestations in art and culture. These are not easy books to write. The victors were more often celebrated than the defeated; the effect of loss on the battlefield could be cultural oblivion. However, that point is not universally true: the British have done more over time to mark their defeats at Gallipoli in 1915 and Dunkirk in 1940 than their conquerors on both occasions. For the history of war to thrive and be productive it needs to embrace the view from 'the other side of the hill', to use the Duke of Wellington's words. The battle the British call Omdurman is for the Sudanese the Battle of Kerreri; the Germans called Waterloo 'la Belle Alliance' and Jutland Skagerrak. Indeed the naming of battles could itself be a sign not only of geographical precision or imprecision (Kerreri is more accurate but as a hill rather than a town is harder to find on a small-scale map), but also of cultural choice. In 1914 the German general staff opted to name their defeat of the Russians in East Prussia not Allenstein (as geography suggested) but Tannenberg, in order to claim revenge for the defeat of the Teutonic Knights in 1410.

Military history, more than many other forms of history, is bound up with national stories. All too frequently it fails to be comparative, to recognize that war is a 'clash of wills' (to quote Clausewitz once more), and so omits to address both parties to the fight. Cultural difference and, even more, linguistic ignorance can prevent the historian considering a battle in the round; so too can the availability of sources. Levels of literacy matter here, but so does cultural survival. Often these pressures can be congruent but they can also be divergent. Britain enjoys much higher levels of literacy than Afghanistan, but in 2002 the memory of the two countries' three wars flourished in the latter, thanks to an oral tradition, much more robustly than in the former, for whom literacy had created distance. And the historian who addresses cultural legacy is likely to face a much more challenging task the further in the past the battle occurred. The opportunity for invention and reinvention is simply greater the longer the lapse of time since the key event.

All historians of war must, nonetheless, never forget that, however rich and splendid the cultural legacy of a great battle, it was won and lost by fighting, by killing and being killed. The Battle of Waterloo has left as abundant a footprint as any, but the general who harvested most of its glory reflected on it in terms which have general applicability, and carry across time in their capacity to capture a universal truth. Wellington wrote to Lady Shelley in its immediate aftermath: 'I hope to God I have fought my last battle. It is a bad thing to be always fighting. While in the thick of it I am much too occupied to feel anything; but it is wretched just after. It is quite impossible to think of glory. Both mind and feelings are exhausted. I am wretched even at the moment of victory, and I always say that, next to a battle lost, the greatest misery is a battle gained.' Readers of this series should never forget the immediate suffering caused by battle, as well as the courage required to engage in it: the physical courage of the soldier, sailor, or warrior, and the moral courage of the commander, ready to hazard all on its uncertain outcomes.

HEW STRACHAN

ACKNOWLEDGEMENTS

It has been a huge pleasure and benefit working with French historians over many years. I would like to thank particularly Professor Philippe Contamine, Professor Bertrand Schnerb, Dr Olivier Bouzy, and Christophe Gilliot of the Centre Historique Médiéval at Azincourt. In the UK there are so many to thank that there is not space to list them here but specific thanks will be given in relevant notes. I am grateful to Mrs Caroline Simpson for passing on materials which her late husband, Professor A. W. B. Simpson, had collected towards a book on the battle. I cannot end these acknowledgements, however, without saying a special thank you to Dr Tim Sutherland, Dr Adam Chapman, the University of Southampton, Dr Sinclair Rogers and Marie Cross, and of course my family who have lived with Agincourt for so many years and still do.

CONTENTS

LIST OF FIGURES

ABBREVIATIONS

AN   Archives nationales de France

BL   British Library

BN   Bibliothèque nationale de France

EEBO   Early English Books Online

PROME   *The Parliament Rolls of Medieval England 1275–1504*, ed. C. Given-Wilson et al. (Woodbridge, 2005)

Sources   A. Curry, *The Battle of Agincourt: Sources and Interpretations* (Woodbridge, 2000; rev. edn, 2009).

STC   *A Short-Title Catalogue of Books Printed in England, Scotland and Ireland and of English Books Printed Abroad 1475–1640* (2nd edn), 3 vols (London, 1986–91).

TNA   The National Archives

V&A   Victoria and Albert Museum

Citations from A. Curry, *Agincourt: A New History* are from the hardback edition (Stroud, 2005).

1

Introduction

At the age of 12, John Lennon—an icon of the late twentieth century—labelled two pages of his notebook 'Agincourt'. On the right-hand page he painted a scene of soldiers fighting in front of a medieval gateway. On the left, along with heraldic shields, clouds, and sun, he wrote out a verse of a poem (see Fig. 1):[1]

> When down their bows they threw
> And forth their bilbows drew
> And on the French they flew
> Not one was tardy;
> Arms were from shoulders sent,
> Scalps to the teeth were rent,
> Down the French peasants went,
> Our men were hardy.

Agincourt, fought on 25 October 1415, has a greater cultural legacy than any other medieval engagement. This book explores why and how this is so. Why should an event of 600 years ago, which lasted little more than a few hours, continue to provoke interest and controversy today? Agincourt was not a decisive battle. It did not force the French to the negotiating table or to acknowledge defeat. In military terms it has many features in common with other battles of the period. Why is it remembered when others are not?

Lennon's verse came from Michael Drayton's 'Ballad of Agincourt' (c.1606), the full title of which was 'The Cambro Britons and their

Fig. 1. At Quarry Bank School, at the age of 12, John Lennon copied extracts from a number of poems, providing illustrations to accompany them, into a school exercise book which he entitled 'Anthology'. Alongside a stanza from Michael Drayton's *Ballad of Agincourt* (c. 1606), he draw a scene from the siege of Harfleur.

Harp, his ballad of Agincourt'. Drayton deliberately wrote in an archaic style. In 1627 he penned the much longer *Battaile of Agincourt*, a historical narrative in verse which projected England's past greatness into the present. The late sixteenth and early seventeenth centuries saw much interest and pride in these medieval glories. Families anxious to prove their antiquity and gentility to the increasingly active College of Arms claimed, accurately or not, the presence of their ancestors at Agincourt. It was in the same spirit that Shakespeare had his *Henry V* (1599) invoke the 'band of brothers':

> For he today that sheds his blood with me
> Shall be my brother, be he ne'er so vile
> This day shall gentle his condition.
> And gentlemen in England, now abed

Shall think themselves accursed they were not here
And hold their manhoods cheap whiles any speaks
That fought with us upon Saint Crispin's Day.
(Act 4 Scene 3, lines 61–7)

Lennon had Shakespeare as much as Drayton ringing in his ears. His drawing was of the siege of Harfleur, the first stage of Henry V's campaign. The siege did not feature in Drayton's 'Ballad of Agincourt' but stimulated one of the most famous lines from Shakespeare's play: 'Once more unto the breach'. In time, Shakespeare's *Henry V* came to dominate popular perceptions of Agincourt and still does today. For many, the battle is Shakespeare's Agincourt rather than the Agincourt of 1415. Agincourt is the only medieval battle which is regularly and repeatedly refought thanks to its centrality to every performance. Shakespeare provided very little dialogue for the battle but the scenes contain his characteristic mix of comedy, bombast, and poignancy. There is ample opportunity for directorial imagination thanks to the simple but well-known stage instruction 'alarms and excursions'.[2]

Stage recreations of Agincourt are inevitably constrained by the theatrical infrastructure, as Shakespeare called to mind in the opening speech with 'this Wooden O'. If he was referring to the newly built Globe Theatre, then further iconic status is achieved since *Henry V is* believed to be the first play to be performed there in 1599. This belief prompted its choice to celebrate the opening of the recreated Globe in 1997. Two mass-market films (Olivier, 1944 and Branagh, 1989) gave opportunities for more 'realistic' battle scenes and have contributed hugely to modern views of Agincourt. Olivier's film has achieved special status through its distinctive interpretation by its equally distinctive actor/director as well as its release six months after D-Day. The 'Band of Brothers' has stimulated its own TV series (2001) concerning the activities of the US Army 101st Airborne Division in the Second World War. Even Drayton had an outing in 1944 with the opening line of his 'Ballad of Agincourt', 'Fair stood the wind for France', forming the title of H. E. Bates's novel in which an RAF crew are sheltered by the occupied French. In turn this generated a spin-off TV series in 1980.

Just as the battle is the crux of *Henry V*, Shakespeare's Agincourt forms a pivotal contribution to this book. Chapter 4 looks at the context in which Shakespeare wrote his play as well as how his work linked back into the century of the battle itself. To what degree is the afterlife of Agincourt the afterlife of Shakespeare's play rather than of the actual battle? That is a key question with regard to the Battle of Agincourt as an expression of English (and after 1714 British) identity. This is what marks it out from the other significant English victories of the Hundred Years War, Crécy (1346) and Poitiers (1356). These battles are much less integrated into the popular psyche even if equally or more significant in historical terms. Crécy was the first major English victory against the French. Poitiers saw the capture of the French king and led to an advantageous diplomatic settlement. Both feature in *Edward III*, but this play, despite Shakespeare's contribution, comes nowhere near the language and dramatic integrity of *Henry V*. Only Agincourt is memorialized.

Chapter 2 sets the scene by looking at the context of the campaign. When Henry became king on 22 March 1413 there was a state of truce. Why did he decide to invade France two years later? An assessment of the preconditions in England and France, and of Henry's war aims, helps us to understand why a battle was fought at all as well as why it was fought in the way it was. These themes are developed in a consideration of the battle, linked to what we know of the two armies. In researching the battle for my *Agincourt: A New History* (2005), I attracted critical comment. How dare I challenge what everyone knew to be true? It is fascinating that Agincourt has come to mean so much that it cannot be debated. The professional historian deals in uncertainties as well as in evidence. It is not easy, and perhaps not even possible, to reconstruct a medieval battle but a possible scenario is suggested as well as the rationale for my arguments on army sizes. What makes Agincourt distinctive? Important here is Henry V's killing of the prisoners. Even Shakespeare hedged his bets, having the royal order linked both to the French attempts to regroup for a new attack and to the attack on the baggage train.

How was the battle interpreted and explained at the time? This question forms the principal theme of Chapter 3. In the modern world, there is a tension between transparency and what governments and media want populations to know and think. Can we detect this concerning Agincourt? Was there a deliberate effort to 'use' the battle? Was this based on national lines? This chapter also considers how the battle was written about as the fifteenth century continued and how changing political circumstances impacted on this. In the Treaty of Troyes of May 1420 Henry V was accepted by the French king, Charles VI, as his heir and regent. Politically this upstaged Henry's triumph at Agincourt. The French were now his people and not his enemy as they had been in 1415. By 1453, however, the English had lost all of their lands in France save for Calais, Edward III's conquest of 1347, which remained in English hands until 1558.

Chapters 2–3 establish the pre-Shakespearean Agincourt. The study of *Henry V* in Chapter 4 leads into the ongoing relationship between the image of Agincourt and national consciousness in the modern period. Chapter 5 considers Agincourt within national consciousness and in particular the impact of later wars on perceptions of the battle. The 400th and 500th anniversaries both occurred in time of war but by 1915 the French were an ally not an enemy. Agincourt is a battle identified with English superiority, but a superiority often based on the role of the common man—the archer—who is contrasted with the arrogant French aristocrat. Yet there are no archers in Shakespeare's play. The 'rise of the archer' marched in step with the rise of the middle and lower classes in later centuries: out of the whole of Drayton's 'Ballad of Agincourt', Lennon copied in 1952 the stanza which most emphasized the role of the archers.

Agincourt has become a thing of legend. Even its name has a significance and use. The battle has inspired literature, art, and music, as well as ancestral claims. A special role for the Welsh has been advanced as well as the invention of the V-sign. A number of objects have alleged associations with the battle. These topics are examined in Chapter 6.

Serious historical study of Agincourt was initially inspired by national pride. The first excavations and mapping by John Woodford in 1818, and the first major documentary study, the *History of the Battle of Agincourt* by Harris Nicolas (1st edn, 1827), were stimulated by British victory in the Napoleonic Wars. The establishment of national archive collections in England and France also played their part. It is the study of the fifteenth-century administrative records, including my own work on the English and French armies and the use of computer databases, which has shed new light on the battle. New techniques are being applied through battlefield archaeology. We now know more than ever but there remain points of contention on location, deployment, and army size. This is the subject of Chapter 7 which also looks at the battlefield, its memorials, and its museum, as is appropriate with the 600th anniversary upon us.

There is more in this book on English/British than French interpretations of Agincourt, because of space constraints but also because there is no parallel in the shaping of French views to the impact of Shakespeare's *Henry V* in the English-speaking world. The different spelling of the battle in English and French causes some problems. For simplicity I have used Azincourt when referring specifically to the location in the Pas-de-Calais.[3]

2

Agincourt

The Battle in Context

On 13 August 1415, ships laden with soldiers, horses, equipment, and supplies stood off the coast of Upper Normandy. A royal proclamation declared that all should make ready to disembark the following morning. No one was to land before the king. As Henry V stepped ashore, he fell to his knees, praying that God might give him justice against his enemies.[1] He was landing as king of France but the French, under their 'so-called king' Charles VI, were unjustly withholding his rights.

The opening of the campaign which ended at Agincourt demonstrates a key point about medieval warfare. Conflict between Christian peoples needed justification. Henry had inherited his right to the French crown by descent from Edward III who had declared himself king of France in 1340, thereby starting what we call 'the Hundred Years War'. Edward had defeated the French at Sluys in 1340 and Crécy in 1346. In 1360 he stopped calling himself king following the negotiation of the Treaty of Brétigny, known as the Great Peace: Edward gained a huge swathe of land in France to be held in full sovereignty without homage to the French king, thereby solving the longer-term problem of the tenure of lands in France by English kings since the twelfth century. Edward's diplomatic success resulted from the capture of King John II by his son, Edward, the 'Black Prince', at the Battle of Poitiers on 16 July 1356.

9 years later

In 1369 the French reneged on the Treaty of Brétigny, invading and recovering many of the lands transferred to the English. In response, Edward III resumed the title 'king of France'. Despite several land and sea campaigns over the next twenty years, the English could not recover the lost lands, but nor could the French remove them from French soil. This stalemate led to a thirty-year truce in 1396. The English still held Gascony, based around Bordeaux, as well as Calais which Edward III had taken in 1347 after a year-long siege.

The state of truce ended in mid-August 1415 when Henry V launched his invasion.[2] He arrived back in England on 16 November. His campaign began with the siege of Harfleur, which surrendered on 22 September. Around 6–8 October he left Harfleur to march towards Calais (see Fig. 2). Arriving at the mouth of the Somme on 13 October, he was not able to cross at Blanchetaque, the fording point used by Edward III en route to Crécy. Fearing there was a large army awaiting him north of the Somme, Henry took his army eastwards along the southern side of the river, shadowed by the French on the other side. On 19 October he succeeded in crossing the Somme between Bethencourt and Voyennes. On the next day French envoys came from Péronne to summon him to battle. Four days later Henry arrived at the plain bordered by Maisoncelle to the south, Ruisseauville to the north, and Azincourt and Tramecourt to the east and west (see Fig. 3). The French were already there. Battle was given on the following day, Friday 25 October 1415. By 29 October Henry was in Calais with his victorious army and its prisoners.

This was the first time for over fifty years that an English king had waged war in person in France; Henry's army of invasion, containing up to 12,000 paid men, was larger than the 10,000 which Edward III had taken in 1359 to besiege Reims.[3] Only the army of 14,000–15,000 which Edward had led in 1346, from the Cotentin to the outskirts of Paris and then to victory at Crécy, was larger.[4] Henry's decision to go to war in person and on a grand scale is worthy of our attention even without Agincourt. The French posed no threat to England: this was simply an act of aggression.

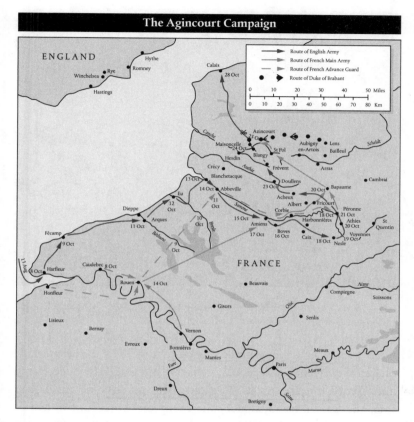

Fig. 2. This map shows the route taken by the English and French armies in October 1415. Henry had planned to move Straight from Harfleur to Calais but, fearing a French army was on the north bank of the Somme estuary, he was forced to march a long way inland to seek a crossing point. The map emphasizes that parts of the French army also had to cover long distances to arrive at Azincourt.

Preparations

Henry's intention to invade France was first made public by the chancellor (Henry Beaufort, bishop of Winchester) at the opening of parliament on 19 November 1414.[5] Beaufort explained that Henry understood that a 'suitable time' had come to accomplish, with the aid of God, the recovery of his inheritance and the rights of his French crown.

Fig. 3. A view of the battlefield today. This view emphasizes the relative flatness of the site as well as flanking woodland.

To wage war the king needed to raise money. As in the previous phases of the Hundred Years War, soldiers expected a daily wage. Henry also needed to raise troops since there was no standing army. Ever since the late thirteenth century the Commons in parliament had to approve direct taxation. Bishop Beaufort expressed his confidence that all would be moved to generosity. After all, if the king could increase his patrimony (i.e. gain lands in France) he could reduce the financial burdens on his subjects at home. 'And when these things have been accomplished, great honour and glory must surely follow from them.'

These statements are key to understanding how Henry was able to gain support for his invasion. They also remind us of the pressure on him to deliver successes in France in order to show that the money had been well spent. The Commons were indeed generous, agreeing a subsidy of £76,000 to be collected in equal instalments on 2 February 1415 and 2 February 1416. On the back of this guaranteed income

Henry was able to raise loans for the campaign. That is how state finance worked, much as today. In the spring of 1415 the City of London was persuaded to make a loan of 10,000 (£666 13s. 4d.) marks for the expedition.

War was expensive for the state. There were many additional costs in terms of shipping and equipment although soldiers had to cover their own victualling costs. In 1415 they were told to take enough food for three months. Their daily wages were dependent upon social status as well as military function. So, for instance, a knight bachelor was paid 2s. per day and an earl 6s. 8d. even though their military role was as men-at-arms. Non-titled men-at-arms were paid 1s. per day and archers received 6d. Wages were paid to the captain for distribution to his troops. There were also well-established arrangements for the division of war booty and ransoms. Such conditions of service, in addition to the excitement and camaraderie of campaigning, made an invasion of France attractive for the military classes.

Parliament was a useful recruiting ground as well as a way of communicating the king's plans back to the shires and towns and uniting the kingdom in the war effort. During or shortly after the parliament of November 1414, lords and knights met with the king. Although they urged that another embassy should be sent to France, they agreed that, in the meantime, 'all works of readiness for the expedition' should begin and declared themselves 'ready with our bodies to do you service to the extent of our powers, as we ought of right to do and as our ancestors have done to your noble progenitors in similar circumstances in the past'.[6] By March 1415 it was apparent that diplomacy had failed. At the end of the next month, contracts (indentures) for the provision of troops were entered into, following a system established in the later fourteenth century. Although made up of many individual retinues—at least 320 men contracted to provide troops—the army was bound together by standard conditions of service and by disciplinary ordinances. These included a requirement that all men should wear the cross of St George on their front and back, an important element in generating an *esprit de corps* and symbolizing a common national purpose.[7]

The size of the army and the large number of indentees reflected the king's presence in person. There was a considerable range of companies, from the largest of 960 men contracted by the king's eldest brother, Thomas, duke of Clarence, to an individual offering his service either alone or with a few archers.[8] As was always the case in medieval armies, the nobility provided the bulk of troops, entering into subcontracts with knights and gentry to make up their large companies. The king also drew on his royal lands: archer companies were raised in Cheshire (650), Lancashire (500), and South Wales (500) (see Fig. 4). Although there were ample precedents for this, 1415 appears to be the first time companies were raised from all three areas simultaneously.

A striking feature is that almost all retinues had a ratio of archers to men-at-arms of 3 to 1. Clarence, for instance, engaged to bring 720 archers and 240 men-at-arms. The latter consisted of himself, his 14-year-old stepson Henry, earl of Somerset, 2 knights banneret, 14 knights bachelor, and 221 'ordinary' men-at-arms. This ratio of 3:1 is first seen in the Welsh wars of the 1400s against Glyndŵr's rebellion. It contrasts with the armies sent to France between 1369 and 1389 which had a ratio of 1:1. Although the archer companies from Cheshire, Lancashire, and South Wales took the overall ratio in 1415 to 4 archers per man-at-arms, the 3:1 ratio was clearly deemed the optimum for individual retinues. It remained dominant in English military organization until the late 1430s when the proportion of archers increased.[9] By Edward IV's invasion of France in 1475 there were 8 archers for every man-at-arms.[10]

Increasing the number and proportion of archers was a way of achieving a larger but cheaper army since archers were paid half as much as men-at-arms. This was important when funds were limited. In 1400, at a time of considerable financial stringency, Henry IV gathered an army of 13,085 men for a twenty-day expedition to Scotland: the ratio of archers to men-at-arms was 7:1.[11] There was

Fig. 4. We know the names of thousands of soldiers recruited for the 1415 expedition to France thanks to surviving muster rolls. Here we see the Welsh archers recruited in Cardiganshire and Camarthenshire (The National Archives, E101/46/20).

also a great pool of men to draw on. Ever since the reign of Edward III there had been a requirement for all adult males to practise at the butts. But there was also ample military rationale. Archers were multifunctional. They were just as useful in sieges as men-at-arms. By this time too, they were normally mounted and therefore able to keep pace when an army was on the move.

Another feature of the indentures in 1415 is the unusual arrangements for payment. Expeditionary armies received pay in advance. Henry contracted his troops for twelve months' service. That is in itself a clear indication of the scale of his ambitions in France. He had conquest and occupation of territory in his sights. Even with loans raised on the back of taxation, however, he had only enough cash in hand to pay for the first quarter (three months) in advance. Half of this was paid at the sealing of the indenture to help the captain recruit his troops, the other half at the muster before embarkation. In order to guarantee payment of wages for the second quarter, an intriguing solution was found: items from the royal treasury were given to the captains as a pledge of payment of cash wages in due course. The indentures obliged the redemption of the jewels within nineteen months (i.e. by 1 January 1417). Henry no doubt hoped that he would be successful in France, and that he would be able to ask the Commons for a new tax grant. He could not afford to fail. Captains had to deposit the jewels with London goldsmiths in return for cash to use as wages. They ran the risk that if the crown could not redeem the jewels, they would be out of pocket. As a result they had a vested interest in the success of Henry's campaign.

As the historian Jenny Stratford points out, although kings had used jewels and plate before to secure loans from corporations and individuals, 1415 is the first, and perhaps only, time when they were pledged directly to captains indenting to serve on a military campaign.[12] Henry was keen to conduct a long campaign. He hoped it might extend beyond the six months for which he had paid in advance. For the third quarter, the indentures guaranteed the captains payment within six weeks of its start. For the fourth, the king was obliged to give surety by halfway through the third quarter. If he could not do so, then the captains would be discharged from obligation to continue in service.

As Bishop Beaufort had explained, Henry thought that this was a good time to invade France. In 1392 Charles VI (1380–1422) had shown the first signs of mental instability. This escalated into competition for control of his government, initially between his brother (Louis, duke of Orléans) and his cousin (John the Fearless, duke of Burgundy). In November 1407 Orléans was assassinated on the orders of Burgundy. By 1410 there was civil war between the Burgundians and the Orléanists (usually called the Armagnacs because the new duke, Charles, married the daughter of the count of Armagnac). Both parties sought the military assistance of the English against their enemy. In return they promised help in restoring to the English their gains of the Great Peace of 1360. In 1411 Prince Henry, in charge of government in England during his father's illness, sent 1,200 troops to assist the duke of Burgundy. In 1412 Henry IV sent an army of 1,000 men-at-arms and 3,000 archers under the duke of Clarence in support of the Armagnacs.[13]

Although the factions had been reconciled almost as soon as Clarence's army arrived, civil war erupted again in the spring of 1414. The Armagnac-controlled government declared the duke of Burgundy a traitor and even the king was present on campaign against him in Artois. The two parties made their peace in the autumn of 1414. As a result the French felt strong enough to repulse Henry V's diplomatic approaches. But it is easy to see why he should have considered this a 'suitable time' to attack France. His decision was also linked to politics in England. He was the son of a usurper. An external war would serve to confirm the dynasty. We should not forget that Henry faced a plot to depose him even as he assembled his troops for embarkation. The 'Southampton Plot' involved his cousin the earl of Cambridge (brother of Edward, duke of York who was to be killed at Agincourt) and other lords in a plan to replace Henry by the earl of March, who had a better claim to the throne but through female descent. For such a plot to be attempted when Henry had many soldiers at hand suggests that not all of his nobility were fully supportive of his plans for war with France.

Henry's reputation was not high at home or abroad. He had a lacklustre reputation in the Welsh wars and was in dispute with his father in the last years of the reign, partly because of differences over which party in France to support in order to gain the greatest advantage. Henry had lost face, in the eyes of the duke of Burgundy, by his father's switch to the Armagnacs. He still courted the Burgundians but there was no alliance or understanding in 1415. The factions were united in opposition to his invasion. Even though the duke of Burgundy was not at Agincourt a large number of his supporters, including his two brothers, the count of Nevers and the duke of Brabant, were killed there. The story of the dauphin sending a gift of tennis balls to Henry in the spring of 1414 or 15 is almost certainly true and was intended as an insult. It reflected Henry's poor reputation and implied that he could not convert words into action. Under these circumstances, it is hardly surprising that Henry issued a challenge to the dauphin for personal combat after the surrender of Harfleur.[14]

Henry wanted, and needed, to prove himself. Even at his accession he was keen to reopen war with France. His father might have done likewise had he lived. But while in 1411 and 1412 the English were sending troops to aid a faction in the French civil war, in 1415 Henry V was launching a full frontal attack on the French. It is worth emphasizing again that this was the first time for over fifty years that an English king had led an army to France in person. His army was large and contracted for a twelve-month campaign.

The Campaign

Henry chose to land in Normandy. In this he was emulating Edward III in 1346 but a major difference needs to be highlighted. Edward conducted a *chevauchée* (mounted raid) across Lower Normandy. Although he captured Caen, after sacking it he had moved on without installing a garrison. His conquest of territory (Calais) only occurred after his victory at Crécy. By contrast, Henry began his campaign with a siege. Harfleur was a strategic location controlling the Seine estuary and was the base for attacks on English shipping and coasts. It was well fortified especially with water defences. The inhabitants flooded the surrounding areas to make the task of a besieging army all the more difficult.

The siege took six weeks. This was longer than Henry had antici-pated, given his army was so large. His departure, originally intended for mid-July, was delayed by the Southampton Plot. Therefore, after the fall of Harfleur he decided to leave France by marching to Calais. His initial intention had been for a campaign of conquest, as is demonstrated by the support staff he took with him—gunners, stone-cutters, carpenters, and other labourers needed for siege warfare. The size of his army permitted this strategy, since there were enough troops to garrison captured places and to make more conquests. Normandy was a sensible target. It was easily reached and revictualled from England. After Harfleur fell, Henry had supplies brought in as well as encouraging craftsmen and settlers to move there. He also acquired reinforcements for some of the troops dead or invalided home by dysentery in the siege camp.

Normandy also had an appeal as the ancient possession of the Norman king/dukes. In his 1417 conquest Henry fanned the notion of the recreation of the duchy, calling himself duke and allocating lands to his troops and administrators.[15] He may already have had this in his mind in 1415. It would make sense of the comment at the parliament of November 1414 that an increase in the king's patrimony would reduce financial burdens at home. Normandy was a fertile and prosperous area and, even better, one from which the king of France gained considerable income. An attack on Normandy was therefore a way of undermining the French monarchy politically and economically.

From the siege camp outside Harfleur on 3 September, Jean Bordiu, archdeacon of the Médoc, and once seen as a possible author of the *Gesta Henrici Quinti* (an important narrative of the campaign), wrote to the city of Bordeaux: 'I have heard that it is not the king's intention to enter the town but to stay in the field. In a short while after the capture of the town, he intends to go to Montivilliers and thence to Dieppe, afterwards to Rouen and then to Paris.'[16] Whilst we cannot be sure Bordiu was expressing official policy, his letter indicates beliefs circulating in the English camp. He also told the Bordelais that it was Henry's intention 'to come thither before he returns to England', a comment interpreted by some historians as indicating that Henry intended to conduct a *chevauchée*-style move from Normandy to Gascony.[17] Such a strategy is very unlikely. Henry had landed on the wrong side of the Seine for that action. No advantage against the French would be gained from it, and the distance was far too long for a large army. Bordiu simply wished to persuade the Bordelais to support the king's Normandy campaign by sending food supplies by sea. No English king had been to Bordeaux since Edward I in the late 1280s. Henry had no military or political reason to go there.

At the surrender of Harfleur on 22 September 1415 Henry wrote to the City of London reporting his success. Kings were accustomed to send newsletters home. Given the City's financial interest in the campaign, this was all the more important. 'We hope by the fine power and good labour and diligence of our faithful people overseas to do our duty to achieve as soon as possible our rights in the area.'[18] This is a vague statement. Henry was already aware that dysentery had impacted upon his army and that he had needed to install a garrison of 1,200 (300 men-at-arms and 900 archers) in Harfleur since the town's fortifications had been damaged by his cannon and he was afraid of French attempts at recovery.

Over the next three weeks Henry debated with his commanders what to do. Sending a summons to the dauphin on 26 September offering personal combat and requiring a reply within eight days also gave him further time to decide what to do. He knew that the dauphin would not respond since this form of summons, used on several occasions in medieval warfare, was never accepted. Its purpose was to give the man who sent it the moral high ground.[19] Henry finally decided to send home those who were too weak to continue and to march the rest to Calais to return to England. It stands to reason that those chosen for the march were not suffering from dysentery. It is common to read that the archers at Agincourt had loose hose because of bowel problems. This is part of the myth. It was simply to allow unconstrained movement as the archers moved swiftly from one position to the next.

Henry chose to abandon his conquest, at least for the time being. He reckoned that it would be difficult to conduct further sieges with winter coming on. Whilst supplies could be brought in from England, there was still a sizeable army as well as a large garrison in hostile territory to feed. Henry was also influenced by the pay arrangements for the campaign. The author of the *Gesta* considered that the march to Calais would take eight days. If the campaign ended in mid-October it would be easier to find money to redeem the jewels since the second quarter would have lasted only a matter of days. As we saw, Henry was not able to follow his chosen route. The march took much longer than anticipated and during it he was brought to battle.

Had Henry envisaged a battle right from the start? It was not an essential element in his strategy. His aim was to take territory both for its own sake and to strengthen his negotiating position. But no commander could ignore the possibility of an engagement. With the king of England present in person, there was an incentive for the French to bring him to battle. Therefore Henry had to be prepared for the eventuality. That was another reason he took as large an army as possible. That way, he could reckon that the French would need time to raise an army sizeable enough to challenge him.

This takes us to the French reaction.[20] An invasion was expected but there was uncertainty over where it would land, which put the French at a disadvantage. Their troops expected pay and therefore there needed to be tax levies to finance the army. Through surviving muster rolls and *quittances* (receipts for payment of wages) we can see that about 2,000 soldiers had been raised by the time of the surrender of Harfleur, certainly not enough to face Henry in battle there. Henry allowed only four days between the treaty of composition with Harfleur (18 September) and the date set for its surrender (22nd). In no way could the

French arrange a large enough army for a *journée* (battle) to save it. Given the short time Henry allowed, nor was he encouraging them to do so.

The French had to anticipate where Henry might move next. As a result, troops were kept in various locations against possible English movements. Marshal Boucicaut, Constable d'Albret, and the sire de Rambures, master of the crossbowmen, were based in Rouen but were also carrying out investigative sorties into the Pays de Caux whilst the siege was in train. Neither the king nor the Dauphin Louis rushed to Rouen whilst Henry was still at Harfleur, indicating French fears that Henry might move his army against Rouen. It was not until Henry left Harfleur that Charles and his son arrived in Rouen, on 12 October. Charles VI had taken the special French battle standard, the oriflamme, from Saint-Denis on 10 September. But it was not to be at Agincourt since it was soon decided that the king would not be there in person. The hereditary bearer of the oriflamme, Guillaume Martel, sire de Bacqueville, was killed at the battle. His lordship lay just north of Harfleur. He was one of many soldiers from Upper Normandy present at Agincourt.

By 8 October we have evidence of 230 French companies in pay. Many of these, as in the English army, were small, commonly containing fewer than fifteen men. As soon as Henry left Harfleur we see French troops shadowing him. From Henry's perspective there was sense in drawing the French away from Harfleur. Whilst he was still in the country the French would be pursuing him rather than attempting to recover the town. But was Henry battle-seeking in his march? This interpretation has been put forward by the historian Clifford Rogers.[21] He is justified in his conclusion that if the French disrupted Henry's march, the king would not shrink from giving battle: he would have no choice anyway. Yet all of the narratives tell us that he did not cross the Somme at Blanchetaque because he heard a large army was gathered on the northern bank. His decision to move eastwards to find a safer crossing is sure indication that he was keen to avoid battle. As Rogers admits, this decision also gave the French more time to raise their army.

All contemporary accounts tell us that it was the French who brought Henry to battle. His route across Upper Normandy was chosen to give the quickest route to Calais. Not surprisingly, given the size of his army, no place he passed through during any stage of his march offered resistance. All bought exemption from attack by providing foodstuffs. This might explain why the narratives do not speak of pillaging by the English army. As the historian Jan Willem Honig points out, the thousands of horses of the English army would have required much feeding, therefore even if Henry was tough on looting, the local population must have been called upon to provide fodder. There were some military actions en route, presumably linked to reconnoitring by both sides. The post-campaign financial records even give the names of the English fatalities since they were no longer entitled to pay.

Whilst at Corbie on 17 October Henry ordered his archers to prepare a 6-foot- (1.8-metre-) long stake sharpened at both ends.[22] Prisoners had divulged that the French had assigned cavalry 'to break the formation and resistance of our archers when they engaged us in battle'. (The fact that prisoners were taken also confirms that there were skirmishes en route.) Henry's action indicates that he was aware that the French were intending to bring him to battle. After he succeeded in crossing the Somme, the French were afraid he would elude them. They therefore sent heralds to him on 20 October with a formal summons to battle. This presumably named the proposed location of the battle.

The French had been forced to change their plans. They had assumed that Henry would cross the Somme at Blanchetaque and had assembled troops at Abbeville and Amiens against this possibility. What better than to defeat him in the same area as Edward III's victory at Crécy? The French plan of battle, discovered by Christopher Phillpotts in the British Library in 1984, belongs to this period of French preparation since it includes only those commanders known to be with the army at this point, and excludes the dukes of Orléans and Bourbon who were present as senior commanders at Agincourt (see Fig. 5).[23]

Fig. 5. This battle plan, now British Library Cotton Caligula DV, f. 44r was drawn up by Marshal Boucicaut, and other French commanders sometime between 13 and 21 October when the French expected to give battle to Henry close to the Somme. How and when it came into English hands is unknown. By the early seventeenth century it was in the possession of Sir Robert Cotton. His library was donated to the nation in 1702 but damaged by fire in 1731.

Two important observations can be made on the plan. It reveals that the French were prepared to give battle with an army smaller than that which eventually assembled at Agincourt. It was to have two main battles but, as the plan outlined, if the English formed only one battle, the two French battles were also to be joined together. There were to be two wings of foot in front of which the *gens de trait* (a term which included both crossbowmen and longbowmen) were to be placed. This did not happen at Agincourt. The second observation is that the plan includes manoeuvres which were used by the French at Agincourt. As the prisoners had divulged to Henry, there was indeed a group of 1,000 heavy horse intended to attack the archers 'and do the utmost to break them'. Another group of 200 mounted men-at-arms—the wording indicating that these troops, unlike the group to break the archers, were not on barded (armoured) horses—was to attack the baggage behind the English lines.

The Battle

The French had chosen the battlefield of Agincourt.[24] Why they had decided on this particular location remains unknown. It may not have been the original choice. Some French narratives suggest that the summons to the English on 20 October was for a battle at Aubigny-en-Artois but that Henry, whilst accepting the challenge, had moved off in a different direction before being intercepted at Agincourt. If this was the case, then the French must have known which route he was taking towards Calais. Burgundian narratives tell us simply that the constable planted the royal banner 'in the field they had chosen in the county of Saint-Pol in the territory of Agincourt'. Marshal Boucicaut knew the area since it was where the royal army had campaigned against the Burgundians in the summer of 1414.

For all of the French troops to gather at the right place to fight against the English, especially if the original plan was for a battle at Aubigny, there had to be a good flow of information. We know that the duke of Brabant arrived after the battle was already under way, perhaps because he had been making for a different location. Other troops, such as those of the duke of Brittany and the duke of Anjou, did not reach the battlefield in time.

Much tends to be made of the length of the English march, overlooking the fact that many French also covered long distances in order to be at Agincourt (see Fig. 2). The duke of Orléans, for instance, is known to have been at Cléry near Orléans on 17 October. The army which had shadowed Henry from the north bank of the Somme covered as long a distance as he did. We might expect the French to find it easier to gain food supplies within their own country, but the local population was hostile to and suspicious of any army.

The English derived benefit from being together for over three months and surviving a 400-kilometre (248.5-mile) march in enemy territory. This engendered cohesion and mutual trust as well as time to discuss possible tactics. A disadvantage for the French was that their troops arrived at Agincourt in dribs and drabs. To those in the Somme plan were added companies under the dukes of Orléans and Bourbon as well as men from Picardy and other northern areas responding to the *semonce des nobles* (a means of calling out nobles and those 'accustomed to follow arms', although such troops expected pay).[25] A new plan of battle had been devised in Rouen around 20 October, inserting the additional lords, but its successful execution depended upon the timely arrival of the troops and opportunity for discussion and coordination. Significantly, an early account of the battle by the Religieux of Saint-Denis comments on the division of opinion between the rash young lords (Orléans and Bourbon) and the more cautious older commanders (Boucicaut and d'Albret).

The French did not give battle as soon as Henry arrived on 24 October, although it was potentially to their advantage to engage before he had time to reconnoitre the field. Henry's army had experienced a challenging final day's march because of the crossing of the River Ternoise. The French delayed because not all of the intended troops had arrived. Henry certainly expected the French to give battle on 24 October. He drew his men up into battle formation and, according to the *Gesta*, went through the pre-battle rituals including an oration. But the French did not attack since they anticipated that more troops would arrive for the following day.

The battle took place on 25 October. The French were definitely in the majority. The moot point is to what degree. Using the financial records I have suggested that, even taking into account losses at Harfleur—whether through death, invaliding home, or garrison deployment—Henry could still have had 8,680 soldiers with him. Further research has suggested that this is a reasonable maximum. Reinforcements were brought from England to Harfleur to substitute for losses. Only a few men were killed or captured on the march.

The crucial point is that the English had a much larger number of archers than men-at-arms. At embarkation the ratio was 4 to 1 but at the battle, because of the losses from Harfleur, it was 5 to 1. Therefore we can suggest around 1,500 men-at-arms and 7,000 archers at Agincourt. This distribution is key to understanding the battle. Henry's skill lay in using his different kinds of troops to maximum effect.

The archers were skilled but tended to be much more lightly armed than men-at-arms in terms of body protection. It is not impossible to use a longbow in full armour, although unusual. Armour is not essential to be an effective archer.[26] Archers were not intended to be front-line troops in the melee so did not need leg protection, gauntlets, etc. but only a helmet and basic body protection, such as a jacket of boiled leather (*cuir bouilli*).

Effective hand-to-hand fighting with swords, staff weapons, and lances took years of training. Men-at-arms had become soldiers from an early age.[27] It was a social as much as a military matter. From the nobility down to the lower gentry it was a sign of social status to have such training, which included handling a horse in a military context. Men-at-arms could be cavalry as well as foot. Both skills would be expected, even if most, if not all, would fight on foot in a battle situation. Training through the foot joust was extremely important, not least as a group activity, since it simulated battle conditions. In these respects, the English and French men-at-arms had much in common. The flower of English, as well as French, chivalry was at the battle. The presence of nobles was strong on both sides.

Archers needed to have their limbs free to use their longbows effectively. They needed to be able to move positions easily. Their value lay in number. Whilst some were the Robin Hoods of their day, their main purpose was mass shooting of arrows, operating much like machine gun fire in later centuries. The archers' long-range shooting covered the men-at-arms as they moved forward to engage with their counterparts on the other side, but it also damaged the advancing enemy men-at-arms. This is precisely what happened at Agincourt.

Archers were also useful at short-range shooting into the flanks of the enemy when the two sides engaged. Because of their ease of movement they could also move to attack from the rear. Henry sent a group of 200 archers into a location behind French lines on the Tramecourt side of the battle. Their purpose was to stir the French into making a forward advance into the trap which Henry had laid. When it was safe to do so, archers could enter the melee with their own weapons. The narratives of Agincourt tell us that they did so, causing much destruction to the already disrupted French men-at-arms through the use of swords, axes, staff weapons of various kinds, and the lead mallets which had been used to hammer in the stakes. They may have deployed the stakes as weapons too.

All of this is evident in the way Henry drew up his troops. His men-at-arms were divided into three groups, with the group on the right, under the duke of York, as the vanguard intended to be the first to engage. This group would encounter the enemy at their freshest and most energetic, and also at their most numerous since the French drew up a disproportionately large vanguard. The post-campaign financial records reveal that mortality rates in York's retinue were the highest of the whole army at the battle. The centre battle was commanded by the king and contained the knights and esquires of his household. The rearguard on the left was under the veteran Thomas, Lord Camoys, 65 years old at the time of the battle. This group needed to hold steady until called upon to engage, and therefore the presence of a seasoned commander was crucial. For any army, the waiting time before fighting is the most unnerving. Once in the fight adrenalin flows. There can be no doubt too that the English would be determined to fight fiercely. They had everything to lose if not.

As for the archers, their number would suggest a wide distribution across the English position, i.e. both on the flanks and in formations in front of the men-at-arms. This also makes sense of the retinue structure. Most retinues had both kinds of troops in them. Some muster rolls indicate that men-at-arms had specific archers attached to them. Archers placed in the front would have to draw back when their men-at-arms made their forward advance but were then available to protect and support their men as the melee developed, for instance, in the taking of prisoners. A reference in one of the post-campaign accounts mentions that the Lancashire archers formed a special bodyguard for the king at the battle.[28]

The remaining archers, the majority, were placed on each flank. Their line would have curved forwards to form a squashed horseshoe shape, aimed at facilitating both forward and flanking arrow-shot against the advancing French. One early French narrative speaks of Henry having his archers 'range themselves in a circle around us to sustain the shock of the enemy'.[29] The impact of the archers was thereby maximized. It was impossible for the French men-at-arms to train for such a situation. They simply had to keep moving forward. The arrow shower, all the more frightening for being intermittent, had the effect of slowing them down, irrespective of whether arrows could penetrate armour or not. Some would be injured, many would fall. The flanking arrow shower also had the effect of funnelling the French so that they pressed into a small space. Narratives tell us that they were so crushed together they could not lift their weapons. They piled up and were easy pickings for the English. Archers could shoot from the rear at short range as well as piling in for the kill.

Agincourt was a horrific battle where many French died from suffocation. The mud contributed to this. Once fallen, it was difficult to get up in such a press and with the suction of the mud. (Without

27

such conditions, men in armour could get back on their feet. This is what they practised in the foot joust.) Such circumstances explain why so many were killed and also why it was possible later to search the heaps of dead for prisoners. Piling up was not unique to Agincourt but was also the fate of the French at Crécy and of supporters of the Scottish king David II at Dupplin Moor (1332). It was an undoubted peril for large armies which found themselves caught in narrow space, much as in a modern crowd disaster.[30]

Henry had deliberately set his deployment in a way which trapped the French. This may have reflected his experience at the Battle of Shrewsbury in 1403; although we do not know the precise size and composition of the royal army, given the ratio of 7 archers to 1 man-at-arms in 1400 and the development of the 3:1 ratio in the Welsh wars, a good proportion of archers is likely, similarly in the army of Hotspur: Prince Henry was wounded in the face by an arrow.

At the beginning of the Battle of Agincourt the French showed a reluctance to make their forward move because they were still hoping for more troops to arrive. Henry therefore moved his lines forward to goad the French into attacking him. He made other decisions which were crucial to protecting his smaller army. The first was to use the baggage as a rear defence, a common tactic in the period. The second was to use the stakes as a protection for the archers. As we have seen from his action at Corbie during the march, he anticipated a French cavalry attack. Stakes were effective protection against this since they enabled the archers to continue to shoot until the horses were very close—their arrow shower completely disrupted the cavalry advance. Panic-stricken horses threw their riders. In their retreat they may have clashed into the advancing men-at-arms, but the phasing of the battle is uncertain in the narratives. It is not clear whether the cavalry charge occurred before the foot advance or simultaneously.

The stakes also served to funnel the French foot advance by forming an outer boundary fence. The use of stakes was not new, being deployed by the Ottomans at Nicopolis in 1396, a battle at which some English, as well as Boucicaut and a number of French, were present.[31] Stakes were a suitable method of protection where it was not possible to dig defences. At Crécy Edward III had time to dig holes against the cavalry.[32] In later centuries caltraps (small three-pronged metal devices) were effective as a way of disrupting a cavalry advance.

We might ask why the French entered the trap. They had no choice once battle had been decided upon, even if Boucicaut and others knew the value of stakes as protection. They were aware of the presence of large numbers of archers, but if archers were in flanking woodland and hidden down the slopes at either side of the field, they may not have been fully apprised of the total English strength. The French tactic was to throw as large a number of men-at-arms as possible at the English men-at-arms: they had many more soldiers of this type and considered that they could overwhelm their English equivalents by sheer weight of numbers. This tactic would naturally involve the attempt to capture Henry and his leading nobles.

However, as they approached the English men-at-arms they were so damaged by the arrows that the impetus of their attack was reduced. As John Keegan notes, the French were forced to a halt. That is always an extremely dangerous position in a battle.[33] Yet their plan had not been unrealistic. They had understood the need to send cavalry against the archers to undermine their impact. Had that happened as planned, Agincourt would have been a very different battle. The narratives suggest that it proved difficult to persuade men to join the cavalry group. This implies weak authority of the commanders who had ordered a cavalry attack on the archers. The explanation must lie in the French assumption that their large foot advance would be successful and would win great gains, not simply noble prisoners but also political advantage in the capture or death of Henry. It also reveals changes since the mid-fourteenth century. At Crécy the French were able to invest much more in the cavalry charge, but the arrow storm had the same effect on horses as in 1415. As a result they had switched to a foot-based advance at Poitiers, but arrows and Gascon cavalry had meant they were defeated there too.

29

The French army in 1415 had a great preponderance of men-at-arms, as was standard in French armies of the later Middle Ages. The tax grant ordered by Charles VI on 31 August envisaged a force of 6,000 men-at-arms and 3,000 *gens de trait*. The requests sent to the duke of Orléans and to the duke of Burgundy were for 500 men-at-arms and 300 *gens de trait*. We know that in general the Burgundians had 70 per cent men-at-arms and 30 per cent *gens de trait*, although as in England it was common for all troops to be mounted.[34] The equipment and armour of the French men-at-arms were comparable with those of the English. Indeed, these soldiers came from the same social origins as their English counterparts. France had a larger nobility and gentry and therefore was able to field a larger number of men-at-arms than the English.

In French armies *gens de trait* tended to be grouped together under the command of the master of crossbowmen. The urban militias were largely crossbowmen. Amiens, for instance, provided 30 crossbow-men and 25 *pavesiers*, who were general infantry with shields also used to protect the crossbowmen, given the longer time needed to reload compared with the longbow. The use of these troops at the battle was minimal, which may seem perplexing but it was not obvious what their target should be. They needed to be used against the English men-at-arms (crossbow bolts were definitely armour piercing) but the forward move of so many French men-at-arms made this difficult, as did the archers fronting the English army at the outset. This rendered the *gens de trait* too vulnerable to be used, since like the English archers they were not in full armour. Against the archers they would not fare well because of the relative speeds of reloading. Similarly, although the French had some field cannon (such pieces being retrieved after the battle by the towns and *baillis* which had brought them), these do not seem to have had any effect against the English.

Narratives give a huge range of figures for the French army. The highest figures are found in English chronicles, sometimes even exceeding 100,000. French figures are lower (10,000–14,000) and Burgundian towards the higher end (50,000).[35] Chronicles always exaggerate. The figures they give were intended to indicate scale not exactitude. We do not have full financial records for the French army in 1415 but we do for earlier occasions. In the late fourteenth century we find royal armies of around 16,600 but also 8,000. During the French civil war in 1414 the king had ordered 10,000 men-at-arms and 4,500 *gens de trait* for service against the Burgundians in an army which Charles VI was to lead in person, even if nominally.[36] The reforms of Charles VII in the 1440s produced the *ordonnance* companies, totalling 7,200 combatants, as well as an infantry of 8,000 *francs archers* levied on local communities, producing over 15,000 in all. These sizes, all authenticated by pay records, serve as useful benchmarks for what might have been possible in 1415. Not until the last quarter of the fifteenth century did French royal armies rise to 20,000–25,000.[37]

Even though the French king had fielded 14,500 men in 1414 there are factors against such a size in the following year. The king was not present in person, which would immediately reduce the size, and troops were kept back at Rouen for his protection. The duke of Berry had 1,000 men-at-arms and 500 archers in his company at Rouen on 12 October. As the king's uncle, his retinue would be one of the largest. The duke was not at the battle so it remains uncertain how many of his troops were present. Other troops had been left in Paris under Tanneguy du Chastel for fear of action by the duke of Burgundy in the king's absence. These factors, along with the highly regionalized nature of recruitment—most troops at the battle were from Picardy and Upper Normandy—explain my suggestion of a total of around 12,000 for the French at Agincourt.[38]

Given the continuing anxieties on whether the dukes of Burgundy and Orléans were fully reconciled, both dukes were ordered in mid-September not to join the royal army. There was a change of mind about Orléans, arising out of the decision that the king, dauphin, and duke of Berry would not be present at the battle. Therefore Orléans, as the next most senior royal, was despatched as the leading commander. The duke of Burgundy was not at the battle, but several of his faction were, as were his two brothers. None the less, the lack of full

Burgundian participation is significant in terms of total numbers. In 1408 against the Liègois, the duke had raised 2,690 men.

French deployment remains uncertain. Some narratives suggest that the French drew up only two battles rather than the customary three but this is not certain. A two-battle formation could suggest fewer troops than expected, or perhaps that the late arrivals, such as the duke of Brittany, were intended to form the third battle. There is no doubt that the first battle was extremely large, containing at least 5,000 men, and that it bore the brunt of the fighting. It was also made more vulnerable by the pressing forward of subsequent lines, which contributed to the pile-up and the impossibility of retreat. We can doubt whether all the troops intended to follow in did so once they saw what had happened to the front formations. In this respect, the size of the French army becomes irrelevant. A large army is only of value if all of its soldiers engage in the fighting. A similar problem had occurred at the Battle of Courtrai in 1302 where the French rearguard fled without engaging.[39] At Agincourt, the French commanders had already chosen not to involve the militias. That is another reason why total size is misleading when evaluating the battle.

As the size of the French army remains contentious, so too does the number of dead and prisoners. Contemporary chronicles give a wide range of incredible figures, a situation not unique to Agincourt.[40] For the Battle of Courtrai (1302), chroniclers give between 5,000 and 20,000 dead although only 60 names are given.[41] High figures indicate that contemporaries saw these battles as especially bloody. For Agincourt, there is the complication of the killing of the prisoners. It is also the case that chroniclers only ever recorded the names of men of status. For Agincourt, chronicles and other kinds of evidence enable at least 500 men to be identified as dying at the battle.[42] It is difficult to know what kind of multiplier to apply but a total between 1,500 and 2,000 is credible. This may seem low compared with the 3,000–12,000 given in the chronicles but it is a very high mortality on one day.

The Killing of the Prisoners and the Aftermath of the Battle

Agincourt is infamous for Henry's order to kill the prisoners. To make sense of this incident, we must accept that Henry had considered the battle over. The heaps of French were being searched through to find those still living and prisoners were being gathered together. Learning that another French attack was imminent, and fearing that he might lose the battle he thought he had won, Henry ordered that the prisoners should be killed. The reminiscence of Ghillebert de Lannoy provides an insight into the mechanics.[43] Lannoy had been pulled out from the bodies of dead and taken to a house where there were ten to twelve other prisoners, all wounded. At the order to kill the prisoners, the house was set on fire but he managed to crawl out and was recaptured by the English.

We can see parallels with the Battle of Aljubarrota (1385). Prisoners had already been captured by the point the Franco-Castilians began a new attack. Because of this new danger the Portuguese commander decided that prisoners would not now be taken. According to Froissart, those French prisoners who had already been captured and disarmed, and who were being held at the rear of the Portuguese lines, were now killed.[44] This is a very similar situation to Agincourt but, being a smaller and less publicized battle, the killing of prisoners at Aljubarrota has not excited the same modern opprobrium as Henry's decision.

Much emphasis has been placed on the incentive of ransoms in late medieval warfare. It has to be remembered, however, that Crécy saw no prisoners taken. It was a fight to the death, or at least to the rout. That was also the common position in the battles of civil wars, such as Shrewsbury (1403) and the battles of the Wars of the Roses. No prisoners appear to have survived alive at Aljubarrota. The battles of Nájera (1367) and Poitiers were very much exceptions in terms of the large numbers of high-status prisoners. On the face of it there was no reason why Agincourt should not have been like those engagements.

As we know, many prisoners had been taken up to the point Henry learned of the danger of a renewed French attack. At the outset of the campaign Henry had issued disciplinary ordinances which envisaged prisoner taking. Such rules were necessary because of the complexities of the matter. One clause, for instance, covered the possibility of a soldier capturing a prisoner but then another soldier coming along and capturing him again. Who was the 'master' (or owner) of that prisoner? The disciplinary ordinances were aimed at clarifying such disputes.

There was no proclamation of 'no quarter' at the beginning of the Battle of Agincourt as there was at Towton (1461) and at Crécy. Therefore it was expected that prisoners could and would be taken. One early narrative of the campaign, the *Gesta Henrici Quinti*, comments that many surrendered themselves several times in the battle but that no one had time to take them prisoner. Almost all were therefore killed either by those who had struck them down in the first place or by others who came later. But the same author makes clear that prisoner taking did occur after the battle was over, when the English searched the heaps of dead for the living, 'intending to hold them as prisoners for ransom'.[45] In other words, in a tight and tough situation, in the early stages of the melee, men were killed. When things eased off, or when it appeared that the enemy had withdrawn, it was possible to take prisoners.

The particular circumstances of Agincourt are relevant here. The French had been driven into a small space and had fallen on top of each other. The rear lines chose not to enter the fray and left the field. It now appeared safe for the English to search for prisoners: they reckoned that not all the French had been killed. Between the English searching for prisoners and the shout going up that the French were regrouping, there had to be a time lag long enough to allow for the prisoners to be found and to be led away, as the reminiscence of Lannoy tells us.

The English had every intention of keeping the prisoners alive until the point they feared the battle was going to restart. The English army had been stood down from its positions and would have removed some of its armour and put its weapons aside. A further French attack would place the English in a very vulnerable position to which they could not respond quickly. Henry could not afford to have his men distracted by their prisoners. The latter might attack their captors, with fists if not weapons, if they thought rescue was at hand. Therefore they had to be killed. The Burgundian narratives claim the owners of prisoners were reluctant to carry out the king's order and that a special posse of archers had to be appointed to do it. This may be true but it is not mentioned in any contemporary English text.

Of the early chroniclers, only Pierre Fenin has the attack on the baggage as the cause of the order to kill the prisoners. All other narratives give the reason for Henry's order as fear of a new French attack, although there is variation as to who was leading that attack. It may have been a new force arriving rather than the rear divisions, previously disengaged, now deciding to attack. Lannoy's testimony has the cause of Henry's order as the arrival of the duke of Brabant. The duke had a long distance to travel on the day of the battle, arriving late and hastily: it is credible that his arrival was the trigger. Yet he did engage in fighting and was killed. Many narratives suggest that there was no more fighting after Henry gave the order. Some are explicit that the French withdrew because of the order, adding that heralds were sent between the two parties. It remains unclear, therefore, whether the final act of the battle was the killing of the prisoners or whether there was further action.

We cannot know how many prisoners were killed. That the leading prisoners survived suggests that they were already housed together and easily exempted. Given that even with the killing there was still a number of living captives (at least 321 can be identified), it suggests that many prisoners had been taken in the first place.

What is missing in all accounts of Agincourt is a rout—a mounted pursuit by the victors against the enemy as it fled. Routs were a common closing move for battles, their purpose being to drive off the remaining enemy and allow the recovery of dead. In routs casualties tended to be high, especially where fleeing troops were on foot and therefore easily hacked down by their pursuers on horse.

The lack of mention of a rout suggests that the French abandoned the field of their own accord. This had been happening even during the melee. The French cavalry, having failed to override the archers, abandoned the field as soon as they saw the vanguard collapse. They had no further role in the battle. The rear divisions of the French also abandoned the field without fighting. If the French were withdrawing in good order voluntarily, there was no need for a mounted pursuit. But this may have encouraged the French to launch a new attack.

It is also possible that, after the killing of the prisoners, there was a negotiated end to the battle—i.e. a formal French surrender. This is surely what the Burgundian accounts imply in their story of Henry summoning the French king of arms, Mountjoye, to ask to whom the victory should be accorded and to decide its name. The scene is placed after the killing of the prisoners and after the French had 'departed in flight to many different locations'.[46] A local chronicle implies confusion, with some French hiding in hedges and bushes but being discovered by local peasants and killed for their money, armour, and horses.

Henry did not linger in the area. He stayed there on the night of the battle but on the morning of the following day he began his march to Calais. He knew that threats of French regrouping had been real but not fully actualized. Therefore there was a possibility of further attacks. His desire to move quickly also explains why he limited the amount of armour booty which his soldiers could keep. The post-campaign financial records reveal no gains of war other than ransoms of prisoners. It is a moot point whether a pitched battle offered much in the way of rich pickings beyond military equipment. Materials left on the field were scavenged by local inhabitants. Some of the towns which had sent their militias returned to the field in later days, finding artillery pieces, tents, and other items.

All of this adds to the picture of both the French and Henry moving away quickly.

A Decisive Battle?

Agincourt has not been seen as a decisive battle, rightly so. Since the king and dauphin were not present at the battle, government continued as before. A number of *baillis* had been killed but there were others to fill their places. In fact, lobbying for offices began immediately after the battle. A large number of nobles and gentry had met their death. Although disruptive for individual families, such losses did not put pressure on the French crown to negotiate with Henry. Whilst prisoners had been taken, none were so significant that they would force the French crown to rush to negotiate and pay ransoms.

At Poitiers, the king of France had been captured. That situation necessitated diplomatic negotiations towards a settlement, although it took several years to bring these to completion, as had also been the case following the capture of David II at Neville's Cross in 1346. There were parallels between Agincourt and Crécy in that neither saw the capture of the king or his heir. But at Crécy Edward III had defeated Philip VI in person. Historians make much of the madness of Charles VI and have also cast aspersions on the capacity of his son, the Dauphin Louis. However, their good sense in *not* participating in the battle with Henry needs to be acknowledged. If Henry had intended his personal summons after the surrender of Harfleur to goad the dauphin into meeting him in battle, then he had failed.

Henry was aware that, great as Agincourt was as a military achievement, it had not brought him advantage save in terms of military damage to and demoralization of the French. This explains why, once at Calais, he considered continuing the campaign. 'The king consulted his men whether, as ought to follow a great victory, he should go on to besiege neighbouring towns and castles.'[47] Ardres, 25 kilometres (15.5 miles) to the south-south-east of Calais, was mentioned as a possible target. Its captain had been killed at the battle. The capture of the town would further strengthen the March of Calais. Towns such as Boulogne feared that Henry would also act against them.

Henry's nobles dissuaded him and encouraged a return to England. They had been supporting their troops for the second quarter out of their own pockets with money raised on the security of royal jewels and plate. Continuing the campaign would have complicated efforts to ransom their prisoners. The lower ranks were already experiencing difficulties in this regard: they could not afford to feed their captives or even themselves. Several had to sell their prisoners to the men of Calais. Keeping a large army in the field would have been costly. Victuals were in short supply. Conducting a winter campaign was never easy. Furthermore, if its only achievements were to be small conquests in the Calais area, it would be using an expensive sledgehammer to crack a nut.

Henry remained unsure as to the likely actions of the duke of Burgundy. It is alleged in the chronicle of Jean Juvenal des Ursins that Duke John sent a challenge to Henry at Calais to avenge the death of his brothers at Agincourt. The truth of this is uncertain but Henry would doubtless have been wary. Even with the death and capture of Burgundians at the battle, Duke John still had significant military resources. If Henry had proceeded to actions in Picardy, these would have been deemed hostile acts towards the duke. None of the major prisoners taken by Henry at Agincourt was Burgundian. Therefore, the king had no bargaining card to play with the duke.

Having his army based at Calais was not helpful if Henry's main objective remained Normandy. He would have been aware that the French would seek to recover Harfleur. Therefore he had to be in a military and financial position to see to its defence. Evidence suggests this was no easy task.[48] As a toehold in enemy territory, Harfleur needed costly revictualling from England as well as a large and expensive garrison, at 1,200 the largest ever installed by an English king on the Continent. Although the captain, Thomas Beaufort, earl of Dorset, carried out successful sorties, the French laid siege to the town by land and sea in April/May 1416. An army of

7,500 had to be recruited in England for two months' service at sea to save it, which was achieved by a naval victory (the Battle of the Seine) on 16 August 1416.[49]

The victory of Agincourt was a moral but not a strategic triumph. Henry had reopened war with France on a large scale. He had shown that, as in 1346 and 1356, an English army could defeat the French in battle. He had demonstrated his own prowess as a warrior. This was a powerful message for his own subjects and for the French. To achieve any lasting success, however, there was much still to do. In this respect, the Battle of the Seine was more significant. Had Harfleur been lost, Henry could not have launched a second invasion of Normandy in 1417. In military terms, Agincourt made the French reluctant to engage in another pitched battle. During Henry's siege of Rouen (1418–19) Charles VI, now controlled by the duke of Burgundy, made preparations to give battle in order to raise the siege, but then decided against it, much as Philip VI had decided against giving battle to rescue Calais in 1347.[50] This failure effectively gave Henry the duchy of Normandy, but it needed the complete breakdown of relations between the Armagnacs and Burgundians, following the murder of Duke John the Fearless in September 1419, to bring Henry the real prospect of a French crown.

3

'The Noble Beginning' or 'The Accursed Day'?

Early Interpretations

And afterwards on leaving Harfleur . . . he encountered a very large army and a great number of soldiers from France . . . he fought with them until God, from his bountiful mercy, gave the victory to him and the enemy was killed and defeated: the aforesaid enterprise, by that noble beginning . . . is clearly determined and approved by God the Almighty.

(Parliament Rolls, 16 March 1416)[1]

Then she said . . . with tears in her eyes . . . 'Ah, cruel destiny, and that accursed day [la maudite journée], sorrowful and ill starred, which turned all my joy into discomfort! Alas, he is taken by death, the man I loved so much and so strongly . . . now he is dead. That is an honour for him but a cause of sadness for me.

(Alain Chartier, Livre des quatre dames, 1416–18)[2]

The first half of the fifteenth century is a truly dramatic period in Anglo-French history and interpretations of Agincourt need to be set against this backdrop. For the triumphalist English, Agincourt provided 'a noble beginning', useful in persuading parliaments to generosity and enabling Henry to wage further war, ending the French blockade of Harfleur by a naval victory in August 1416, launching a systematic conquest of Normandy from the autumn of 1417, and threatening Paris by the late summer of 1419.

By contrast, the French were demoralized. The defeat exacerbated existing political divisions between Armagnacs and Burgundians. Each blamed the other for the disaster. Chartier's poem put forward four female victims of the 'accursed day . . . so painful that it could not be named'. The widow was indeed to be pitied as also the wives of the prisoner and the soldier missing in action. But the most wretched was the woman whose husband had not engaged but fled the field as a coward. For Chartier, he was a Burgundian but for other writers it was the Armaganacs who were the traitors of Agincourt.

Over the following years, the French saw two dauphins die from natural causes (December 1415 and April 1417), Charles VI become increasingly incapable of an active role, and John the Fearless, duke of Burgundy, seize Paris and the royal government in May 1418. On 10 September 1419 a final effort was made to reconcile Duke John and the new leader of the Armagnacs, the Dauphin Charles, but so deep-seated were divisions that instead, the dauphin's henchmen assassinated the duke on the bridge at Montereau. Rightly did a Carthusian friar show Duke John's skull to Francis I in 1521, pointing out the hole through which the English entered France.[3] The new duke of Burgundy, Philip the Good, immediately allied with Henry, making it possible for the English king to dictate terms. By the Treaty of Troyes of 21 May 1420, Henry was acknowledged as heir to the French throne as well as regent for Charles VI, marrying the latter's daughter, Catherine. Save for a short visit to England in the spring of 1421, Henry was personally involved in the government of France from the sealing of the treaty to his death on 31 August 1422. The dauphin was formally disinherited, having already fled south of the Loire when the Burgundians took Paris in 1418.

Shakespeare's *Henry V* takes us directly from the victory at Agincourt to the Treaty of Troyes, omitting the murder of Duke John. It is easy to see why later centuries made this simple connection between the battle and French acceptance of the English claim. In reality, the crucial factor was political division in France. The Treaty of Troyes superseded Henry's success at Agincourt. In 1415 the French were the

41

enemy. From 1420 they were Henry's people. The treaty committed the English and French to live in peace and harmony under the man who expected to be king of them both. As it transpired, Henry V died before his father-in-law. It was the 9-month-old Henry VI who became king of the double monarchy of England and France at the death of Charles VI on 21 October 1422.

The Treaty of Troyes obliged military action until the 'so-called' dauphin and his supporters were totally defeated, thereby transforming Henry's international war into a continuation of the French civil war. Anglo-Burgundian cooperation and success in the 1420s included battle victories at Cravant (1423) and Verneuil (1424). Many English benefited from settling in Normandy and Maine, which also moved the emphasis away from Agincourt. Only in 1429 did the tide begin to turn with the inspiration of Joan of Arc and the coronation of the dauphin as Charles VII at the traditional French crowning place of Reims. A coronation of the young Henry VI at Paris in 1431 was no substitute. In 1435 the Burgundians defected from Henry to Charles. The double monarchy was irrevocably undermined. The English lost control of Paris in 1436, Normandy in 1449–50, and Gascony in 1451–3, leaving only Calais in their hands. Such military disasters, and a mentally unstable king of their own, led the English into the Wars of the Roses. By contrast, the French monarchy grew more powerful, boosted by the recovery of territory.

Interpretations of Agincourt were influenced by the context in which authors were writing. The changing fortunes of England and France were a significant influence. Hiram Johnson allegedly observed in a speech to the US Senate in 1917 that 'the first casualty when war comes is truth', an observation no less true in the fifteenth century. The population at large only knew what the powerful chose to tell them, as is particularly noticeable in England in the immediate aftermath of the battle. Henry V was an adroit user of propaganda.

Before we explore this more fully, it is interesting to see how the battle was reported outside England and France. Evidence from Italy and Spain suggests that Agincourt was deemed notable for the high numbers of French dead and prisoners. Take, for instance, a letter sent on 30 October 1415 from Paris to Venice: commenting on the losses, the writer concluded that 'never had such bad fortune or such a great defeat been heard of'. Thirteen prisoners were mentioned by name along with 26 dead.[4] Including this letter in his chronicle, the Venetian Antonio Morosini added that, according to another messenger, 10,000–12,000 were dead or prisoner. Numbers of this scale should always be treated cautiously: they simply mean a strikingly large number. To put this in context, Morosini had heard that Henry had landed at Harfleur with 30,000 men and 6,000 had died during the siege. A letter written in Venice on 27 July 1416 claims French losses of 6,000.[5] The large number of dead and prisoners is also remarked upon by a Castilian chronicle of the 1450s.[6]

The report received by Morosini emphasized that battle had been given at the behest of the French. That this was the common international perception is confirmed in a Scottish chronicle of the 1440s. This also claims that the French army totalled 200,000 of which 12,000 were killed.[7] We can detect other ideas circulating in Europe. Duarte, king of Portugal, commented in his *Leal Conselheiro* (pre-1438) that Henry V declared before the battle 'that the royal house of England would never have to pay ransom for him since he would either conquer or die in the battle. And God was pleased by his good effort and so he defeated the main power of France with no more than eight thousand warriors.' When advising his brother, Henry the Navigator, during the latter's attack on Tangiers in 1437, Duarte urged him to follow the example of the English 'who mainly for keeping good order in their fights are many times the winner . . . even when they are few . . . and in a small space, they are put in such an order that they make their enemies very afraid'.[8] Family connections (Duarte was Henry V's cousin) go some way to explaining these comments but they also show the high reputation of English soldiers as well as of their king.

England: The Noble Beginning

Henry had considerable control over how his victory at Agincourt was reported. Following well-established precedents (eight newsletters are known for the Crécy campaign) the king had sent a letter on 22 September to the City of London explaining that the French king had not come to relieve Harfleur by the appointed date.[9] Therefore the town had surrendered and an English garrison been installed under the earl of Dorset. The king urged that thanks should be given to God for this good news, adding that 'we hope by the power, labour and diligence of our faithful people to do our duty to achieve our rights in this area as soon as possible'.

News of the victory at Agincourt was received in London by early morning of 29 October 1415, the same day that Henry and his army arrived in Calais.[10] The Letter Book of the City of London records that a trustworthy report had arrived 'to refresh all the longing ears of the city'. The wording suggests that this was an oral despatch and not a full royal letter but we can reconstruct the gist of the message. Henry had, by God's grace, gained victory over the French who had assembled to prevent his march to Calais. The report continued that the majority (a clear exaggeration) of his opponents had been 'delivered to the arbitration of death or had submitted to his gracious might'. The City made public proclamation of the victory at 9 a.m. on 29 October at the customary place, St Paul's Cross, arranging also the ringing of bells and the singing of *Te Deums* in churches. Later in the day, the mayor and others processed to Westminster Abbey to offer thanks at the shrine of Edward the Confessor.

Three elements are evident in this report and in the speech given on 4 November at the opening of parliament by Henry Beaufort, bishop of Winchester and chancellor of England: divine support for Henry; his personal courage; and the scale of the victory in terms of dead and captured. Such was the official line on the battle. Beaufort also provided an outline narrative of events.[11] Harfleur had surrendered to the king after a short siege without the shedding of English blood. This was a deliberately positive statement on a siege which had taken longer than hoped. Henry had left a large garrison in the town and a good part of his army had succumbed to illness or had been invalided home:

> Henry had travelled through the heart of France towards Calais. As a result of his most noble and most excellent courage, with a small number of men compared with the might of his enemies, he encountered and fought with a large number of dukes, earls, barons and lords of France and other lands and countries overseas [a reference to the involvement of Brabant and Lorraine] and with all the chivalry and might of France and of these lands and countries...finally, with the Almighty's help and grace, all the French were defeated, taken or killed, without great loss to the English.

Henry had moved on safely to Calais 'with his men and prisoners, praise be to God, with the greatest honour and gain which the realm has ever had in so short a time'.

At the time parliament opened, Henry was still in Calais.[12] For the king there was advantage in giving the impression that the campaign might be extended: he needed new tax grants to repay the loans raised for the initial invasion and also to redeem the jewels pledged for the second-quarter wages.[13] Publicizing his success had the necessary effect. In one of the shortest parliaments ever, lasting eight days, the Commons not only granted a new subsidy to be collected by November 1416 but also brought forward to 13 December 1415 from February 1416 the collection of the second instalment of the subsidy agreed at the parliament of November 1414. Henry was also granted the wool subsidy and tonnage and poundage for life instead of having to ask each new parliament for renewal.

Secure in these grants, Henry returned to England, landing in Dover on 16 November. In March 1417 it was agreed that soldiers' wages should be paid for eight days after the king's arrival in England. The end of the campaign and the official demobilization of the army were therefore established retrospectively. Soldiers had been returning home in dribs and drabs over preceding weeks. What they told their families and communities about the battle is, alas, not documented. The sole example of a soldier's narrative, written by John Hardyng, is problematic. In the second version of his rhymed chronicle (1464), Hardyng presents a heading 'How the king came homeward through Normandy and Picardy and smote the battle of Agincourt, where I was with my master'. What follows is thirty-five lines of generic comment on the numbers of dead and prisoners. Hardyng wrote an earlier version of his chronicle in 1457 in which he did not mention his presence at the battle. His lord, Robert Umfraville, had been ordered to stay in England for the defence of the north. Hardyng does not appear in any of the muster rolls for the campaign. Given his reputation as a forger and fabricator, we cannot be sure Hardyng was at the battle at all. He may have invented the story (although that indicates that Agincourt still had some cachet in the 1460s).

A passage in a guide to learning French reads as if written shortly before the king returned to England. If so, it is the earliest known text in England to mention Agincourt as the place of battle (since neither the London Letter Book nor the Parliament Roll gave a location), and also to hazard army sizes:

> I have heard tell that the lords of France with 50–60,000 met Henry en route and that the king with 10,000 men fought with them at a place called Agincourt...I tell you for certain that the French who were captured at the battle of Agincourt, the duke of Orleans, the duke of Bourbon and many other counts, knights and valiant esquires, both of other foreign lands as of France, will be brought Thursday after the feast of St Martin to London [14 November].[14]

The Letter Book of the City of Salisbury also includes a short text on the battle. This must post-date Henry's formal reception into London on 23 November since it recounts that event. It also gives the place of battle as Agincourt and the size of the English army as 10,000, but the French as 100,000. It contains the earliest known mention of the date of the battle as 'Friday the feast of St Crispin and Crispinian'. The names of 75 dead are given along with the claim that there were also 4,000 valiant knights and esquires slain 'without counting the rest', whilst English losses were of the duke of York and the earl of Suffolk 'and of lords no more, but of their men about 15'. Seven of the French prisoners are named, with the addition 'and other gentlemen'. The text ends, 'A great victory. Glory to God in the highest.'[15] It reads as though it derives from a communiqué sent out after Henry's entry to London. When news was brought to Winchester College, although we do not know precisely when, the capture of dukes, counts, barons, knights, and other nobles of France was again emphasized. The date was given as the feast of the Crispins and the place as Agincourt with 'in Picardia' inserted above.[16] You can almost hear the 'where on earth is Agincourt?'

Focus was on the king, not on the nation or the army. We see this also in accounts of the welcome given to Henry in Kent and Canter-bury which followed customary forms.[17] The reception into London on 23 November was in the tradition of royal entries where the king chose 'to honour his city of London with his personal presence', as the author of the *Gesta* puts it.[18] It was not a triumphal procession of the whole army. Indeed, the *Gesta* comments on the king's modest retinue, emphasizing that only a few trusted members of his house-hold were in attendance. The procession did include, however, the six principal French lords captured at the battle 'under a guard of knights/soldiers [*militum*]'.[19] In this respect it paralleled the entry to London of Edward III and his son in May 1357, where the French king and other leading prisoners were displayed and where the Gold-smiths' Company provided a pageant.[20] As then, orchestration of the event was in the hands of the Londoners who took every opportun-ity to elevate their city. As Coldstream observes, 'they thankfully acclaimed their king as a successful soldier but the triumphalism was theirs'. The pageant contained no direct allusions to the battle. The *Vita Henrici Quinti*, written in the late 1430s, emphasized that Henry 'did not wish his crowned helmet which had been broken in the battle or his armour to be shown to the people, shunning all this popular praise'.[21] The procession culminated in religious devotion at Westminster.[22] Whether the famous 'Agincourt Carol' (Fig. 6) was written for the entry remains uncertain. In a recent study, the musicologist Helen Deeming concluded that 'a performance of *Deo gracias Anglia* at the London Pageant cannot be proven but it lies within the realms of possibility'.[23]

As in the written circulations, the emphasis in the entry was on God's support for Henry. This theme was also emphasized in a letter addressed to the king between the opening of parliament on 4 November and of the Canterbury convocation on 18 November. The author urged the king not to fall into the sin of pride because of such a great victory but to thank God for it:

> Thy royal majesty deems and firmly holds, as I presume, that not thy hand, but the outstretched hand of God, hath done all these things, for His own praise, the honour and glory of the English nation, and the eternal memory of the royal name ... Moreover, it is fitting that your royal highness should not boast of the past, but be anxious for the future; neither let the power of our enemies drag us back; let not their astuteness disturb us; nor let any fair promises seduce any one.[24]

The author is unknown but Henry Beaufort, bishop of Winchester and chancellor, has been suggested. If so, it raises the question of why he was concerned that the victory would go to Henry's head and that little advantage might be gained from it. In this context, and given the emphasis in all reports of God's support for Henry, celebration of the victory was inextricably linked to religious practice. The convocation of the clergy of the Canterbury province met from 18 November to 2 December, concluding with a mass at St Paul's Cathedral for all of the English who had died at Harfleur and the battle. The assembly also agreed the elevation of St George's Day into a double feast. In the announcement made in early January, St George was referred to as 'the special patron and protector of the nation'.[25] Although the battle is not mentioned it seems likely that the decision was prompted by it: after all, Henry's soldiers had worn, at royal order, the cross of

Fig. 6. The 'Agincourt Carol' (Bodleian Library MS 3340 f. 17v-18r) may have been composed for Henry's entry to London. Even if this was not the case, it is an early commemorative composition in both words and music, written within the king's lifetime.

St George. Invocation of, as well as the support of, St George at Agincourt is a strong feature of the early texts, the *Liber Metricus* and the *Gesta Henrici Quinti*.

In the modern age we are accustomed to officially orchestrated celebration of anniversaries. Commemoration of the victory on 25 October 1416, however, appears to have been private to Henry's chapel. The *Gesta* tells us that Henry, 'not unmindful of God's goodness, renewed praises to Him in the hymn *Te Deum laudamus*, solemnly chanted in his chapel before Mass'. Henry's constant emphasis on divine assistance at Agincourt is also reflected by various carols and motets written for his chapel which allude to the victory.[26]

A parliament had been called to commence on 19 October 1416 so that its session would include the first anniversary of Agincourt, although this was for political rather than commemorative reasons. The opening speech, given by Bishop Beaufort, mentioned the God-given victory as well as the high death and capture rates. Despite this success, 'the French, full of pride and thinking nothing of their defeat or weakness, have refused to reach any agreement'. This reminds us that Agincourt had not forced the French to the negotiating table. The prisoners were not politically important enough for the French crown to need to do so. Therefore Henry was obliged to go to war again for his just cause. As the chancellor announced, 'let us make war so that we might have peace, for the end of war is peace'.

At the March 1416 parliament Henry had simply requested that collection of the previous tax grant should be brought forward. Such funds had helped to pay for an army of 7,500 raised for three months to rescue Harfleur, achieving victory at the Battle of the Seine on 16 August 1415. Now in October 1416, as in November 1414, Henry needed a large grant on which to raise loans so that a second major invasion of France could be prepared. A double subsidy was granted but not without conditions. As Christopher Allmand points out, 'the shoe was now clearly beginning to pinch'.[27] There was a rebellion in Cheshire in September–October 1416 against collection of taxation.[28]

The 'Agincourt legacy' was part of this financial challenge. The campaign indentures had promised redemption of the jewels used for the second quarter's wages by 1 January 1417. This did not happen. Scarcely any campaign accounts had been settled by then and there were still many questions outstanding about wages, including basic matters such as the agreed start and end dates for the campaign. That the king finally was persuaded to give some answers to these matters on 6 March 1417 has much to do with pressure from those who had indented in the previous month to serve on his next campaign to France, which, as in 1415, was intended to last twelve months.[29]

It is in this context that the 'victory card' was revived towards the end of 1416 at the king's behest and with the support of Henry Chichele, archbishop of Canterbury. In December 1416 the Canterbury convocation agreed to a broad programme of commemoration for 25 October in future years. Orders to the clergy indicate that prayers were to be shared between Crispin and Crispinian, St John of Beverley, and other martyrs.[30] In contrast to the earlier elevation of the feast of St George, the wording of the December 1416 order invoked the battle explicitly: 'the gracious victory granted by the mercy of God to the English on the feast of the translation of the saint [St John of Beverley] to the praise of the divine name and to the honour of the kingdom of England'.

The banner of St John of Beverley had been taken by Edward I on his campaigns in Scotland. St John was a particular favourite of the Lancastrians: he had shown his approval for them by emitting oil from his tomb at the point of Henry Bolingbroke's landing in 1399, and again on the day of Agincourt. Convocation in April 1416 had already agreed special commemoration of his main saint's day (7 May). Henry had visited the shrine as prince in 1408 and was to do so again in 1421. His personal devotion was therefore consciously linked to the commemoration of the battle. It is possible that the orders also sought to channel popular recollections of Agincourt linked to the Crispins. The latter feature much in Latin jingles and in English poems, as well as in the English vernacular chronicles of the *Brut* tradition which are the closest we get to 'popular' works. The *Brut*, which took the story of England back to Trojan foundation myths, was the basis of several continuations in the fifteenth century. One version of the 1450s alludes to a poet who wrote, 'By Crispin the English race laid low many French'. After Henry V was dead, the link of the battle with St John of Beverley declined but the link to the Crispins persisted (although by the time of Shakespeare they had merged into one St Crispin).

It is hardly surprising that Henry should deliberately invoke the memory of Agincourt to encourage support for future expeditions. Every parliament from the victory until October 1419 included mention of the battle in the chancellor's opening speech.[31] In reporting the speech made in March 1416, the *Gesta Henrici Quinti* adds that the chancellor referred to three occasions on which God had made known his support for the English claim to France: the victory at Sluys, at Poitiers, and at Agincourt.[32] Agincourt was portrayed as a parallel to past victories. By October 1419, when Rouen and virtually all of Normandy was in Henry's hands, recent successes could be added: God had shown His support by 'the glorious victory over the French people at Agincourt' as well as by the conquest of Normandy. Significantly, however, the battle is not mentioned at all in parliamentary texts after Henry became heir and regent by the Treaty of Troyes. Henry's achievement at Troyes overtook all other successes. At the parliament of December 1420 the chancellor's speech brought to mind how Henry had recovered his royal rights in France and brought peace between the two nations.[33] A similar pattern is revealed in the use of an Agincourt herald. The office had been created by at least late February 1416, its use for overseas missions a means of bringing Henry's victory to mind on the international stage. The last known reference to 'Agincourt herald' dates to March 1419. The title was consciously dropped thereafter because of Henry's desire to appear an acceptable ruler, initially to the Normans and, after the Treaty of Troyes, to the French as a whole.[34]

Henry's emphasis on Agincourt as a divinely ordained victory is echoed in the earliest narratives. These were in Latin and were written by churchmen whose interest in, and understanding of, military and political causation was limited. The *Gesta Henrici Quinti* is considered the best early prose account because it was written by an eyewitness—a priest present on the campaign and on whose identity there has been considerable speculation.[35] Sometimes described as a campaign diary, it does indeed contain a chronologically arranged narrative of the whole expedition. Its account of Agincourt, from the eve to the end of the battle, takes up twelve of the ninety pages in the modern printing of the text. However, about half of this wordage is religious invocation. For instance, Sir Walter Hungerford's supposed wish for more men and the king's response is situated on the eve of battle, but this is simply a vehicle for the king to express his faith in God and for the author to link Henry to Judas Maccabeus. 'For those I have here with me are God's people whom he deigns to let me have at this time. Do you not believe that the Almighty, with these His humble few, is able to overcome the opposing arrogance of the French.' Invocations of Jesus, the Virgin Mary, and St George precede the English advance. During the battle the author and his fellow priests recite their prayers. At every point in the military narrative God is mentioned as the arbiter. The battle ends because the French have been utterly wasted 'at God's behest'. Before the listing of prisoners and dead, there is a long passage on God's anger against the French 'whom He has delivered up, indiscriminately, to flight, capture and the sword' through 'that little band of ours that was striving for justice'. In all of this Henry is supremely wise and God's chosen one.

To understand the *Gesta* we need to remember that the work is not simply an account of the 1415 campaign but provides a selective narrative of the reign from Henry's accession to the end of the parliament of October 1416. Taylor and Roskell suggested that the work was written between November 1416 and July 1417 with an 'immediate purpose... to justify the king's second French expedition and encourage support of it'.[36] If this is correct, who was the work intended to persuade? Its choice of language and constant emphasis on Henry's piety as well as on divine support indicate a clerical audience. That would suggest that the *Gesta* was written to encourage church support in the renewal of the war. There is strong evidence that the clergy were not happy with the king's repeated demands for clerical taxation.[37] In addition, the clergy had not been inspiring their congregations in the war effort as much as the king wished. On three occasions (August 1416, May 1417, and June 1417) the archbishop of Canterbury complained that both the clergy and laity were tepid in their participation in prayers and processions for English success.[38] We can see why it had been considered necessary to establish a new programme of religious commemoration for 25 October involving St John of Beverley and the Crispins, and to constantly remind the English of God's support for the king in his wars.

It has been suggested that the *Gesta* was written to justify Henry's aggression against France to the Council of Constance, a Europe-wide church assembly in process from 1414 to address the problem of the papal schism. Such a purpose would explain why Henry's monastic foundations, his defeat of Lollards, and the visit of Emperor Sigismund are included in the work. Sigismund came to England in the spring of 1416 to bring about peace between Henry and the French king for the sake of joint crusading action, but instead Sigismund agreed an alliance with Henry. The *Gesta* may have been written to vindicate that decision also, by showing the degree to which God was on Henry's side. Significantly, the work ends with a crusading vision: Henry had already triumphed twice (at Agincourt and at the Battle of the Seine), 'so may he triumph yet a third time [i.e. with further success in his forthcoming expedition to France], to the end that the two Swords, the sword of the French and the sword of England, may return to the rightful government of a single ruler, cease from their own destruction and turn as soon as possible against the unsubdued and bloody faces of the heathen'. In this context the wording of the killing of the prisoners is significant since it is expressed without any indication of royal agency:

But then, all at once, because of what wrathfulness on God's part no one knows, a shout went up that the enemy's mounted rearguard (in incomparable number and still fresh) were re-establishing their position and line of battle in order to launch an attack on us, few and weary as we were. And immediately, regardless of distinction of person, the prisoners, save for the dukes of Orléans and Bourbon, certain other illustrious men who were in the king's battle, and a very few others, were killed by the swords either of their captors or of others following after, lest they should involve us in utter disaster in the fighting that would ensue.

Was the wording chosen to distance the king from the decision? If the work was intended for the church's Council of Constance, was it anticipated that the killing of the prisoners might be an issue? This can only remain speculation. English arguments put forward at Constance for superiority over the French did not invoke the outcome of the battle or the divine support which it indicated for Henry.[39] The *Gesta* is undoubtedly a religious rather than a military interpretation of Agincourt. Its purpose was not to provide a narrative of the battle but rather to deploy the victory to enhance Henry's reputation and to encourage ecclesiastical support for his future ventures.

Since God was believed to control the affairs of men, it was easy to interpret events as God-given, even in battle. This had been a central theme in the presentation and reception of Agincourt in England all along. The *Gesta* emphasizes that it was the French who had caused the battle, sending heralds to Henry on 20 October to inform him that they intended to give battle before he reached Calais. Henry is made to accept this 'as an act of grace on God's part'.

The *Gesta* describes the deployment of the French as a large vanguard with squadrons of cavalry on the flanks 'to break the formation and resistance of the archers'. The English have three battles with 'wedges [*cuneos*]' of archers in between, protected by stakes; Henry has his troops move forward in order to stimulate the French into attack. The essential elements of the battle are established: the failed cavalry attack, the impact of the English arrows, and the piling-up of the French men-at-arms as they advance. The order to kill the prisoners follows when it is thought the French rearguard, implicitly not yet entered into the battle, is regrouping.

Existing only in two manuscripts, one a copy of the other, the *Gesta* was not widely known or circulated in the fifteenth century nor was it used by sixteenth-century historians.[40] It was only when it was translated by Harris Nicolas in his *History of the Battle of Agincourt* (1827) that it came to prominence but it has dominated Agincourt studies ever since, especially in the numbers game. Its 900 men-at-arms and 5,000 archers have been widely accepted as the size of the English army. No other narrative gives such low figures: the author may have deliberately underestimated for the sake of making Henry's victory all the greater, thereby emphasizing further divine assistance. For the French the author claims 60,000 'by their own reckoning', also saying that the vanguard was thirty times larger than the whole English force. This is mathematically challenging, to say the least. Totalling all the references to the French dead we come to 5,598, but with vagueness on the prisoners. Only 6 are named, with the addition 'and few others of gentle birth'. English losses add up to 14.

Better known in the fifteenth century was the *Liber Metricus de Henrico Quinto* of Thomas Elmham, which survives in nine manuscripts and was used by several other writers in the fifteenth century.[41] Elmham had been a monk at the Benedictine house of St Augustine's Canterbury but in 1414 became prior of Lenton (Notts). The *Liber's* complex Latin elegiac verse suggests a clerical audience. It may have been derived from the *Gesta* but it continues into 1418 with a bare narrative of Henry's conquest of Normandy. The battle account is shorter but follows the same troop deployments and actions. Again there is no direct involvement by Henry in the killing of the prisoners. As the *Gesta*, the French are numbered at 60,000 but the English are claimed at one point to be 7,000 strong. The *Liber* gives a higher total of French dead (9,310) and names 8 prisoners, giving English losses as York, Suffolk, and 'scarcely thirty others'. It includes elements not in the *Gesta*: the breaking of a fleuron from the king's helmet by a French axe, and in Henry's pre-battle speech, the king's assertion that he would not be ransomed but was ready to die in the conflict.[42] The *Liber* is more explicit that the narrowness of the field acted against the French and has the French weighed down by their armour, a comment not found in the *Gesta*.

Whilst the *Liber* emphasizes God's support for Henry, it is less overwhelmingly religious in tone than the *Gesta*, nor is it so xenophobic towards the French. The differences between the works indicate anecdotes and reminiscences circulating about the battle. The *Liber* recounts that the French threw dice on the eve of the battle for the prisoners they planned to take on the following day. The *Gesta* mentions the penalties which the king announced for those who did not keep silence in his host on the eve of battle. Both texts include the wounding of the king's youngest brother, Humphrey, duke of Gloucester, in the groin. This was a story which was to be expanded in later writings, encouraged no doubt by the political prominence of the duke as protector of the realm for the young Henry VI.

Another early account, again in Latin, is by Thomas Walsingham, a Benedictine monk who continued the tradition of the monastery of St Albans for historical writing, compiling several chronicles for the period from 1376 to his death in 1422. As he grew older he farmed out much of his writing to others, but he chose to compose the account of Agincourt himself.[43] Its exact date of composition is uncertain but it was definitely within Henry's lifetime. A basic narrative is present, indicating themes which were dominant in English knowledge of the battle. For instance, reference is made to the French strategy of destroying bridges to disrupt Henry's march from Harfleur to Calais, a comment we also find in the *Gesta*, the *Liber Metricus*, and the *Chronicle* of Adam Usk, also composed within Henry's lifetime.[44] This emphasized that it was the French who had forced a battle on Henry. Walsingham mentions Henry's preparations on the evening of 24 October and that on the day of the battle, he made the first forward move to goad the French into attack. English archers (although with no mention of stakes) drove back the French cavalry advance. Their arrows continued to have a damaging effect against the main French advance. The French were an easy target, felled like animals. Henry himself was supremely brave, 'offering an example in his own person to his men by his bravery in scattering the opposing battle lines with a battle axe'.

Walsingham does not mention the killing of the prisoners but does include the attack on the English baggage, ascribing this to 'French thieves' who took a royal crown, the showing of which was used to claim that Henry had been captured. Jubilation follows, with bells being rung and canticles sung, until the truth was learned 'from the downcast herald': 'their song was turned into one of lamentation and rejoicing was turned into mourning'. The *Gesta* (but not the *Liber Metricus*) also included the sacking of the baggage but mentioned simply that a sword and crown were taken. The inclusion of this story in these early narratives suggests that it was circulating in England soon after the battle, and that it was elaborated as a means of mocking continuing French presumption. In some late versions of the *Brut* chronicle, the truth of the outcome of the battle is revealed by the return to Paris of 'much wounded' soldiers. When the inhabitants asked them what had happened, they replied 'nos som to mors, we be killed and overthrown'.[45] The inclusion of their supposed actual words in French is a literary technique to create a spurious sense of veracity.

Although Walsingham's chronicles include narratives of other battles in the late fourteenth and early fifteenth centuries, his account of Agincourt is unique since it is the only one where he used classical quotations. There are at least thirteen, drawn from Virgil's *Aeneid*, Lucan's *Civil War*, the Latin *Iliad*, Persius' *Satires*, and Statius' *Thebais*. For instance, 'every dart finds its mark...no stroke was without wounds', used to describe the effect of English arrows, was taken from Statius. Walsingham's purpose was surely to place Henry on a par with classical heroes. He wished to portray Agincourt as special and distinct from any other battle he had narrated. This may reflect hindsight that Henry had gone on to further triumphs, events which were also included in Walsingham's chronicles, including a special work triggered by the conquest of Normandy (the *Ypodigma Neustriae*). Walsingham's narrative gives a strong sense of a victory against the odds, placing the French army at 140,000 and the English at 8,000, with 700 French prisoners and 3,069 French noble dead, very different figures from other early accounts. He heightens the sense of English weakness by claiming that soldiers had to eat nuts and dried meat since they had no bread. This reads like another story circulating in England, not simply from soldierly reminiscence but also an official line. The opening speech of the chancellor at the March 1416 parliament commented that the English army had been 'severely weakened from lack of food'. But as both narrators emphasize, God would always provide for those he favoured.

All of these early narratives place Henry centre stage. There were only two extensive narratives of the battle written in England after his death: these also focused on Henry, being Latin lives of the king—the *Vita Henrici Quinti* by the Italian Tito Livio Frulovisi and the anonymous *Vita et Gesta Henrici Quinti*, customarily called the *Pseudo-Elmham* from a now-discredited idea that it was written by Thomas Elmham. The dating and relationship of these Latin lives has been a matter of debate. The traditional view was that the *Vita et Gesta* was a later and expanded version of the *Vita* but historian David Rundle has argued that Livio's work was derived from the *Pseudo-Elmham*.[46] The *Vita* is customarily dated to 1438 which could mean that the *Pseudo-Elmham* belongs to the mid-1430s, and had been stimulated by the completion of Henry V's chantry chapel in Westminster Abbey which revived interest in the king. It includes long invocations on how fortunate England had been to have such a king, especially because of Agincourt: 'He it is who renews and increases with his industry the ancient fame of your nobility, which had been shrouded in the midst of oblivion . . . who brought terror to the enemy and crowned you with the glory of supreme victory. Delight in the Lord, O Britannia, who provided this most noble prince and monarch of your kingdom.' Emphasis on the glories of Henry's reign had been stimulated by reverses in English fortunes, especially the defection of the Burgundians to Charles VII in 1435.

Livio was in the employ of Humphrey, duke of Gloucester, Henry's youngest brother, who was protector of England during the minority of Henry VI. This has led to claims that the *Vita* was written to glorify the duke, a veteran of Agincourt, as well as to inspire the young king, who came of age in 1437 and to whom the work is dedicated, to emulate his father. Gloucester's wounding in the battle is mentioned in both Latin lives. The incident is expanded by mention of the king standing astride his brother to protect him.

Henry's unswerving emphasis that his victory at Agincourt was God-given is acknowledged, as is the point that it was the French who had forced a battle, but both works are more pragmatic because of their use of reminiscences from veterans such as Duke Humphrey. They provide fascinating details of contemporary military practice. At the commencement of the battle, for instance, they tell us that the English knelt and took a small piece of earth into their mouth (as a manifestation of their mortality) and that the heralds were ordered to their duties. The *Pseudo-Elmham* adds uniquely that Henry ordered them to do so without arms.

Both Latin lives emphasize Henry's generalship, mentioning, for instance, that he sent out scouts on the eve of the battle to study the location: 'from their report he derived information the better to enable him to array his forces'. Both mention last-minute negotiations between the French and English before the battle, something not found in narratives written closer to the battle but which have a ring of authenticity since they are common in other battles. Both describe the English army as having three battles, with their line, four men deep, stretching across the field. The French had a wider front because they had two cavalry wings 'like horns': the *Pseudo-Elmham* puts the French at twenty deep, the *Vita* thirty-one. Both mention the late arrival of the duke of Brabant and his improvisation of a standard. This is the first occurrence of this in narratives written in England. Being written in the 1430s, their accumulated knowledge of the French side of things was greater. They also include much more on the immediate aftermath, including discussions at Calais on whether the campaign should continue—surely the reminiscence of Humphrey and others present.

There are some interesting differences, however. For Livio all of the English had stakes, not simply the archers. He gives a lesser place to the archers. This reveals the predominant input of reminiscences of Humphrey and others who fought as men-at-arms. Although Livio admits that the English would have been thrown into disarray had not many French been killed or wounded by arrows, his main emphasis in fighting is of the fierce melee and he makes no mention of the involvement of the archers in this stage of the battle. By contrast, the *Pseudo-Elmham* has the archers continue to darken the air with their volleys during the melee.

Livio obfuscates Henry's role in the killing of the prisoners. The decision is collective: 'they feared that they might have to fight another battle against both the prisoners and the enemy so they put many to death'. In the *Pseudo-Elmham*, however, Henry's role is explicit: he sends a herald to enquire of the French whether they intended to continue the fight, since if they did, he would kill both them and the prisoners. No length is given for the battle in the *Pseudo-Elmham*, whereas Livio cites three hours. The *Gesta* has the battle lasting two to three hours. This may be an accurate reflection but it is interesting that the fourth-century *De re militari* of Vegetius, still the main military treatise used in the fifteenth century, defined a pitched battle as lasting three hours. Authos may have found it difficult to escape the battle topoi they knew from classical and biblical texts.

Save for the *Liber Metricus*, none of these Latin texts had a wide readership or circulation. A contrast can be drawn with the English *Brut* chronicles of which at least 172 manuscripts are known for the fifteenth century, although the earliest known is from 1430.[47] Many versions were produced later in the century. Accounts of Agincourt in all *Bruts* are eulogistic of Henry as the inspirer of his troops and as a valiant warrior. That he announced he would die rather than surrender is a common inclusion. Another story is unique to the *Brut*—a supposed exchange during the preparations for battle. The king asks what the time is. At the reply 'Prime', he comments that this is propitious since 'all England will be praying for us'. References to

St George are also more frequent in the *Brut* than in the Latin texts. In one late fifteenth-century version St George is seen in the air fighting for the English.

Other than the personal action of the king there is little reference to the activity of men-at-arms but the role of the archers is prominent in all *Brut* versions. Their skill is emphasized, with the anecdotal comment that they were 'shooting that day for a wager'. Much is made of the stakes which prevented the French in their plan to override the archers and caused them to pile up. In addition archers are explicitly said to have used the stakes to enter the melee. An increased emphasis on the duke of York—in later versions he rather than Henry orders the provision of stakes—reveals the impact of regime change in 1461 when his nephew, Edward IV became king. The killing of the prisoners is in most, but not all, versions of the *Brut*: where included it is at the behest of the king at hearing that a new force of French is poised to attack. The *Brut* tends to give very high numbers for the French—120,000—and 7,000 for the English. Low fatalities on the English side are also emphasized (commonly expressed as 26 to 28), in contrast with claims of French losses as high as 11,000–12,000. All English narratives exaggerate French numbers and losses, but this tendency is especially marked in all versions of the *Brut*.

One of the most frequently used images of the battle is found in a *Brut*, Lambeth Palace Library MS 6 (Fig. 7). This was a large-scale, finely produced manuscript covering the period from the Trojan Brutus to the 1436 siege of Calais by the Burgundians. It is associated with the Arundel family, later forming part of the library of John, Baron Lumley. Many copies of the *Brut* were owned by men of noble, gentle, or bourgeois status. It is therefore difficult to claim that the *Brut* represents a popular or lower-class view of the battle, but the quantity and distribution of the *Brut* manuscripts suggests that they reveal the most widespread view of the battle. The image in Lambeth Palace M6 needs to be treated with caution, however. Illustrations of other battles show the same forms and landscapes. Even Julius

Fig. 7. This representation dates to *c.*1450 and is found within a version of the English *Brut* chronicle now in Lambeth Palace Library MS 6. It places Agincourt in a landscape which is imagined rather than an accurate reflection of the terrain.

Caesar is portrayed as invading Britain with soldiers who wore the cross of St George and fighting with a lake and mid-fifteenth-century buildings in the background.[48]

Closely linked in content to the *Brut* were the *London Chronicles*, also in English but structured by the City's mayoral year. One version of the early 1440s draws on a poem about the battle, initially rendering it into prose but finally quoting it verbatim.[49] This and others separately surviving are the only sources which ascribe actions in the battle to individual lords and knights. The prose accounts of Agincourt, whether in Latin or English, rarely mention anyone by name other than the king and his closest associates, such as the duke of York. However, the references in the poems to individual actions are so generic that they were no more than literary creations: in the poem found in one of the *London Chronicles*, for instance, we have lines such as 'Huntingdon and Oxford both, were wonder fierce in that fight'. Personalities and speeches were invented for the French commanders too. These poems, written to be recited, continued the epic tradition. They focused on the deeds of the upper classes: the archers are only mentioned in passing.

All narrative accounts of Agincourt written in fifteenth-century England were triumphalist, but other kinds of sources reveal that the battle generated costs and disadvantages for the victors. After the death of Henry V veterans put forward petitions that they had never been fully paid for their service. Surviving indentees as well as the executors of those who had died, used the earliest possible opportunity—the first parliament of Henry VI in November 1422— to ask collectively for the jewels used as security for the wages of the second quarter to be redeemed. The new government issued a statute in their favour but there were further individual petitions after this point, such as that of Thomas Strickland in 1424, who had borne the banner of St George, and of the earl of Salisbury and the duke of Gloucester in 1427.[50] Henry's financial arrangements for the campaign, and his reluctance over the rest of his reign to divert funds away from his new ventures, had caused difficulties for captains. Salisbury and Gloucester noted that they had had to pay soldiers out of their own pockets, implying that they had not been able to raise funds on the royal jewels. Furthermore, the campaign had been brought to an end halfway through the second quarter even though, as their petition notes, 'they were then prepared to remain in the realm of France in accordance with the terms of their retaining'. (This implies that it was Henry who had decided to return home, a version of events contrary to that given in the Latin lives where he had been keen to continue but his lords had persuaded him otherwise.) The petitioners were out of pocket as well as being hassled by the Exchequer to settle their account. Many accounts were never terminated. The general pardon issued when

Henry VI came of age in 1437 allowed those still holding jewels simply to keep them.

Agincourt was not a profitable campaign for the majority of its participants. There were no war gains other than ransoms, and many ransoms proved difficult to collect as well as generating disputes. The initial euphoria on the capture of leading French lords, so much publicized in the immediate aftermath of the battle, subsided. The king was not keen to compensate those who had captured them even though the indentures required this.[51] Sir John Cornwall had handed over the count of Vendôme but the case was only settled after Henry's death when the prisoner was given back to Cornwall with all arrears and costs. The Treaty of Troyes changed the political situation fundamentally. Thereafter, it proved impossible to fix ransom terms. Two of the leading prisoners died in England, Boucicaut in 1421 and Bourbon in 1434. The duke of Orléans was released in 1440 but without real advantage to the English. In addition, English reversals, such as the capture of English lords at the Battle of Baugé in March 1421, led to some ransoms being offset against those owed by the English.[52]

Narratives of Agincourt written in England were closely tied up with the image of Henry V. During his lifetime he used the battle to encourage support for his future wars and to emphasize divine approval of his cause.[53] After his death, he and his victory stood as exemplars of model kingship, stimulating compilations of *Brut* and *London Chronicles* and poems.[54] Two Latin works containing accounts of Agincourt have as their intended recipient Henry VI: the *Vita Henrici Quinti* of Tito Livio and the *De Illustribus Henricis* of John Capgrave (*c.*1446–53). Capgrave strikes a chord when he writes, 'I shall remain silent about the archers and the stakes, how they were ordered, and also on many other related matters, for they deserve a lengthy explanation'.[55]

By the time Capgrave was writing, memories of the battle were fading and the Agincourt generation dying away. In the wake of the French victories of 1449–53, Agincourt was memorialized as a past golden age. It is no coincidence that the Commons of the parliament of November 1449, after Rouen had already surrendered to Charles VII, chose as Speaker Sir John Popham, the only MP present who had served at the battle. Although he declined the post, his election was a criticism of the failure of the government to maintain the conquests of Henry V. When the duke of Suffolk was impeached later in the same parliament for the failures in France, he cited in his defence the death of his father (Michael de la Pole sen.) at the siege of Harfleur and of his elder brother (Michael de la Pole jun.) at the battle. He could not mention his own presence since he had been invalided home from the siege. When a petition was put forward in the early 1450s to redeem the reputation of Humphrey, duke of Gloucester, who had been arrested for treason in 1447, dying within days afterwards, it began with mention of service at Harfleur and Agincourt: 'there grievously wounded unto the point of death'.[56]

A chronicle written in French shortly before the death in 1457 of Sir John Fastolf, a well-known participant in the wars, took the 1415 campaign as its starting point and continued with other English conquests to 1428.[57] Its authors were soldiers although neither can be shown to have been on the campaign. The text emphasized the cult-like status of Henry V, calling him the 'tresvictorieux prince' every time he is mentioned. Although Fastolf was invalided home from Harfleur, the short account of the campaign and battle may reflect reminiscences. This is the only text which tells us of knightings during the march to the Somme, and which says explicitly that the killing of the prisoners was the reason why so many nobles died at the battle.

Agincourt was a noble beginning but was seen in a wider context. The All Souls College which Archbishop Chichele founded in 1438 memorialized those who had died in the wars of the period as a whole, and did not mention Agincourt by name.[58] The window which Sir Thomas Erpingham sponsored in the Austin Friary in Norwich was in memory of the lords, knights, and esquires of Norfolk and Suffolk who had died without male issue. No building or memorial in England commemorated or invoked Agincourt. Brasses or tombs for around forty Agincourt veterans are known to survive. None mention the battle and only one the campaign—the brass of Sir John Phelip at Kidderminster which notes his death at Harfleur.[59] Agincourt was one of the memorable dates added to glosses in religious and secular texts but so too were other battles such as Shrewsbury.[60]

The secretary of Sir John Fastolf, William Worcester, wrote the *Boke of Noblesse* in the 1450s to inspire Henry VI to renew the war, subsequently at the change of dynasty readdressing it to Edward IV. Agincourt is recalled three times.[61] The first is within a list of English successes but with the added remark that many prisoners were taken 'that bene in remembraunce at this day of men yet living'. The second mentions Agincourt in the same breath as the loss of English lands, indicating a falling-away from past successes. The third occasion claims that at the battle Henry gave counsel not to seek treasure, jewels, gold, and silver 'but only to his right and to own worship'. This emphasized the popular notion that the final losses of 1449–53 had arisen out of individual greed and covetousness. Political divisions in England made any invasion impossible until 1475. On that occasion Edward IV chose to spend two nights at the field of Agincourt.[62] As far as we know, Henry V never revisited the battlefield after 1415.

France: The Accursed Day

How did the French seek to explain their defeat? What did Agincourt mean to them? Not surprisingly, French responses are closely entangled with the Armagnac–Burgundian contestation and with further English successes after 1415. John the Fearless, duke of Burgundy, had not been at the battle but two of his brothers and several supporters had given their lives there. By contrast, whilst the Armagnacs also had many dead, their leaders had been captured and taken to England. As a pro-Burgundian Parisian writer observed, 'it was widely said that those who had been taken prisoner had not been loyal or true to those who died in the battle'.[63] We saw at the beginning of this chapter Alain

Chartier's poetic response blaming the Burgundians. This was soon matched by *Le Pastoralet*, an allegorical poem produced in the early 1420s, which blamed the Armagnacs. The 'lions' (Burgundians) stood their ground whilst the 'wolves' fled the field. The absence of Duke John (Léonet) from the engagement was because he suspected treachery, not because of his fear of the enemy, for no one was braver than he or more feared by the English.[64]

As in England, all French accounts of the battle placed emphasis on the losses suffered by the nobility, whether by death or by capture. All narratives provide some names. The Burgundian chronicler Enguerran de Monstrelet lists 273 dead by name. Historians have used this as the main guide to the Agincourt dead but research indicates that other casualties were excluded in order to emphasize the heroism of the Burgundians at the battle.[65] The dislocation caused to individual families and to the northern regions of France, the area from which many casualties hailed, has yet to be studied in detail. We should not forget the burden on estates caused by ransoms, nor inheritance disputes arising out of deaths and by the problem of those missing believed dead. The killing of the prisoners exacerbated this problem since some seen alive after the first phase of the battle met their end in this action.

The high level of post-battle confusion is revealed by the first known royal order after the battle issued from Rouen on 29 October 1415. The French king was lobbied, 'even before we had certain knowledge of the outcome', by requests for appointment to offices of those rumoured but not proved to be dead.[66] This is the only evidence of an official response. The University of Paris held a mass on 12 November in memory of relatives who fell at the battle but there were no special religious services when the king returned to Paris on 29 November. This contrasted with the official mourning in the wake of Nicopolis (1396) and reflects the political uncertainties exacerbated by defeat at Agincourt.[67]

The *Histoire de Charles VI*, written by the Religieux (monk) of Saint-Denis (Michel Pintoin) provides the earliest written account of the battle which can be dated to 1417.[68] His explanations follow well-worn precedents in medieval responses to disasters: the French were defeated because of their sinfulness.[69] The Religieux developed this line at length in a separate chapter following his narrative of the battle, claiming debauchery, blasphemy, and luxury had turned God from the French. At the battle the nobility had been overconfident and full of self-pride, just as they had at previous French disasters (Courtrai, Poitiers, and Nicopolis). They had not taken the English seriously because they were smaller in number. The caution urged by older and wiser participants had been ignored by younger hot-heads. This again was a line found in accounts of earlier defeats, including Crécy. The *Chronique de Ruisseauville*, written in the 1420s or 1430s at a monastery close to Azincourt, adds a further point. The battle ought to have been fought on 24 October but the court-iers said it would be better to wait until the next day, 'and thus was their cause ruined'.[70]

The Religieux makes the specific point that too many wanted to be in the vanguard and that its huge size was to its disadvantage. Other accounts give the same interpretation with minor glosses. Pierre Fenin adds that there were so many nobles in the vanguard that the remain-ing parts of the army were leaderless. Another comment found in the Religieux and elsewhere is that the crossbowmen and other 'lower ranks' (such as the *gros varlets* mentioned by the *Chronique de Ruisseau-ville*) were not used in the battle because the nobility wanted to win it on their own. This folly, and the failure to wait for all troops to arrive, were seen as significant factors in causing the defeat.

Such explanations were commonly held and widely circulating but we should be cautious about considering them 'officially approved'. There are no royal texts providing explanations of the defeat. As with English texts, all French narratives agree that it was the French who chose to give battle, a stance which made authors keen to try to explain what had gone wrong. The Religieux's response was to men-tion the practical difficulties which the French faced, presumably reflecting reminiscences which he had picked up directly or indirectly.

One was bivouacking on the eve of battle in newly worked ground which became a quagmire. English and French accounts agree that it rained during the night but only French accounts use the weather to explain the defeat. With little sleep, and forced to march up to their knees in mud, the French were exhausted by the time they reached the enemy.

The Religieux also emphasizes cowardice in the face of English tactics. Mounted troops fled at the first volley of arrows, leaving their leaders stranded and blocking the forward advance of the vanguard by crashing into the centre of it. This spread 'terror and confusion'. English arrows obscured the sky and wounded a great number of the French, allowing the English to enter the melee with confidence. There, the French were too tightly packed to wield their weapons.

Significantly the *Chronique d'Artur de Richemont*, completed by his servant Guillaume Gruel in the late 1450s, also noted that the field was too restricted to fight with so many men, adding that Richemont had been pulled out from under the piles of dead to be taken prisoner. This comment was surely triggered by personal communication. Gruel tells us that in the middle of 1436 his master passed through Agincourt when returning from a journey to lands of the duke of Burgundy and that he 'explained to those who were with him how the battle had been'.[71] Gruel is the only chronicler of any nationality to claim that two men dressed like King Henry were killed, suggesting that Henry used doubles for his own protection.

The Religieux follows the comment on the tight packing of the French front lines by claiming that the divisions following in were terrified when they saw what was happening to the vanguard and simply fled the field. 'This ignominious flight brought upon them eternal opprobrium.' In this account, it was the manoeuvre of some to 'withdraw from the blind fury of the victors' which made Henry think the French were intending to regroup and which led to the killing of the prisoners.

The Religieux made little effort to name and shame. Although three of those commissioned to lead the cavalry to disperse the archers are named (Clignet de Brabant, Louis Bourdon, and the sire de Gaule), they are portrayed as being left stranded by their cowardly companions. Similarly the commanders of the vanguard, given by the Religieux as the count of Vendôme and Guichard Dauphin, were forced to retreat when they had lost too many men. Only the duke of Alençon, 'who until then had enjoyed a great reputation for wisdom', was assigned mild opprobrium for leaving the main body of the army to throw himself into the melee. The Religieux also draws comparison between the indisciplined conduct of the French soldiers of the period and the good order of the English. This is a theme found in several texts, even those written well after 1415. The civil war in France was an influence, especially in the light of the violent sack of Soissons by the Armagnacs in 1414. The way Henry V governed his subsequent French conquests generated further admiration for his leadership. The control of his army after the taking of Harfleur was noted and contrasted with the way French troops often behaved. This also influenced the advice which Jean de Bueil gave in the 1460s. Henry had won because he kept up the morale of his men, saying the overnight wait on 24 October would refresh them. The French, on the other hand, were forced to sleep in a muddy field and then to march to meet their enemy, which exhausted them.[72]

In his post-battle peroration, the Religieux emphasizes the damage caused by divisions in the kingdom. For Pierre Cochon writing in the early 1430s the division between Orléans and Burgundy was key: he adds that the duke of Burgundy had an agreement with Henry which he broke off immediately after the battle. Even if the accusation was unjustified, it reflected suspicions at the time and was still being mentioned when Thomas Basin wrote his chronicle in the early 1470s. An anti-Burgundian line is also seen in an anonymous chronicle which claims that only one lord from Flanders and Burgundy was at the battle: the lists of dead prove this was not the case. The *Chronique de Ruisseauville* claims that some thought Constable d'Albret (an Armagnac) had been killed at the battle by the (pro-Burgundian) Picards on suspicion of treason.

Other writers were keener than the Religieux to emphasize the folly of individuals. In the *Geste des nobles françois*, the duke of Bourbon was to blame for failing to wait for the Bretons to arrive before giving battle. For Perceval de Cagny, in the household of the duke of Alençon, it was the duke of Brittany's concern for his own interests which explained his non-arrival. Some writers name those to blame for triggering Henry's order to kill the prisoners. In French narratives there is never opprobrium against Henry for this act but only against those who caused it to happen. Self-criticism dominates French accounts alongside acceptance of military necessity and of English political dominance after 1420. For Pierre Fenin, Isambart d'Azincourt and Robert de Bournonville were to blame through their attack on the baggage; for the *Chronique de Ruisseauville* it was Clignet de Brabant by gathering men together for another assault on the English army. Clignet and others were also singled out as traitors by the Berry Herald for failing in the initial cavalry attack against the English and for fleeing the field. Jean Juvénal des Ursins, writing in the 1430s and 1440s but influenced by the Religieux on the desire of so many to be in the vanguard, is more specific on the division of opinion between the French commanders: Marshal Boucicaut and Constable d'Albret had urged caution but the dukes of Alençon and Bourbon had urged attack.

The military element in most of these accounts is thin. The writers were mainly clerics, although other than the Religieux they wrote in French. Much more detail is provided in accounts written by laymen. The *Chronique des ducs de Brabant* written in the mid-1440s by Emond de Dynter, secretary of Duke Anthony of Brabant, is interesting for its detail on the duke's response to letters sent by the French lords at Péronne on 19 October concerning their plans to fight the English. We see him raising troops in the towns of his duchy but then hearing on the morning of 25 October that battle was to be given that day. He rushed to reach Azincourt, improvising his armour, but was killed. For the Burgundian Ghillebert de Lannoy, reminiscing about the battle in later years, the arrival of the duke of Brabant prompted Henry's order to kill the prisoners. Lannoy had been wounded in the first stage of the battle and lay with the dead until pulled out by the English. He was taken to a house with ten to twelve other prisoners. When the king feared a new attack, the house was set on fire but Lannoy managed to crawl out only to be recaptured and taken to England, where he was put to ransom by Sir John Cornwall.[73]

Two Burgundian chroniclers were also present at the battle. Jean de Waurin (or Wavrin) whose father and half-brother were killed in the battle, claimed to have been present on the French side aged 15. He compiled his chronicle in the 1450s and 1460s. Jean Le Fèvre, who completed his in the 1460s, was mentioned by Waurin as present, aged 19, at the battle but he was a non-combattant who accompanied the English as a heraldic observer from Harfleur to the battle. In 1431 Le Fèvre became king of arms of the Burgundian Order of the Golden Fleece.

The chronicles of Waurin and Le Fèvre provide the military detail lacking in other accounts but we cannot assume this was based on their presence at the battle. For the majority of their narrative they simply copied the *Chronique* of Enguerran de Monstrelet, a work already completed in 1447 when it was presented to Duke Philip of Burgundy as a continuation of the *Chroniques* of Jean Froissart.[74] Monstrelet's *Chronique* exists in several copies, some illustrated (see Fig. 8).[75] The military detail may have come to Monstrelet from other informants. The relationship between the accounts of Monstrelet, Waurin, and Le Fèvre remains problematic. All three mention Sir Thomas Erpingham throwing a baton in the air but only Monstrelet and Waurin give his cry, *necieque/nestroque* (possibly meaning 'now strike'), and only Waurin glosses it with 'which was the signal to attack'. All three have Henry after the battle enquiring the name of the nearby castle and saying that 'as all battles ought to take their name from the nearest fortress, village or town where they happened, this battle from henceforward and for ever more will be called the battle of Agincourt'. The story is unique to their accounts; whether it is true is impossible to know. Only Monstrelet, however, mentions the presence of the French herald Mountjoye at this juncture. We can detect occasions when

Fig. 8. This representation dates to the 1470s and is found within a copy of the chronicles of Enguerran de Monstrelet in the Bibliothèque nationale de France. It imagines both armies as similar in composition and appearance, even giving the French a large number of longbowmen.

the two battle participants drew on their own experiences. Le Fèvre's presence with the English army explains his unique comment, echoing the *Gesta*, that Henry lined up his men and had them kneel to pray on 24 October, thinking that battle would be given. Le Fèvre and Waurin clearly exchanged information: they are the only French writers to tell us that heralds were sent from Péronne to Henry on 20 October to assign a place of battle.

All three Burgundian writers claim the French had 50,000 men at the battle. For Monstrelet and Waurin this was six times the English army, for Le Fèvre three times. Monstrelet has 2,000 men-at-arms and 13,000 archers on the English side, Waurin and Le Fèvre 900–1,000 and 10,000. All emphasize the importance of the English arrow storm in disrupting the French attack. 'In the opinion of the French it was precisely what injured the most their enemies which assured the English of victory, especially the continuous way in which they had rained down on our men a terrifying hail of arrow shot.' The value of archers in the melee, through their lead-covered mallets, is also emphasized in all three chronicles, along with the claim that Henry sent 200 archers secretly to a meadow near Tramecourt behind French lines, 'so that when the French marched forward, they could fire on them from the side'. Waurin and Le Fèvre add a perplexing remark: 'I have heard and had certified as true by a man of honour who was there that day in the company of the king of England that nothing like this happened.' Did they say this because an attack from the rear would be considered an abuse of military conduct or simply because in a battle no one knew quite what had happened?

All three ascribe the killing of the prisoners to Henry's fear of the French regrouping. However, Monstrelet follows this with a comment that John the Fearless later imprisoned those deemed responsible for the attack on the baggage (Robinet de Bournville and Isembart d'Azincourt). This juxtaposition caused confusion when Monstrelet's account was used by sixteenth-century writers since it made the attack on the baggage appear to link to the killing of the prisoners. The pro-Burgundian leanings of all three chroniclers are apparent throughout, not least in giving examples of heroic deeds performed by men within the Burgundian group. Waurin and Le Fèvre give detail of a suicidal attack on Henry himself by eighteen men under the banner of the sire de Croy, claiming they had all taken an oath before the battle to carry out this endeavour. They blamed the Armagnac Clignet de Brabant for failing to have enough cavalry to override the English archers. Waurin and Le Fèvre judiciously describe the men who regrouped and triggered the killing of the prisoners as 'French, Bretons, Gascons, Poitevins and others', omitting any mention of Burgundian areas.

That they were writing after Duke Philip of Burgundy had abandoned the English in 1435 explains why they all recount how Duke

John had prevented his son (then count of Charolais) from participating in the battle. His absence was a matter of embarrassment for Philip now he was a loyal Frenchman. Monstrelet adds that it was 'Philip of Charolais' who organized the burial of the French dead. The accounts of Duke Philip's receiver-general in 1431 note a payment to Monsieur de Berthelon, his councillor and confessor, 'for the mass which has been said weekly at Lille since the Battle of Agincourt; after the mass the Passion has been read'.[76] This suggests the commemoration began under Duke John. The pro-dauphinist chronicler Jean Juvénal des Ursins claimed that Duke John sent a defiance once Henry reached Calais because of the death of his brothers, the duke of Brabant and the count of Nevers, adding that Henry replied that if the duke came to Boulogne on 15 January he would show him, by the confessions of prisoners, that Nevers had been killed by the French not the English.[77] The Burgundian chronicles do not include this story and the truth of it must be doubted but it shows the suspicions and rumours circulating even twenty years or more after the battle.

Just as the pro-Burgundian stance of Monstrelet, Waurin, and Le Fèvre is apparent, so too we see the effect of the revival of French fortunes by mid-century. Although later writers never ceased to see Agincourt as a disaster or to blame French folly, after 1450 there is a tendency for narratives to increase the size of the English army. In the *Chronique d'Artur de Richemont*, written in the late 1450s or early 1460s, the English, at 11,000–12,000, outnumber the 10,000 French. The Berry Herald (1450s) also puts the French at 10,000 but the English higher, at 1,500 knights and 15,000–16,000 archers. In texts of this period French mortality rates tend to decrease and those of the English to increase.

By 1453 the English had been driven out save for Calais. A French text of 1458–61 admitted that the English had been victorious at Agincourt and at other engagements but that, at the end of the day, the French had the conquest and victory. Besides, the author noted, the English tended to forget that they lost battles too. He pointed to parallels with Hannibal who won battles but was eventually defeated by the Romans.[78] This sense of recovery, which revived French pride,

Fig. 9. This representation dates to 1484 and is found within the *Vigiles du roi Charles VII* (Bibliothèque nationale, MS français 5054), a celebratory poem by Martial d'Auvergne on the life of this French king who eventually succeeded in booting out the English from most of their French possessions.

is apparent in the *Vigiles de Charles VII à neuf psaumes et neuf leçons* by Martial d'Auvergne, dated to the 1480s–90s.[79] The work contains another famous image of the battle featuring prisoners being led away with their wrists tied (see Fig. 9). The purpose of the work was to celebrate the recovery of France under Charles VII. To this end, it also contained many images of Joan of Arc's successes and of the entry of Charles to Rouen in November 1449. In the French psyche, these events redeemed the disaster of Agincourt.

4

'Alarms and Excursions'

The Enduring Influence of Shakespeare's Agincourt

The rehanging of the funeral achievements of Henry V in West-minster Abbey in 1971 was accompanied by Lord Olivier reciting the 'St Crispin's Day' speech from Shakespeare's *Henry V* (Act 4 Scene 3).[1] For many, Shakespeare's play *is* Agincourt, and Lawrence Olivier's film of the play, premiered on 22 November 1944 six months after D-Day, is the quintessential portrayal of the battle and of the king. Under such circumstances it is easy to see why it was rumoured, incorrectly, that Olivier's hands were used as the model for the missing hands on Henry's effigy in Westminster Abbey. Olivier's film is the single most important shaper of modern perceptions of Agincourt. It was the first time that the battle had reached a mass audience.

The dedication of the film, proclaimed after the opening titles, linked the present to the past: 'to the Commandos and Airborne Troops of Great Britain, the spirit of whose ancestors it has been humbly attempted to recapture in some ensuing scenes'. History was being put to a practical purpose, but what history was this? The film was produced more than five centuries after Shakespeare had penned his play. *Henry V* is believed to date to 1599 and may have been the first play performed at the newly built Globe Theatre. The play was written 184 years after the actual battle. This was an imagined Agincourt, influenced by the events and ideas of the late sixteenth century. There has been much discussion on the context of the play as well as how its performance in subsequent centuries was modified by changing tastes and audience expectations. This is a fascinating story, as we shall see in this chapter.

Shakespeare used Raphael Holinshed's *Chronicles of England, Scotland and Ireland* (1577, 1587) as a source. These printed works, more properly seen as the production of a team than an individual, were the most widely read histories of their period, providing a complete historical narrative from earliest times.[2] Their account of the battle reflected the state of knowledge of the literate community in the late sixteenth century. Therefore, to understand how they portrayed the battle, we need to examine the sources of their information. How, if at all, were they informed by works written in the immediate aftermath of the battle? What direct or indirect lines can be detected between 1415 and 1599?

Sixteenth-Century Histories and the Battle of Agincourt

The development of printing from the late fifteenth century onwards plays an important part in this story. When Caxton included an account of Agincourt in his *Cronycles of England* (1480) and his *Continuation of the Polychronicon* (1482) he simply used the basic narrative found in the *Brut* chronicle tradition of the fifteenth century.[3] His choice was not surprising since there were so many manuscript copies of the *Brut* in existence. He followed the numbers given in the majority of *Brut* versions: the French at 120,000, of whom 11,000 were slain and captured, and the English at fewer than 7,000, with 26 dead. Other salient elements of the battle account in the *Brut* are present. With a loud invocation of God and St George Henry ordered the advance. The French moved forward, but 'God and our archers' made them stumble. The stakes caused the French to fall over and pile up. The men-at-arms and archers then laid on with weapons and stakes, with the king fighting manfully. When Henry heard that a new French division was regrouping, he ordered the killing of the prisoners, which continued until the French withdrew. Whilst we cannot speak of a mass readership in these early days of printing, access to knowledge was greater than in the days of manuscripts alone. Therefore this account, with its emphasis on the impact of arrows and on royal leadership, encapsulates the 'standard' view of the battle around the turn of the century.

Caxton drew solely on the *Brut*. The next printed account, in Robert Fabyan's *New Chronicles of England and France* (1516), also looked to past precedents by following the format of the *London Chronicles*, where each section was preceded by the names of the City officers elected for the year.[4] Fabyan's battle follows the same basic line, including the killing of the prisoners, but there are some differences. For instance, for Fabyan only the archers were ordered to have stakes whereas in the *Brut* it tended to be the whole army. Whilst Caxton, following the *Brut*, mentions French riotous behaviour in the camp on the eve of battle, Fabyan comments instead on the prayerfulness of the English camp. He gives the French army as 40,000 strong, of which 10,000 were cavalry, figures not found in any known fifteenth-century source. He gives the number of prisoners as 2,400 to which he adds an interesting gloss, 'as witnesseth the book of mayors'. This is an apparent reference to the records of the City of London but, as yet, the actual source Fabyan refers to has not been identified.

Fabyan's account contains the first evidence of the use in England of French sources, in this case the work of Robert Gaguin (1423/33–1501).[5] Following the *Brut* tradition, Fabyan puts the size of the English army at 7,000 but adds that Gaguin spoke of 1,500 spearmen and 18,000 yeomen and archers. He notes also that English writers speak of 10,000 French dead but that Gaguin gives 4,000 men of name 'besides others which he numbered not', an indication that Fabyan was trying to explain why there were differences in the figures. He also includes a description of the archers' loose clothing which facilitated their drawing 'bows of great strength' and shooting 'arrows of a yard long, beside the head'. This is not found in any fifteenth-century English text and is most likely inspired by French tradition. The *Chronique* of Monstrelet, for instance, mentions the appearance of the archers with 'their hose loose round their knees'. Fabyan also claims that when Henry ordered the killing of the prisoners, it was the (already captured) duke of Orléans and his fellow lords who sent word, 'by licence of the king', to the French, with the result that they withdrew. No English account includes this story and its inclusion may reflect French influence or else Fabyan's desire for a rational explanation. This also explains why he includes a rout after the battle, even though earlier English accounts do not mention it. Routs were an action which an early sixteenth-century writer would have expected in a battle situation.

Fabyan's work is the first example of the mingling of English and French sources to establish a narrative, thereby marking a transition from chronicle to history. The printing of Edward Hall's *Union of the Two Illustre Families of Lancaster and York* in 1542 is a second significant stage in this process.[6] Hall's work had a great influence on Holinshed to the extent that the latter's account of Agincourt follows that of Hall almost verbatim. Hall's work was shaped by the political turmoils of the fifteenth century and their redemption under the first two Tudor kings. Eight reigns are covered. That of Henry V is presented under the title 'the victorious acts of Henry V'. Hall's narrative begins with the duel between Henry Bolingbroke and Thomas Mowbray in 1398 which triggered events culminating in the deposition of Richard II in 1399. Via Holinshed, this duel was exactly the point that Shakespeare used to start his play *Richard II*, written in 1595.

Hall includes as a preface a long list of the Latin, French, and English sources, both printed and manuscript, which he had consulted. These include Polydore Vergil, Monstrelet, the *Chroniques de Normandie*, Hardyng (printed in 1543), Fabyan, the *London Chronicles*, Caxton, and Basset. It was from Basset's Chronicle (now College of Arms MS M9) that Hall must have drawn Henry's dubbing of knights at Pont-Saint-Maxence during the march along the Somme, since this is not known in any other English or French source. The same chronicle was certainly a major source for Hall's account of campaigns in France between 1417 and 1429, especially for the long lists of appointments to captaincies and battle presences which are a characteristic of Hall's narrative for those years. Basset's account of Agincourt, however, was brief and not a major influence on Hall's lengthy narration of the battle, which, at almost 7,000 words, was the longest written to date.

It has been claimed that Hall drew heavily on Polydore Vergil's *Anglia Historia*, a work begun under commission from Henry VII and completed in 1513 but not printed until 1534. However, Polydore's account of the battle, originally in Latin, is much shorter than that of Hall, stretching to just over 3,000 words in translation. Polydore gives Henry's army as 2,000 cavalry and 13,000 archers. He does not provide a total for the French army but claims that there was 3,000 cavalry in the first line and that 10,000 perished, with almost as many taken prisoner. His comments on the English dead are interesting and reflect the rationalization which we would expect of an Italian humanist scholar of the early sixteenth century. 'If we believe those who recount miracles scarcely a hundred perished . . . I am sorry not to be of their opinion for when the battle was hard fought for more than three hours, it is undoubtedly fair to believe that the English who were involved in armed conflict also received wounds of their own.'[7] As a result, Polydore inclined to believe writers who placed the English dead at 500–600.

Polydore was influenced not only by his reading of battle narratives in classical texts but also by his understanding of contemporary military practice. For him, all of the archers were on the right flank of Henry's army, with the cavalry on the left and around the sides. The stakes formed fences behind which the infantry stood. The cavalry were placed on the flanks beyond the stakes. 'Even now the English keep this method of forming their battle array,' he tells us, 'although other machines [i.e. field artillery] have been invented for this purpose.' Polydore's solution of how the English could make a forward advance despite the stake wall is seen in his comment that 'to certain soldiers of the common sort Henry gave the task of refixing the stakes as chance and the situation required, and fixing them again at that point of the location to which the infantry moved in the fighting'.

For Polydore the battle began at midday, and lasted for three hours. This timing reflected the influence of Vegetius' *De re militari* where three hours was the length for a pitched battle. Polydore assigned the same length to the Battle of Bosworth in 1485. Polydore claims that, at the signal 'given at the same point of time from both sides', the armies rushed towards each other. He does not follow the fifteenth-century line that Henry had to move first to goad the French into an attack but he nonetheless sees English archers as damaging the French cavalry and infantry and also joining the melee: 'a good part of the English archers, having quickly thrown away their bows, as is their custom, and taken up the daggers and swords which they always have ready to hand, rushed at a great pace into the advancing enemy'. The French on the right strove to counter this 'with their shields held before them'. This again betrays classical influences since shields do not feature in the medieval narratives and were not carried by men-at-arms in 1415.

For Polydore it was the attack on the baggage by Robert de Bourne-ville and the French cavalry which made Henry afraid the French were regrouping and which triggered the order to kill the prisoners. The source of this must have been a French account since this explanation is not found in any fifteenth-century English narrative. Polydore made significant use of Enguerran de Monstrelet's *Chronique*, which had been printed by Anthoine Vérard in France in 1500 and 1508.[8] This also explains Polydore's mention of divided opinions amongst the French at Rouen on the best course of action and on deployment at the battle.

Hall's claim that Henry's vanguard on the right was made up wholly of archers is derived from Polydore, but Hall also drew directly and intensively on Monstrelet. Indeed, the real importance of Hall's narrative is that it brought Monstrelet's account of the battle, in detail and in English, to a wider audience. Readers were alerted to elements of Henry's supposed actions which had never before appeared in English accounts. These included two significant claims, that Henry had sent 200 archers to a meadow behind the French lines, and that Sir Thomas Erpingham threw a baton in the air to signal the attack. Erpingham is not mentioned in any English chronicle or in Polydore Vergil's narrative. There is some irony that this commander, Shakespeare's 'greybeard', who features prominently in popular views of Agincourt today, became known in England, thanks to a French source, over a hundred years after the battle.

Hall tells us that arrows from these 200 archers and those 'in the forefront' 'so galled the horses and so cumbered the men of arms that the footmen durst not go forward . . . so at the first joining, as the Frenchmen were clearly discouraged, so the Englishmen were much cheered'. Like Polydore, Hall follows Monstrelet on the entry of the archers into the melee but adds the more contemporary 'bill' to the list of weapons. In describing the stakes he glosses Polydore: 'this device of fortifying an army was at this time first invented but since that time they have imagined caltraps, etc.'. The attack on the baggage by Bourneville is similarly the cause of the king's order to kill the prisoners, but Hall adds the involvement of Rifflart de Clamas and Isambert d'Azinourt from Monstrelet. Hall also uses Monstrelet's account of the king's interview with Mountjoye herald which establishes the name of the battle by reference to the nearby castle. This quintessential tale of Agincourt, as with Erpingham, was therefore introduced to English audiences only in the 1540s.

For Hall, the English army comprised '2,000 horsemen and 8,000 archers, billmen and of all sorts'. The French vanguard contained '8,000 healms of knights and esquires, 4,000 archers and 1,500 crossbows', with two wings of 1,600 and 800, and a further 800 'to break the shot of the English'. These figures were taken by Hall from Monstrelet's chronicle. The 'middle ward' (again note the sixteenth-century terminology) contained as many as in the first battle, and in the rearguard were all the rest. Many names of French commanders are given—the first time most of these men would have been known to an English audience.

Oddly, Hall has the duke of Exeter commanding the rearguard. Since Holinshed simply copied Hall this explains why Shakespeare's play has Exeter present at Agincourt when in fact he had been appointed captain of Harfleur and had remained in the conquered town. But whilst Polydore has the duke of Clarence present at the battle, Hall does not: he had here followed another source which noted that the king's eldest brother had been invalided home from the siege.

What is most striking about Hall's account is his invention of lengthy pre-battle speeches for Henry, for the French constable, and for the herald Mountjoye after the battle. That for d'Albret is a marvellous example of creative writing, imagining the French national stereotype of the Englishman:

> for you must understand, ere keep an Englishman one month from his warm bed, fat beef and stale drink, and let him that season taste cold and suffer hunger, you will then see his courage abated, his body wax lean and bare, and ever desirous to return to his own country . . . Such courage is in Englishmen when fine weather and victuals follow them.

Hall's imagination runs riot on other occasions for the sake of verisimilitude. We see this in his fabrication of discussions within the French camp about what they would do when they captured Henry, and on the variety of means used by the English to kill the prisoners: 'sticked with daggers, some were brained with pollaxes, some were slain with mails, others had their throats cut and some their bellies paunched'.

The use of Monstrelet by Hall is also evident in lesser emphasis on divine intervention than in English sources. None the less, Henry's acknowledgement of his debt to the Almighty is mentioned and there is an envoi at the end of the narrative:

> This battle may be a mirror and glass to all Christian princes to behold and follow, for king neither trusted in the puissance of his people, nor in the fortitude of his champions, nor in the strength of his barded horses, nor yet in his own policy, but he put in God (which is the corner stone and immovable rock) his whole confidence, hope and trust . . . and He sent him this glorious victory, which victory is almost incredible if we had not read in the Book of Kings that God likewise had defended and aided them that only put their trust in Him and committed themselves wholly to His governance.

The few differences between Hall and Holinshed need mention since they link to Shakespeare's play. Holinshed dropped the envoi and the invented speeches (which is significant when considering Shakespeare's own creation of speeches). This largely explains why Holinshed's account is 2,000 words shorter than Hall's. Although Holinshed follows Hall's numbers for the French he says nothing on the size of the English army. He includes new elements which derive from additional sources, as the marginal notes of his text indicate. Use of Fabyan explains inclusion of a comment on the looseness of the English archers' clothing. Holinshed (and hence Shakespeare in Act 4 Scene 2, line 59) mentions the late arrival of the duke of Brabant which is omitted by Hall. There are also novelties, such as that the French cast away their armour on fleeing.

The most notable difference is Holinshed's inclusion of the wish of one of Henry's captains for more men, which was taken up by Shakespeare to create one of the most famous scenes of the play, triggering the St Crispin's Day speech:

> 'I would to God there were with us now so many good soldiers as are at this hour within England!' The king answered: 'I would not wish a man more here than I have. We are indeed in comparison to the enemy but a few, but, if God of his clemency do favour us, and our just cause (as I trust he will) we shall speed well enough.'

This story came to Holinshed through John Stowe who had lent him a copy of the *First English Life of Henry the Fifth*, a work written in 1513–14 but which existed only in manuscript. The *First English Life* drew on Tito Livio's *Vita Henrici Quinti* as well as Monstrelet. We shall return to the importance of this work shortly.

Holinshed also drew on Stowe's own work which was to be published in the latter's *Chronicles of England* (1580) but he did not accept all of Stowe's ideas. For instance, Holinshed chose to follow Hall's narrative that the killing of the prisoners was triggered by the attack on the camp. Stowe, following the *First English Life*, attributed it to the threat of the French regrouping. Holinshed also ignored Stowe's story of

English soldiers kneeling and taking a piece of earth into their mouths before the advance.

Sixteenth-century narratives were much influenced by the selection policy of their authors. Also important were Anglo-French relations. England and France were still enemies and English kings still called themselves kings of France. Henry VII had gone to war in 1492; Henry VIII in 1513, 1523, and 1544. It has been claimed that Henry VIII sought to emulate Henry V. Some historians even suggest that he was obsessed by him.[9] Henry VIII had declared soon after his accession that he would assault the king of France. In 1513 he landed in Calais with an army of 30,000. This was not an independent English campaign, however, but part of a joint attack with the Emperor Maximilian on France. The increase in army size was in response to similar trends elsewhere in Europe. The English army still had a high number and proportion of archers, in fact more in 1513 than in 1415: during his time at Calais, Henry VIII entertained ambassadors by displaying his own prowess with the longbow.[10] But his army had a wider array of infantry in terms of billmen and gunners, as well as German mercenaries. Henry won a small-scale cavalry engagement with the French at the Battle of the Spurs near Thérouanne on 16 August 1513, only 22 kilometres (13.7 miles) to the north-east of Agincourt.

Historians have not emphasized the geographical proximity of Henry VIII's campaign but have based their argument on the anonymous *First English Life of Henry the Fifth*.[11] This was largely an English translation of Tito Livio's *Vita Henrici Quinti* but the author also drew on Monstrelet and Caxton as well as reminiscences of James Ormond, fourth earl (1392–1452), transmitted by the earl's descendants. Since Ormond served on the 1415 campaign, this could have provided a participant's viewpoint but none of the Agincourt narrative in the *First English Life* was based on these reminiscences.[12] At the end of the *First English Life* the author quotes four lines which he claims were on the standard of the earl of Stafford at the Battle of Agincourt. However, no one of that name was at the battle: this story seems to belong to the Battle of Shrewsbury of 1403 where Edward, earl of Stafford died.

In the prologue of the *First English Life* the author claims that he had been moved to write the work so that Henry VIII,

> hearinge, seeing or readgine the vertous manners, the victorious conquests and the excellent sages and wisdoms of the most renowned prince in his daies, Kinge Henry the Fifte, his notable progenitor...his grace maie in all things concerning his person and the reigement of his people, conforme himself to his life and manner...and...by knowledge and sight of this pamphile should partly be provoked in his said war to ensue the noble and chivalrous acts of this so noble, so virtuous and so excellent a prince, which so followed, he might the rather attain to like honour, fame and victory.

This wording indicates that the work had not been commissioned by the king but it has not stopped some historians claiming that it was.[13] In this they have assumed that the work was written before Henry's campaign and served as a stimulus to it. In fact, the next sentence reads as follows:

> But, praised be God, it is nowe much better for us, for that mortall war and hatefull discension is nowe chainged into an amiable, toworde, and peace honourable, and also profitable (as wee believe both to the kings Highness and to this Realme).

This shows that the author was too late to inspire the king. Although he had *started* the work in time, it was not ready for presentation until after Henry had come to a peace settlement with the French in 1514. The work exists only in two seventeenth-century manuscript copies and we cannot know whether Henry ever received it or, if he did, what he made of it. It cannot be used as proof of the king's wish to emulate Henry V. That 'proof' is that Henry VIII renewed invasions of France, but so had Henry VII. The influence of the *First English Life* on other writers was not extensive save for the fact that John Stowe had a copy which was used in the writing of Holinshed's *Chronicles*, most significantly in the story of the English captain who expressed a wish for more men.

There is a handful of other early sixteenth-century invocations of Agincourt. The itineraries of John Leland (1538–43) include two references.[14] The first is linked to the burial place of the duke of York, in the middle of the quire at Fotheringhay parish church, with an effigy on a tomb chest. The duke's request to have command of the vanguard and his death in the battle is noted, as well as the fact that his body was brought back for burial. What is more intriguing is Leland's transmission of a popular belief about the duke's size: 'in the foreward where be much hete and y thronged, being a fat man, he was smouldered to death'. A second entry arising out of Leland's visit to Farleigh Hungerford leads to the statement that 'there is a common saying that one of the Hungerfords built this part of the castle by the praye of the duke of Orleance whom he had taken prisoner'. This suggests an oral tradition linked to Sir Walter Hungerford. The *Gesta Henrici Quinti* named him as the captain who asked for more men. He was present at the battle and held a number of prisoners, but there is no evidence that he was the captor of the duke of Orléans.

In connection with the religious change of Henry VIII's reformation we find an interesting reference to Agincourt. Richard Morrison, in 1538–9, urged Henry VIII to inaugurate annual triumphs against the pope.[15] He cited as a precedent the celebrations of Agincourt at Calais:

> For the victory that God gave to your most valiant predecessor, King Henry the Fifth, with so little a number of his countrymen against so great a multitude of the Frenchmen at the battle of Agincourt, your retinue at your noble town of Calais and others over there yearly make a solemn triumph, going in procession, lauding God, shooting guns, with the noise and melody of trumpets and other instruments, to the great rejoicing of your subjects who are aged, the comfort of those who are able, the encouraging of young children.

It has not proved possible to know how far back in time these Agincourt processions went. They may even have been a recent 'tradition' stimulated by Henry VIII's invasion of 1513.

In October 1549 John Coke, who had been appointed clerk of the Staple at Calais in 1536, wrote a fictional debate between the heralds of England and France, stimulated by sight of a mid-fifteenth-century French version noted in Chapter 3.[16] In his desire to emphasize English superiority, Coke mentioned Agincourt along with all of the other English victories of the fourteenth and fifteenth centuries. 'The myghty and puissant conqueror kyng Henry the fyfte, with nyne thousand Englyshemen wan a mighty battayle at Agyncourte in Normandye, against a hundred thousande Frenchemen.' The deaths of the dukes of Bar, Lorraine, and Alençon and 1,500 knights are noted along with the capture of the dukes of Orléans, Brittany (an error), and Bourbon, the earls of Vendôme and Eu, the marshal of France, 'with many other lords and knights'. It is important to note that it was not only Agincourt which was singled out as an example of an English victory against the odds. Coke mentions the Battle of Poitiers 'byng ten Frenchmen against one Englyshman'. For Crécy a mortality of 80 barons, 1,200 knights, and 100,000 Frenchmen is claimed. The wars of Henry VIII are included as evidence of continuing success. This suggests that links with the past were being drawn in men's minds as a result of recent invasions of France.

Shakespeare's Agincourt Created

There were no more formal wars with France after 1544. Anglo-French hostilities were not a direct stimulus to Shakespeare's *Henry V* but longer-term memory of them contributed to the continuing sense of English patriotic endeavour. By the time *Henry V* was written, Shakespeare had already produced three plays concerning Henry VI (1590) as well as *Richard III* (1592). Given that *Richard II* (1591) and the two parts of *Henry IV* had also been written (1597), *Henry V* followed naturally. Agincourt was bound to be a key element within it. Battles had featured in many plays already. Crécy, Neville's Cross, and Poitiers were all in *Edward III* (1592–4), a play in which Shakespeare certainly had a hand. History plays were very popular in this period, fanned by patriotic fervour stimulated by the Armada (1588). In the same year as Shakespeare's *Henry V*, for instance, we find a two-part play on Edward IV by John Haywood as well as a play concerning Sir John Oldcastle.

Shakespeare's *Henry V* was not the only, or indeed the first, play to be written on the king. An anonymous play, *The Famous Victories of Henry V: Containing the Honourable battle of Agincourt*, was entered in the Stationers' Register on 14 May 1594 but is believed to date to 1583–7, being performed by the Queen's Men at the Bull Inn in Bishopshithe. It was printed in 1589 but this text was a cut-down touring version. A second fuller printing followed in 1617.[17] Literary critics consider this play's sources to be Hall, Holinshed, and Stowe. However, there is also a good deal of invention. For instance, we hear of a French army of 60,000 horsemen and 40,000 foot, including Normans, Braban-ters, Picards, Danes, Hainaulters, and Burgundians, with a claim that 12,600 were killed at the battle. The English army is numbered at 2,000 horsemen and 12,000 foot, with 25 or 26 killed. Interestingly, Shakespeare never felt the need to mention any army sizes in his play.

The *Famous Victories* has a stronger 'military' feel than Shakespeare's *Henry V*. For instance, archers and stakes are to be found whereas they are both completely missing from Shakespeare. After the battle one soldier is made to remark, 'didst thou see what a pollicie the king had, to see how the Frenchmen were kild with the stakes of the trees?'. Henry's pre-battle comment on how he would not be ransomed (in other words, that he would fight to the death) is influenced by the battle speeches in Hall and Holinshed but is derived from a longer English tradition. There are oddities, such as the earl of Oxford, rather than York, asking for command of the vanguard. But the *Famous Victories* knew that Exeter was not at the battle and omitted him from the dramatis personae.

As in Shakespeare, there is no detail in the *Famous Victories* on how the battle should be fought on stage. The directions are 'Strike Drum-mer. Exeunt omnes. The French men crie within, S. Dennis, S. Dennis, mount joy, S. Dennis. The Battle.' Three scenes follow: the closure of the battle involving the herald and the naming after the castle of

Agincourt, which had first entered English texts with Hall; and soldiers reporting an attack on the camp, but with no killing of the prisoners mentioned at all. The third is a comic scene. A Frenchman captures the English soldier Dericke, who cleverly offers to give as ransom as many crowns as will lie on his sword. Tricking the French man to put down his sword, Dericke picks it up and with a mighty swing tries to cut off his enemy's head. The text suggests that the sweep of the sword must be excessive and wholly amateurish since it causes Dericke to turn 180 degrees and the Frenchman to escape—an interesting demonstration of how slapstick might be made to fit into a portrayal of Agincourt. Shakespeare also includes a comic scene between Pistol and his would-be prisoner, Monsieur le Fer, but it is reliant on verbal than physical dexterity.

Other Henry V plays were in existence in the 1590s. The diary of Philip Henslowe mentions 'a play of Henry the Fifth' performed by the Admiral's Men at the Rose in 1595–6. This included the Battle of Agincourt, but otherwise we know nothing of its content.[18] There is also a reference to a 'play of Henry V' in Thomas Nashe's *Pierce Penniless* of 1592, probably performed at the Theatre or the Curtain. This is not the *Famous Victories* since the description mentions a scene not in that play: Henry attacks the French at Agincourt, takes the French king prisoner, and forces both him and the dauphin to swear fealty to the crown of England. To modern eyes, this appears gross historical ignorance. None of the fifteenth- or sixteenth-century narratives ever mention the presence of the king or dauphin at the battle. But it reminds us that dramatists might rewrite history for the sake of dramatic effect. Shakespeare also has the dauphin at the battle. Think what we would lose if Shakespeare was not able to place the dauphin and Henry V in direct juxtaposition throughout, from the tennis balls to the defeat. The dauphin is conveniently dropped thereafter.[19] Shakespeare's scenes concerning the Treaty of Troyes make no mention of the disinheritance of the dauphin.

Was there a specific context for Shakespeare to produce a *Henry V* in 1599? Various thoughts have been expressed on this. There were fears of French invasions in 1598–9 after Henri IV had made peace with Spain. Attending Edmund Spenser's funeral on 13 January 1599 at Westminster Abbey, Shakespeare may have been inspired by sight of Henry's tomb and funeral achievements. The prologue to Act V in the Folio Edition refers to 'his [i.e. Henry's] bruised helmet and his bended sword'.[20] More significant, however, is the specific military context. This was the Irish campaign led by Robert Devereux, earl of Essex. Chorus (Act 5 Scene 1, lines 28–32) compares Essex to Henry V on his triumphant return from France as a 'conquering Caesar', defeating 'rebellion broachèd on his sword' while in the service of 'our gracious empress . . . as in good time he may'.[21]

This last reference suggests Devereux was still in Ireland when the play was first performed. The earl led his army out of London on 27 March 1599 and returned to England in late September. A second quotation used to date the play is in the opening speech of Chorus in Act 1. This is a reference to the place of performance—'this wooden O'. Critics are divided, however, as to whether this was a comment on the poor facilities of the Curtain Playhouse or a 'mock-modest' description of the newly built Globe.[22] The land for the latter was secured in February 1599 and the theatre was in use by September. Devereux's failure and subsequent rebellion might explain why the first printing of the play in the Quarto Edition in August 1600 ('The Cronicle History of Henry the fift, with his batell fought at Agin Court in France. Together with Auncient Pistol') omits Chorus and his speeches: it would hardly have been appropriate to include his hopes of the earl's success when by the time of printing it was known that he had failed spectacularly. The Quarto Edition contains a play text of 1,600 lines. The First Folio Edition of 1623 ('The Life of King Henry the Fift') is 3,380 lines long. The famous 'once more unto the breach' speech at Harfleur (Folio, Act 3 Scene 1) is not found in the Quarto Edition. This is part of an effort in the Quarto Edition to portray Henry more positively and as less bloodthirsty. In terms of the Battle of Agincourt, however, there is only one difference between the Quarto and Folio versions—minor variations in the discussions between the French lords just before the battle.

In terms of structure, the battle is the crux of the play in both versions. Yet much is left to the playgoers' imagination, stimulated by 'alarms' (the noise of drums and trumpet) and 'excursions' (rushings on- and offstage). The only scripted fight is the comic scene between Pistol and Monsieur le Fer. The script does not require any of the main protagonists to engage in combat, which is a contrast with other Shakespearean plays. No use is made of Holinshed's account that the king was nearly felled by the duke of Alençon or that Henry 'with plain strength' slew not only Alençon but two of his company. The duke is not even chosen by Shakespeare as one of the French characters. By contrast, as noted, the dauphin was in the dramatis personae even though Holinshed, accurately, did not have him present at the battle.

Holinshed informed the basic narrative: this is revealed in the critical editions of the play which identify the links. But Shakespeare was not constrained by his historical source. Dramatically, the dauphin's presence was necessary since he had sent the insult of tennis balls to Henry. By contrast, the presence of English archers was not essential. The juxtaposition of the demeanour of the English and French lords was crucial to the dramatic effect, as was Henry's style of command. His night-time tour of the camp is not taken from any historical source. Furthermore, as critics have pointed out, Shakespeare does not glorify war in the play. There are some speeches, admittedly put into the mouths of common soldiers, which query the validity of war and the use of violence. As Shakespeare portrays it, the battle is patriotic but not militaristic. The literary specialist Baldo makes an interesting point with reference to the king's pre-battle speech. Neither St Crispin's Day nor those who had shared in the victory had been 'rememberèd', despite Henry's certainty that they would be. England had lost its Continental possessions completely by 1558. It was Sir John Oldcastle, the Lollard heretic of Henry V's reign, and not Agincourt that John Foxe had suggested for commemoration in a new Protestant calendar.[23] Samuel Johnson later lamented astutely that 'we are apt to promise ourselves a more lasting memory than the changing state of human things admits', adding that the English Civil War had 'left this nation scarcely any tradition of more ancient history'.[24]

The text of *Henry V* also reveals Shakespeare's dilemma on what triggered the killing of the prisoners. This stemmed from having two authors from whom to draw—Stowe and Holinshed. At the end of Act 4 Scene 6 an alarm sounds, presumably a trumpet. The king speaks (lines 34–7): 'But hark, what new alarm is this same? | The French have reinforced their scattered men. | Then every soldier kill his prisoners. | Give the word through.' This gives the impression that the king has been moved by fear of the French regrouping to attack, the causation given by Stowe. Lines 7–10 in the next scene (Act 4 Scene 7), spoken by Captain Gower, indicate that it was the attack on the camp which caused the royal order: 'they have burned and carried away all that was in the king's tent, wherefore the king most worthily hath caused every soldier to cut his prisoner's throat'. This followed Holinshed's version.

Henry V was performed at court in 1605. The Quarto version was reprinted in 1602 and 1619, and the play was included in the major compilation of Shakespeare's plays in the Folio Edition of 1623. There were two further other important works on Agincourt in the early seventeenth century, both by Michael Drayton (1563–1631). His 'Ballad of Agincourt', a short poem of 120 lines, was printed around 1606. It was this poem which stimulated John Lennon's drawings, as noted at the beginning of this book. Drayton's 'Ballad' was consciously archaic in construction, using what the poet called 'the old English garb', and may have been inspired by sight of fifteenth-century texts through John Stowe. Henry's pre-battle speech occupies several stanzas, including his refusal to be ransomed. The archers are prominent as is Henry himself, with a number of nobles mentioned in passing (for instance, 'Suffolk his axe did ply'). In 1627 Drayton published a longer poem of 2,250 lines, the *Battaile of Agincourt*. Both works were part of a much larger output of 'historical' poems by Drayton, beginning in 1593 with *Piers Gaveston* and including *The Barons Wars* (1596, 1603) and *Sir John Oldcastle* (1599).[25] In the same volume as *The Battaile of Agincourt* was *The Miseries of Queen Margaret* (Margaret of Anjou, queen of Henry VI). This juxtaposition was deliberate: *Agincourt* illustrated the good fortune of England when united against a common foe, the *Miseries* the bad fortune when disunited and fighting a civil war.

The medieval past was being used for didactic purposes as well as literary pleasure. Drayton's works, those on Agincourt included, inculcated English patriotism and national identity, themes paramount in late Elizabethan and early Jacobean culture. Drayton addressed his two poems of 1627 to 'You those Noblest of Gentlemen, of these Renowned Kingdomes of Great Britaine: who in these declining times, have yet in your brave bosomes the sparkes of that sprightly fire, of your couragious Ancestors; and to this houre retaine the seedes of their magnanimitie and Greatnesse'. In his adulatory verses added as preface to the *Battaile*, Ben Johnson urged:

> So shall our English Youth vrge on, and cry
> An Agincourt, an Agincourt, or dye.
> This booke! it is a Catechisme to fight,
> And will be bought of euery Lord, and Knight,
> That can but reade; who cannot, may in prose
> Get broken peeces, and fight well by those.[26]

In the same period we see a huge expansion of interest in genealogy and heraldry. The first copies of the 'Agincourt Roll' date to the late sixteenth century, as we shall see in Chapter 6. This was part of a rediscovery of chivalric culture not only by the gentry but also at the early Stuart court. The last stanza of Drayton's 'Ballad' had asked when England might breed again 'such a king Harry'. In fact, one was in the wings. James I's eldest son, Henry, who was invested as prince of Wales in 1610, inspired comparisons with Henry V. In 1606 Robert Fletcher wrote, 'The nine English worthies: or, Famous and worthy princes of England being all of one name; beginning with King Henrie the first, and concluding with Prince Henry, eldest sonne to our Soueraigne Lord the King'.[27] He saw Henry V as the greatest of these because of his battle victory. A drawing by Inigo Jones of a costume design for Prince Henry echoes early Tudor portraits of Henry V. Ben Jonson also alluded to the military accomplishments of Henry V, 'to whom in face you are so like'.[28] Interest in the *First English Life* in the early seventeenth century was linked to the prospect of another King Henry. It was in 1610 that the first copy was made for the antiquarian Sir Peter Manwood.

We can only assume that Drayton knew Shakespeare's play. He was linked to a rival theatre (The Rose) and his interest in Agincourt may have been linked to a desire to 'correct' Shakespeare. He had already been involved with Antony Munday in an Oldcastle play of 1599 which was a rebuff to the travesty of Oldcastle in the Falstaff of the *Henry IV* plays.[29]

The outline narrative of the battle in Drayton's *Battaile* is standard. Henry advances to goad the French into attack, the English archers wreak damage (although Drayton sends 300 archers into the meadow rather than the 200 in Holinshed), and the melee is hard fought. The killing of the prisoners is linked to the attack on the English camp. Drayton's imagination knows no bounds. His inventiveness would be impressive were it not that later centuries took what he said as an accurate reflection of what actually happened. In order to have the army assemble, ships come from every port at home and abroad, and are described in Homeric catalogue form. (In this, as in the style of the *Battaile* more generally, Drayton was heavily influenced by the English translation of Homer's *Iliad* and *Odyssey* by George Chapman (c.1559–1634), which had been published by 1616.) Similarly each supposed county force is mentioned, following its own banner, reminiscent of the heraldry on John Spede's county maps in *The Theatre of the Empire of Great Britain* published in 1610–11.

Drayton drew on Spede's *Historie of Great Britaine* (1611, 1623), which rivalled Holinshed on the library shelves of the nobility and gentry. Indeed, Raymond Jenkins has suggested that Drayton used Spede to correct Holinshed, and that he may not even have read Holinshed at all.[30] Spede's narrative of Agincourt was influenced by Holinshed, although more selective, but not distinctive enough to merit longer discussion here. Spede also drew on new materials, including the works of Alain Chartier and a life of Henry V (probably the *First English Life*) to which he had access through Robert Cotton (d.1631).[31] Cotton was building up his large collection of manuscripts at this very time: it was sold to the nation in 1702 and is housed in the British Library. But no one was making use of these documents when writing their histories at this time.

Drayton invented special roles at the battle for Davy Gam and John Wodehouse, as we shall discuss in Chapter 6. Indeed he invented stories for virtually everyone. Each French nobleman is given a stanza in which to die or be captured just as each English captain is given a stanza to act heroically. There are some excesses of imagination, such as in stanza 295 where the wounded English force the French to carry them on their backs. The weapons are early seventeenth century. There is a rout and even a fort which mysteriously appears for the English to attack in stanza 264. The battle is exceptionally violent. Blood flowing from veins is enough to create a flood. The images invoked would grace a horror movie:

> Slaughter is now desected to the full,
> Here from their backs their batter'd Armours fall,
> Here a sleft shoulder, there a cloven scull,
> There hang his eyes out beaten with a mall,
> Vntill the edges of their Bills growe dull,
> Vpon each other they so spend their gall,
> Wilde showtes and clamors all the ayre doe fill,
> The French cry 'tue' and the English kill.
>
> (stanza 279)

Even though individual French lords are portrayed in acts of courage, the general tone is xenophobic:

> Ignoble French, your fainting Cowardize craves
> The dreadfull curse of your owne Mother earth,

Hardning her breast, not to allow you graves,
Be she so much ashamed of your birth.

(stanza 258)

Given the patriotic tone, it is not surprising that Drayton chose to draw overt links with Crécy and Poitiers. This is achieved by means of an old man who recalls stories of archers who could pin a Frenchman to a tree from 'twelve score away' (240 yards). Archers and common soldiers feature in the *Battaile* more than in any previous narrative of Agincourt.

Whilst Shakespeare's play has had an enduring impact on views of Agincourt, Drayton's poem has passed into obscurity and has little appeal for a modern audience. Yet it was more influential in the past. In 1672 it was cited in an 'Address to the Lord Mayor of London' and was frequently reprinted in the eighteenth century, as advertisements show.[32] Its patriotic and dramatic tone influenced perceptions of the battle and introduced several of the legends which have continued to the present day, as we shall see in Chapter 6.

Shakespeare's Agincourt Replayed

Shakespeare is now such a key part of Britain's heritage that it is hard to imagine a time when this was not the case. In reality, few of his plays remained in theatrical repertoire as the seventeenth century progressed. *Henry V* fared particularly badly. No performances are known between 1605 and the end of the century. Samuel Pepys mentions in his diary that he saw *Henry V* in 1664 and 1668. This was not the Shakespeare play but a verse version by Robert Boyle, earl of Orrery (1621–79) in which the Battle of Agincourt is not portrayed at all but is simply deemed to have taken place between the opening scenes.

The fate of *Henry V* from the early seventeenth century to the early twenty-first century was much affected by changing tastes for the theatre, affecting both the popularity of *Henry V* as a play as well as the way it was presented.[33] This was also the result of external influences, especially wars, whether against the French or other enemies. Today we are accustomed to different interpretations of *Henry V* according to the whim of a director but we expect the text to be that of the Bard. This was not deemed necessary in earlier centuries. Playwrights drew on Shakespeare's text but added in new words, characters, and plots to make the play more appealing. An excellent example is Aaron Hill's *King Henry the Fifth: or, The Conquest of France, By the English: A Tragedy* (1723). Here Henry's spurned mistress, the totally fictional Harriet, niece of the traitor Henry, Lord Scrope, follows the king to France. Catherine de Valois is in love with Owen Tudor but is forced to marry Henry without even meeting him. 'Her brother the Dauphin tries to stop the marriage, and so the Battle of Agincourt is explicitly figured as a fight for Catherine ... the play becomes an account of the king's loves, not his wars.'[34] This solves the problem of the lack of women in Shakespeare's play, a considerable disadvantage in Restoration and Georgian theatre. Hill transformed the play into a tragedy by having Harriet commit suicide when she realized she had lost Henry's love even though she had betrayed her uncle's plot in order to save Henry's life.

Agincourt itself is not portrayed by Hill. Instead recourse is had to the techniques of the masque. A new character, 'the Genius of England', sings a poem of patriotic praise for the victory:

> They bend, they break! The fainting Gauls give way
> And yield, reluctant, to their Victor's Sway.
> Happy Albion!—strong to gain!
> Let Union teach Thee, not to win, in vain.[35]

The battle is also used to serve a literary purpose akin to the debate between music and poetry in *The Beggar's Opera*. As Smith observes, 'Hill identifies his work as engaged in a commercial and dramatic Agincourt with other, implicitly Frenchified, entertainments: a struggle which is both aesthetic and nationalistic.' In this respect the play consciously reflects the Anglo-French tensions of the early eighteenth century. The re-establishment of France as the principal enemy of England (or, more accurately, Britain following the Act of Union with Scotland in 1707) fanned interest in past victories. This is epitomized in Thomas Goodwin's book of 1704, *The History of the Reign of Henry the Fifth* which we will consider in Chapter 7. Suffice to say here that its author saw the book's dedicatee, John, Lord Cutts, a hero of the Boyne and Blenheim, as reviving past glories so that 'our Black Prince's and Fifth Henry's Wars are now no longer acted only in our Theatres'.[36]

There was an important revival of 'the historical play King Henry V with the memorable battle of Agincourt' at the Theatre Royal Covent Garden in 1738 'at the desire of several ladies of quality'. The *London Daily Post and Advertiser* of 22 February noted that the play had been 'acted but twice these forty years'. This was Shakespeare's play and led to a series of performances over the 1740s. That the play was linked to perceptions of Shakespeare within the pantheon of English heroes, of which King Henry V was also a member, is revealed by the fact that, when the playwright's monument was placed in Westminster Abbey in 1741, a bust of Henry V was included as well as those of Richard III and Elizabeth I. This did not prevent the continuing performance of bowdlerized versions, however. When Aaron Hill's adaptation was revised into a one-act version in 1746, *The Conspiracy Discovered*, it was given the subtitle 'French Policy Defeated', a reference to the Jacobite rebellion of the previous year as well as to continuing Anglo-French hostilities.

The impact of the opening of the War of the Austrian Succession in 1740, in which Britain and France were again in conflict, is seen by the addition of a new prologue to the play as well as musical additions, 'Songs to Arms' and 'Britons Strike Home'.[37] In 1749 we see the first evidence of separate printing for sale of 'the Speech of Henry V before Agincourt'.[38] When France and England were again at odds in the Seven Years War (1756–63), Shakespeare's *Henry V* was frequently performed. Surviving playbills show it as commonly subtitled 'With the Conquest of the French at Agincourt'. On the eve of war in 1755 an anti-French polemic had Shakespeare's ghost urge the revival of 'a work of mine: You need not fear it will miscarry', 'What Play d'ye mean, Sir'—'My *fifth Harry*'.[39]

There were few performances between 1773 and 1789.[40] The play was much promoted by the French Revolution and the Napoleonic Wars as was the use of the battle in other contexts, as we shall see in Chapter 5. Charles Kemble, a frequent player of the role of Henry, staged an anti-French Revolution version between 1789 and 1792, again subtitled 'the Conquest of France'.[41] The *Morning Post* of 28 October 1803 expressed delight that *Henry V* was playing in one theatre and *Edward the Black Prince* at another: 'what better examples of the unfaded and inextinguishable glory of our forefathers'. This year saw a special performance of *Henry V* to raise money for the Patriotic Fund as well as to encourage recruitment to the volunteer forces to defend England against the expected French invasion. A review in *The Times* praised this production for its efforts 'to convince our Gallic neighbours that in the midst of all their triumphs they are but mere mortals'.[42] The *Gentleman's Magazine* also had Shakespeare's ghost encourage English resistance, drawing on some of the famous speeches from Henry V but with a contemporary twist: 'Cry God for us! for England! And King George!'[43]

In Kemble's productions we see the first attempts at spectacle through special backdrops for the battle scenes which included an impressive castle of Agincourt. This emphasis on visual impact grew as the nineteenth century advanced. A high peak was William Macready's production of 1839, which established the 'Victorian Agincourt'. This fitted with contemporary interest in medievalism: a tournament held in the same year at Eglington castle, Ayrshire, attracted 100,000 spectators, although it did not feature any Agincourt elements.[44] Macready used seventy actors, the first evidence of attempts to create a real scale for the battle. There was also an effort towards authenticity in armour. Elaborate dioramas were painted as backcloths by Clarkson Stansfield. At the battle 'a litte smoke was made to obscure the stage, and by a pantomime trick process, the troops painted, as if in the distance, were converted into the same troops engaging'.[45] This style of production was reprised by Samuel Phelps in 1852 who boosted his forty-strong cast by dummies from Madame Tussaud's so that he could have soldiers marching three abreast. He also added the singing of 'The British Grenadiers'.[46] Further lavish productions followed. In 1876 the Horse Guards provided extras for the battle and other key scenes.[47]

Charles Kean's production of 1859 used 200 extras. We can see something of the research which went into his production thanks to the surviving playbill and his specially edited text of the play which provides detailed notes drawn from Harris Nicolas's *History of the Battle of Agincourt* (1827) and other works.[48] Kean appropriated medieval music and created lavish scenery even for the various parts of the battlefield. He also included an entry to London which used twenty-four dancing girls. There was, of course, no entry to London in Shakespeare's play: it is only alluded to by Chorus. But in the lavish productions of the Victorian age anything was possible (see Fig. 10). This production made an important contribution to the solidification of popular ideas on history and Englishness in the 1850s and 1860s.[49]

Another major production by Charles Calvert in 1879 was influenced by the Franco-Prussian War.[50] This turned the French into victims and was an early effort to bring out the horrors of war. One reviewer mentioned how a group of women was made to scrutinize the group of returning soldiers at the royal entry to London to see if their menfolk had survived.[51] However, attempts at verisimilitude were mocked when Calvert's production was performed in New York. Henry James complained about the hobby horses used in the battle scenes as well as the lack of protective armour on the actors' rears, all too apparent when they moved offstage. Where possible, however, it had become de rigueur for Henry to sit on a real white horse to deliver his speeches. Open-air productions in Stratford and Burlington Gardens even allowed real campfires.[52]

Fig. 10. This print from the *London Illustrated News* of 23 April 1859 depicts the entry into London as enacted in Charles Keen's production of *Henry V* at the Princess Theatre, London. This was an invented scene interpolated into the play to meet the nineteenth-century taste for lavish and spectacular productions, including live horses.

From 1897 *Henry V* was regularly performed at the Shakespeare Memorial Theatre at Stratford on St George's Day, usefully also Shakespeare's birthday. This reveals that it was by now well established as 'the cultural auxiliary of English imperialism'.[53] It was also taken to the provinces by Frank Benson's touring company. After one performance of the play in a rural town, an old farmer commented, 'God bless you sir for showing us them 'istory plays; they've taught me 'ow we English became what we are, and 'ow we can keep so'.[54] Benson (d.1939) played the role on many occasions, including at the Shaftesbury Theatre in 1914, and managed the Shakespeare Festival at Stratford from 1886 to 1916, when he was knighted. His production in

London in 1900 added dancing girls to emphasize the dissolute nature of the French camp on the eve of battle.[55]

The play proved eminently suitable in the context of the Boer War—the right play, as the *Illustrated London News* reported in February 1900, for 'this hour of national excitement and patriotic fervour'.[56] *Henry V* was also seen as a patriotic play in the First World War. Benson staged the play in London at Christmas 1914. The first known silent film version was produced in 1913 using the boys of Shakespeare's old grammar school in Stratford.[57] In 1916 a silent film of around fifteen minutes, *England's Warrior King*, was produced by 'Eric Williams' (the actor-manager Bransby Williams).[58] The film is lost but consisted of a series of speeches from the play delivered by Williams as Henry to a cast of medievally clad Royal Scots Greys stationed in York. When shown in a cinema, it allowed a reciter to dub the narrations, thereby combining theatre and film. By 1916 the War Office had realized the benefit of reaching wider audiences for the sake of recruitment and publicity for the war effort. Cinema exhibitors were also looking for material that could be related to the war but which would pass the close scrutiny of both the censor and the local authorities where the films were shown. The style of delivery to 'massed' troops also enabled emphasis on the common soldier as well as on the leader himself. In this respect the film fitted with other 'roll of honour' presentations of the Great War.

By the end of the First World War there were signs that war-weariness was rendering *Henry V* less popular. The fact that France was now an ally rather than enemy also had an impact. Progressives such as Bernard Shaw complained how Shakespeare had 'thrust such a jingo hero as his Harry V down our throats'.[59] In the professional theatre, the play was less frequently performed but in the schools of England, *Henry V* was a much-studied play, as a survey of 1906 revealed.[60] The memorizing of its key speeches was deemed to contribute to the development of a manly British identity. This was not new: *The Preceptor* ('containing a general course of education wherein the first principles of polite learning are laid down'), published in

Dublin in 1786, included as lesson VII 'the speech of Henry V at Agincourt where he gained that glorious victory'.

A brief glance at school books of the late nineteenth and early twentieth centuries shows that their portrayal of the king and battle was drawn exclusively from Shakespeare. Even if people had not seen the play, their images of Agincourt were those of Shakespeare. This was stimulated by the *Pictorial Shakespeare* published by Charles Knight in parts between 1838 and 1841. A second major illustrated edition was produced by Howard Staunton, also initially in parts, between 1856 and 1858. This included images provided by Sir John Gilbert (1817–97), whose depictions of medieval and chivalric scenes earned him the epithet 'the Scott of painting' and who also produced major oil paintings of the battle.[61]

Olivier's Agincourt (1944)

In the Second World War, the individual *Henry V* speeches remained popular and well known. Lawrence Olivier had played the role at the Old Vic in 1937 before going to Hollywood. Shortly after his return, he toured the UK, performing scenes from this and other Shakespeare plays. Dallas Bower, who had already proposed *Henry V* in 1938 for the recently established BBC TV, produced a BBC radio broadcast 'Into Battle' in May 1942 where Olivier gave the 'Once more unto the breach' and 'St Crispin's Day' speeches. Bower was an important influence on Olivier's decision to direct the film and to star in it.

Olivier's *Henry V* was not an official government film although the Ministry of Information followed it with interest and Olivier was released from Fleet Air Arm service to make it.[62] In November 1944 a special showing was arranged for the Prime Minister and his family. John Colville, private secretary, recorded that Churchill went into ecstasies about it.[63] The combination of wartime conditions and the star quality of Olivier, as well as the novel use of Technicolor, made the film remarkable both in artistic and historical terms. At the time of its release in November 1944, victory in Europe, triggered by the Allied liberation of France, was assured. The film's dedication to the

Commandos and Airborne forces, who had paved the way for D-day, established a clear link between 1415 and the present. The premiere at the Carlton Theatre in London was in aid of benevolent funds for the same troops.[64]

The British population was by now devoted to the cinema. Olivier's film made Henry V and Agincourt known to a wider public on a scale hitherto unprecedented. Eagle-Lion distributors also issued material 'for use in factories and schools in connection with the Laurence Olivier presentation of Henry V'. The lecture text and accompanying illustrations drew analogies between the archer of 1415 and the 'Tommy Atkins' (the common soldier) of 1944.

The Olivier Archive at the British Library contains much fascinating material on preparations for the film, including a typed copy of the battle chapter from Wylie's Reign of Henry the Fifth (1914) and a copy of Stothard's Monumental Effigies (1876), both of which were used to underpin the film's attention to history. This was particularly relevant to Agincourt, where even in the initial synopsis prepared by Alan Dent, we read that the battle scenes should 'follow history as closely as possible'.[65] The film was made between 9 June 1943 and 12 July 1944: the battle scenes were the only ones filmed on location and were the first to be shot.[66] The site chosen, Powerscourt Park in County Wicklow, was not accurate in terms of landscape (Azincourt is much flatter) but offered advantages the embattled UK could not, including extras from the Eireann Home Guard. The horses were problematic but John Betjeman's wife came to the rescue: her knowledge of breeds avoided Olivier being seen on a white Arab charger, a type not known in medieval England.[67]

The battle sequences were extremely expensive to film, consuming £80,000 out of a total budget of £300,000, but are very impressive, especially in the cavalry charge and arrow shower. This was the first portrayal of mass arrow shooting on screen. The battle was a very long sequence without dialogue, and in that respect a new way of treating Shakespeare. Particularly effective was the panning from one group to another and then back again, to create mounting tension.

This was assisted by Walton's score, including the sight-and-sound combination of on-screen drummers and the increasing pace of the music as the charge quickened. The music was played at the Proms in 1945 and has continued to have a special status of its own, even being chosen for the announcement in July 2005 of London's victory over Paris for the 2012 Olympics.[68]

It is fair to say, however, that no one gets killed or even wounded in Olivier's Agincourt save for the Boy killed in the camp. There is no blood nor is there any mention of the killing of the prisoners or of the plot against Henry before departure. This was deliberate, not simply because of the reluctance, in a period of war, to show the more horrific side of it.[69] It fitted with the theatricality of the rest of the production, which used a mock-up of the Globe and painted panels modelled on the 'Très Riches Heures' of the duke of Berry. Furthermore, the sun shone throughout the battle. There was no rain or mud. The portrayal of Henry was as a strong and untroubled leader. Indeed, it was commented at the time that the king was made to demonstrate 'the qualities attributed to the ideal officer by current service journals'.[70]

The film's enduring image lives on. When the Society of West End Theatre Awards, introduced in 1976, were renamed the Olivier Awards in 1984, they took the form of the bust of Olivier as Henry V, although it was modelled on his performance of the role at the Old Vic in 1937 rather than in the film itself (see Fig. 11). Esmond Knight (d.1987) who played Fluellen in the film, and who lost most of his sight in naval service against the *Bismarck* in 1941, went on to perform a one-man show, *Agincourt: The Archer's Tale* in the early 1970s.[71]

We can add an interesting tailpiece on initial reactions in France. Olivier's film had been passed by French censors in January 1947 but there was pressure in the Ministry of Foreign Affairs to prevent its release on the grounds that it might damage Franco-British relations.[72] What was at issue was the 'depiction made . . . of the moral faults and weaknesses of the French', especially the way the French nobility were portrayed on the eve of battle: 'their inability to bother themselves with what matters, that is to say the victory of the next day'. The worry

Fig. 11. In 1976 the Society of West End Theatre Awards were introduced, becoming the Olivier Awards in 1984. The bronze statuette received by the winners is modelled on Olivier as Henry V at the Old Vic in 1937, later reprised in the film of 1944, demonstrating the dominance of the performance in both the actor's own career and the public imagination.

was that the scenes might be considered 'not as the representations of the faults and errors of a past age, but . . . the permanent traits of our character'. The writer was well aware of the success of Vichy propaganda about English aggression towards France. One of the most famous posters of Vichy France is that of Joan of Arc tied to the stake with a burning bombed Rouen in the background and the title 'Murderers always return to the scene of their crime'.[73] But the minister decided not to intervene: the film was released.

Branagh's Agincourt (1989)

In his 1989 film of *Henry V*, Branagh's battle is quite different from Olivier's. There is much more hand-to-hand fighting and much more gore and mud. This betrays the time of its making. Philip French commented in *The Observer* that it was 'made for a generation that has the Indo-China war and the Falklands campaign just behind it and is wary of calls to arms'.[74] Branagh intended a portrayal critical of violence. As Branagh himself wrote on 5 December in a special diary which he kept during the filming, 'There would be no question about the statement this movie was making about war.'[75]

Here Branagh was following contemporary trends. Michael Bogdanov's production of the play for the English Shakespeare Company in 1986 had emphasized the brutality, even within the confines of a traditional stage and using the limited dialogue Shakespeare had provided: 'Pistol filled a shopping cart with plunder from dummy corpses, savagely beating Le Fer.' Bogdanov had the killing of the boys in the English camp as revenge for Henry ordering the killing of the prisoners. This may be good drama but is bad history. There was no heroism in this play at all. It had earlier invoked the Falklands War directly, with Chorus bearing the banner 'Gotcha', The Sun headline at the sinking of The Belgrano.[76] In Branagh's film, however, Henry and his soldiers remain cerebral and heroic. As Smith puts it, Branagh portrayed the 'parable of personal decency and bravery in a brutal situation'.[77] Branagh had played the role on stage in Adrian Noble's RSC production in 1984, giving some of the signs of angst which coloured his subsequent performance on screen. The influence of the Falklands was also apparent in Noble's production. The battle was fought on a dark, smoky stage with strobes and loud martial music. The London performances used a curtain smeared with blood.[78]

The desire to produce a film of Henry V was Branagh's own. It was his first experience as director and he also wrote the screenplay. The battle scenes were filmed between 31 October and 5 December 1988 at Thames Water Field near Shepperton. Branagh was keen to portray, as he described it, 'the brutal, savage scrum of Agincourt'. Fortuitously it rained heavily and the mud deepened. This gave the battle a certain veracity, assisted by efforts towards accuracy in costumes, weapons, and fighting styles. As Branagh recorded, 'I wanted to reveal as much of the devastation as possible... Tim Harvey and his team had constructed a terrifying battlefield, where our 300 extras would mingle, wounded and dead, with horses and large numbers of dummy horses and people.' At the end the victors march in exhaustion across the field, with Branagh, mud-spattered, carrying the dead Boy on his back. A French woman makes to attack him, one of several women who have appeared to seek their loved ones.[79] As Branagh commented on the day he finished filming the battle scene, 'I felt as if I had come back from the war'.

Intriguingly, like Olivier, he omitted the king's order to kill the prisoners. In a film to be seen by millions, and a successful candidate for an Oscar, that aspect of Agincourt remained a step too far for modern sensibilities.

Conclusion

The image of Agincourt which people have in their minds is Shakespeare's Agincourt. The language of Shakespeare is what rings in their ears. The separation of truth and fiction proves difficult. Some believe that what Shakespeare has Henry say at the battle is actually what he said. This idea has affected our written culture for over 250 years. The earliest use I have found of Shakespearean wording about the historical Henry V is in the London Evening Post of 25–7 October 1757, which includes four quotations from the play to illustrate elements of the campaign. The year is significant since England and France were at war. Although the anniversary of the battle is not mentioned in the article, it is invoked in the Lloyds Evening Post and British Chronicle of 26–8 October 1759, which provides the whole of the St Crispin's Day speech, as it was also to do in the following year.

Not surprisingly the St Crispin's Day speech is the most cited. Charles Dickens drew the title of his magazine Household Words from it (Act 4 Scene 3, line 52). It even got into a debate in the House of Lords in November 1801 when Lord Mulgrave declared that 'the conduct of our army in Egypt would entitle them to immortal fame, and those that have outlived the siege of Alexandria, might say with our Henry the 5th, speaking of the battle of Agincourt, "He that shall live this day...tomorrow is St Crispian"'.[80] The whole of the St Crispin's Day speech was printed in *The Times* on the 500th anniversary of Agincourt on 25 October 1915. The leading article on the same day, headed 'St Crispin's Day', brought to mind Henry V's victory but moved on immediately to declare that 'the greatest of all poets has told the legendary story of that splendid feat of arms in verse that has stirred the blood and moved the pride of them who speak our tongue from generation to generation'.

Other speeches from the play also had their value. In May 1758 the Chorus prologues to the second and third acts were used in an article in *Owen's Weekly Chronicle* aimed at inspiring young men to serve in a forthcoming expedition. The *True Briton* in November 1798 pointed out that the manifestos then being put forward by the French so resembled the demeanour which Shakespeare ascribed to them on the eve of Agincourt 'that we trust the same presumption is a prelude to the same disgrace'. *Henry V* is still used 'in the direct service of militarism'. The Dover edition of the play was issued to US soldiers going to Afghanistan and Iraq. The Attorney General John Ashcroft quoted the St Crispin Day's speech before announcing that 'six hundred years later, history beckons yet again'.[81] As on the battlefield, so also in sport. In support of England's efforts in the 2010 Football World Cup, the comedian Rik Mayall recorded a track 'Noble England': 'Once more onto the pitch, dear friends, once more, invoking the spirit of the Battle of Agincourt'. As Mayall put it in an interview, 'That battle was basically very few Englishmen against the rest of the world.'[82] So too football?

The play has also been deployed in management training. This is best exemplified in a book written in 2001 by Richard Olivier, one of Laurence Olivier's sons, *Inspirational Leadership: Timeless Lessons for Leaders from Shakespeare's Henry V*. Agincourt is particularly useful for the 'dark night of the soul' on the eve of battle as well as 'hardening the resolve' on the day. Killing the prisoners raises 'the hardest choice' as well as 'leadership might not be good for you'. It has also stimulated further analogies linked to the modern business world. In March 2014 a 'multimedia opera', *Steve 5* (*King Different*), was premiered in Lyons. The creators claimed that it brought together 'two great figures of history, Steve Jobs, the king of computers, and Henry V, king of England... Both fought hard, draw out battles for their crowning victories, be it against company boards and Microsoft or the French at Agincourt.'[83] Inevitably the material for Henry V was entirely Shakespeare's.

Life has also been made to reflect art in mock trials of Henry for war crimes. The first, in the Shakespeare Theater Washington in 2004, was stimulated by debate over American engagement in the war with Iraq and by the involvement of Kenneth Adelman, well known for his use of Shakespeare in executive training.[84] In 2010 a more elaborate process was staged in the same location with an imagined backstory. The initial trial of Henry and the archbishop of Canterbury by the 'Global War Crimes Tribunal' had found them not guilty: Henry's war was legal, no non-combatant had been killed unlawfully, and Henry bore no criminal responsibility for the death of the prisoners. The 'French Civil Liberties Union' then sued in a civil court. Since the judge there and in the ensuing appeal deferred to the decisions made in the original suit, the case went to a 'Supreme Court of the Amalgamated Kingdom of England and France'. (Henry would surely have loved that title.) There modern-day judges sitting in a fictional court ruled that his slaughter of the French prisoners was legally unjustified and awarded damages to the estates of the prisoners killed.[85] This was all great fun and good publicity. Quotations from the play rather than from chronicle sources were used in the case, as they had been in an article published in 2000 by John Sutherland.[86] This had pointed out several anomalies in how Shakespeare portrays the incident, suggesting he left the audience uncertain because he was too: as noted, Shakespeare found it difficult to reconcile the two traditions of causation between French regrouping and attacking the baggage train.

It was not until 1999 that Shakespeare's play was performed in French. The production did not receive acclaim, one reviewer commenting that it aspired to Monty Python but only reached Asterix. The problem, as in 1947, was the negative portrayal of the French at the battle. The actor playing Henry hardly helped with his comment, 'Shakespeare portrays the French as a bunch of pretentious cretins. Yet I'm afraid my compatriots [are] pretty much the same today—which is to say rather more arrogant than effective on the field of battle.'[87] Even so, the voice of Shakespeare was used when the Centre historique médiéval was opened at Azincourt in 2001 by making the Henry V mannequin deliver the battle speech from the play.

The cultural legacy of Shakespeare's Agincourt is immeasurable but it commonly places Henry V centre stage. When Royal Mail stamps were designed by David Gentleman for Shakespeare's 400th birthday in 1964, the 1s. 6d. stamp portrayed Henry praying in his tent on the eve of Agincourt. Leading actors remain keen to play the role and audiences to watch them to so. Directors continue to use their imagination in the portrayal of the battle, the contrasting armies, and the king. To cite but one example: the 2007 production of the RSC used explosions and put the French on trapezes, as well as having 'a boyishly vulnerable Henry weighed down with public responsibility' (or, as one critic put it, 'a smug schoolboy').[88] Without Shakespeare's *Henry V*, it is impossible to believe that Agincourt would be so well known and such a quintessential element of English-speaking culture.

5

'France's Bane and England's Glory!'

Agincourt, War, and National Identity

> From Cressy, Poitiers, Agincourt
> Fields renown'd in ancient story
> Hither spirits blest, resort
> France's bane and England's glory!
>
> See, your sons again in arms!
> Frenchmen's blood again shall flow:
> Sound with us War's loud alarms:
> Strike with us the deathful blow!

These are the words for a new song 'written for a corps in the north' published on 28 June 1798 in the newspaper *True Briton*, to be sung to the tune of Handel's 'See the Conquering Hero Comes' from *Judas Maccabeus*. At this point Britain was once more at war with France in the Revolutionary Wars. The song did not have quite the same ring as the Marseillaise of 1792 but it evoked the same spirit. What better than to link the glories of the past, such as Agincourt, to the hoped-for glories of the present?

This chapter considers how Agincourt has been used to invoke national identity from the early seventeenth century onwards. Not surprisingly the battle has most often been recalled in military contexts but its use has also extended into politics as well as into cultural contexts. Agincourt appealed to the spirit of manliness central to

British education from the eighteenth to the early twentieth century. The notion of the humble English archer outwitting the arrogant French aristocrat was fanned by the pride of the British in their democratic traditions and their sense of superiority over other nations. This is also revealed by attitudes of nineteenth-century British visitors to the battlefield.

In 1904 Britain and France signed the Entente Cordiale ending centuries of enmity. Ten years later they were fighting as allies. The 500th anniversary of the Agincourt fell in the midst of the First World War. The 400th anniversary had occurred five months after the British had defeated the French at Waterloo. This chapter considers how the anniversary of the battle was approached on both these occasions.

The Seventeenth Century

In the late sixteenth and early seventeenth centuries, Agincourt was mentioned in several political and military treatises. Henry V was applauded in Richard Crompton's *Mansion of Magnanimite* (1599) for his willingness to expose his royal person to danger.[1] The anonymous 'Of the knowledge and conduct of the wars' (1578) praised his use of the stakes as an example of the virtue of prudence in a captain. It was all the more laudable because it protected foot against cavalry attack and was 'of the kynges owne deuisinge'. This idea was reiterated until, in Robert Ward's military treatise of 1639, Henry was credited with inventing a whole new weapon: a stake tipped at each end with an iron pike, which was further developed by the Swedes as the 'Swines-Pike'.[2]

In 1642 Prince Rupert used the example of Agincourt to urge Charles I to recruit large numbers of foot soldiers:

> for unlesse that be done there is no hope of keeping the field against the Parliaments forces so numerously strong in infantry, which in all the ancient warres of this Nation hath alwayes done the best service; as those battells against the *French* at *Crossie* and *Poyctiers* under the conduct

of *Edward* the third, and his sonne *Edward* the blacke Prince can testifie; but more especially that of *Henry* the fifth at *Agincourt*, where by the vertue and valour of the *English* foot, being but a very small number, but well resolved and ordered, hee overthrew the whole flowre of the *French* horse, and atchieved as great a victory as is memorable in any history whatsoever.[3]

It is interesting that the prince does not refer to archers. Eight years earlier, Gervase Markham had urged in *The Art of Archerie* a return to increased use of archers, citing Agincourt as the prime example and making the point that the English only seemed to win battles when they used the bow.[4]

The first known mention of Agincourt in a newspaper occurs in *Mercurius* in the issue for 13–20 January 1648, reflecting the impact of the English Civil War. War can bring glory, as it did for Henry at Agincourt, but

> most sure it is, if once againe,
> we dare to manage steel,
> we may a place in Story gaine,
> But quick destruction feele.

During the Commonwealth there was a still place for the battle as a mirror of Christian devotion. Agincourt features in sermons of the mid-1650s by the pro-parliamentarian John Trapp (1601–69), emphasizing the damage of self-pride for the French and the benefit of reliance on God for the English: it was the latter which made the archers hit their mark.[5] After the Restoration, Agincourt featured again in military treatises, such as in 1665 when it was cited as precedent for the success of the duke of York's naval actions.[6] We have here an early example of what was to become a common phenomenon: the inclusion of Agincourt in the pantheon of English (and subsequently British) military achievements. This became more apparent as relations with France deteriorated. In 1678 Marchamont Nedham invoked the battle in his *Christianissimus Christianandus, or, Reason for the reduction of France to a more Christian state in Europe.*

The French were not to be trusted but nor was their bragging to be feared. Witness what happened at Agincourt. Patriotic feeling is also evident by the inclusion of Agincourt in *Victoriae Anglicanae: Being an Historical Collection of all the Memorable and Stupendious Victories obtain'd by the English against the French, both by Sea and Land, since the Norman Conquest* (1691).[7]

In 1682 Sir William Wood produced *The Bowman's Glory or Archery Revived*.[8] This spoke of a victory 'that can scarce if ever be paralleled in any history'. The archers were to be thanked for this. Wood was not suggesting a revival of their use in English armies but rather the celebration of historical and, increasingly, sporting traditions. This had the effect of 'gentrifying' the archers. A major contribution to this was the foundation in 1652 of the Society of Finsbury Archers which used the grounds of the Honourable Artillery Company and claimed a place in City of London parades.

The Eighteenth Century

Thomas Goodwin produced his *History of the Reign of Henry the Fifth* in 1704, in the midst of the War of the Spanish Succession. He dedicated it to John, Lord Cutts who had fought at both the Boyne and Blenheim, thereby protecting the liberties of his own country and those of Europe as a whole.[9] Goodwin's account of Agincourt, based on a wide range of chronicles, was garbled, putting both the dukes of Exeter and Clarence at the battle but, as Allmand comments, the book 'went far beyond the language of the "deeds"...of a single man. It was the history of a national enterprise, guided and led by the king.' That Agincourt also featured in military education is revealed by a small handwritten booklet probably dating to the early eighteenth century, where Holinshed's account of the battle was copied alongside other military materials, including how to build a bridge of boats.[10]

The War of the Austrian Succession (1740–8), the last war in which a British king served in person, boosted interest in Agincourt as a battle as well as in Shakespeare's play. A letter in the *General Advertiser* of 3 April 1744 made the crucial link to past triumphs as a motivation for present-day vigour:

Agincourt! O glorious day! How great a reverse of fortune didst thou produce...that our arms may be successful; that when Britons strike, they may strike home: that our mildness and lenity misconstrued by the enemy fear, may turn to the enrag'd fury of the lion; and that British valour and the terror of our nation may shine forth with its accustomed eclat is the hearty wish of Sir yours, etc.

The relative lack of English success in this war, however, also elicited regretful comparisons with such past successes. As Horace Walpole put it, 'having learnt to spell out the reigns of Edward the third and Harry the fifth and begun lisping with Agincourt and Cressy, one uses oneself awkwardly to the sounds of Tournay and Fontenoy'.[11] Even allowing for poetic licence, Walpole's comment suggests that Agincourt was part of childhood inculcation. The battle was regularly included in histories from the 1720s onwards, and was often chosen for pictorial illustration, as in *The New History of England by Question and Answer* of 1746 where it was one of thirty prints covering the period from Alfred the Great to Blenheim.[12]

The study of history, an essential element in the education of a gentleman, communicated a sense of British superiority through reference to past achievements. Even if David Hume (*History of England*, 1754–62) criticized Henry and Edward III for invading France 'without any object of moment, merely for the sake of plunder', he also saw, for Agincourt as well as Crécy and Poitiers, 'the same presence of mind, dexterity, courage, firmness and precaution on the part of the English; [and] the same precipitation, confusion and vain confidence on the part of the French'.[13] By the 1750s many felt that the French were gaining the upper hand in the colonies in particular. Fears that the soldiery was a pale reflection of past times prompted waves of invocations of Agincourt as of Crécy and Blenheim: 'These are the times that Britain expects where her sons shall be reverenced by their allies and dreaded by their enemies.'[14]

Agincourt, Crécy, and Poitiers were often mentioned together as a trinity of triumphs, but Agincourt emerged as the strongest thanks to the possibility of seeing it on stage. This gave 'an uncommon pleasure in the exhibition of their ancestors' glory and patriotism and their enemy's overthrow and eternal disgrace', according to the *Public Advertiser* of 7 May 1756, eight days before war with France began again (the Seven Years War, 1756–63). Initial reverses increased such outpourings: 'will the laurels gained at Cressy and Agincourt... make amends for this national disgrace: to what end does the record of such exploits serve but to convince our rivals how much we are degenerated from our forefathers?' This became a political argument too: 'there is no doubt but that the radical fortitude, which is natural to the British Isles, inspires the heroes of Agincourt, Poitiers and Cressy; strengthened and directed the great assertors of our liberties'.[15]

On 25 October 1757 we find the earliest public invocation of the anniversary of the battle, used to demonstrate a falling-away from past greatness and encouraging an aggressive attack on mainland France. As a letter in the *London Chronicles* lamented: 'it makes my blood run cold when I think of the great disparity there is between us and our ancestors'. Significantly, the writer included the whole of Shakespeare's St Crispin's Day speech as well as Henry's answer to the French herald when asked whether he would compound for ransom. The anniversary of the battle in 1757 was also noted in the *London Evening Post*, declaring that, since the period of Agincourt, 'corruption had chased away all the glorious spirit of this nation'. Such views were frequently expressed over the following year with increasing anti-French venom and often including short narratives of the campaign and battle.

A letter of February 1759 in the *Universal Chronicle* alludes to historical toasts, claiming that the earliest the writer had heard was to Magna Carta, and 'then no more before Good Queen Bess than Crécy and Agincourt'.[16] The victory at Minden on 1 August 1759 caused several invocations of Agincourt in newspapers. The anniversary was soon in the public gaze again since fortuitously it coincided with the accession of George III on 25 October 1760.[17]

Interest in Agincourt from a military perspective had not completely subsided. In May 1761, with war against France still under way, Colonel Dalrymple's 'Military Essay' in the *London Chronicles* urged emulation of older ways of raising troops, such as had given victory at Crécy, Poitiers, and Agincourt. A military guide for young officers published in 1776 in Philadelphia, and *A Military History of Great Britain from Julius Caesar to the Present* produced in 1777 by the Society of Military Gentlemen, both used Agincourt to illustrate how commanders had coped with difficulties. In a later volume in the *British Military Library* of 1798–9, there was a letter comparing the relative benefits of arrows and shot. The author concluded, 'I can admit of no advantage arising in favour of the bow, from the possibility of discharging two arrows for one ball.'[18]

The Revolutionary and Napoleonic Wars

Wars with France in the late eighteenth and early nineteenth centuries, and the impact of the Revolution, had a marked effect on allusions to Agincourt. A letter to the 'People of England', published in *The Times* on 16 October 1794, began 'Countrymen, remember Agincourt!'. The battle was used to emphasize post-Revolutionary French degeneracy as well as British resilience. Witness the *True Briton* on 9 November 1798:

> The French preserve their character. The events of this war show we are not degenerated for we think we may without arrogance assert that in the hour of severest trial we have proved ourselves worthy of our glorious ancestors.

Such medieval successes were used as examples of when the British had been outnumbered yet had still succeeded, thereby boosting confidence in similar situations now arising:[19]

If there were any historians in their number, they might ruminate over a long succession of brilliant exploits, for five or six hundred years past, not forgetting the deeds of Wolfe and Marlborough, or the scenes which were exhibited at Agincourt, Poictiers and Cressy.

As the wars continued, new successes were paralleled with those of the past. As the Lord Chancellor said at the Pitt Club on 28 May 1811,

> The battles of Cressy and Agincourt find a parallel in some of the late splendid achievements of our arms. We have only to pursue the same course to raise our national fame and character still higher than it ever has been before, whilst, under Providence, our exertions and our example may lead to the general DELIVERANCE OF EUROPE.[20]

The 400th anniversary of Agincourt in 1815 was not emphasized in the press, however. By then, Waterloo, fought on 18 June, had taken pride of place. Yet when the duke of Wellington was thanked in the Commons for his victory, Sir Thomas Ackland declared, 'we saw renewed the splendid days of Cressy and Agincourt'.[21] The Lord Mayor's Day (now Show) in November 1815 gained the attention of the crowd by its ancient knights, the first of whom was clad in the armour of Henry V:[22]

> It was a happy coincidence which reminded us at the same instant of two of the most distinguished epochs in British history, which at once made us exult in former triumph and present glory by placing in the forefront of this national picture the valued relics of Agincourt with the honoured trophies of Waterloo.

This may not have been the first time Henry V had been seen at the Lord Mayor's Day. The *Morning Post* of 21 December 1811 included the rather scurrilous 'Pun on seeing the drunken man at what was called the Lord Mayor's Feast, in the armour worn by Henry the Fifth at the Battle of Agincourt':

> Our modern hero clad in steel
> With Henry's arms and martial port

> Prov'd at Guildhall by many a reel
> That he had been at a-Gin-court.

A desire to communicate with the glorious past is evident in the presentation of Waterloo medals to the 12th (Prince of Wales) Light Dragoons at Azincourt on 17 May 1816. The report in the *Caledonian Mercury* commented on the appropriateness of this 'highly gratifying military spectacle' honouring the gallantry of modern heroes being held 'on plains so celebrated for British valour'. A surgeon with the troops, Dr John Gordon Smith, reminisced on the event in a talk to the Royal Society of Literature in 1827. He also emphasized 'the mark of their sovereign's approbation on the very spot which, nearly four hundred years before, was the scene of the scarcely less glorious triumph of Harry the Fifth of England'.[23] Lieutenant Colonel John Woodford, a commander in the Army of Observation placed in the Pas-de-Calais after 1815, carried out excavations at the battlefield in 1818. These will be discussed in more detail in Chapter 7.

1815–1914

In the fifty years or so following Waterloo, Agincourt is mentioned frequently in several different contexts, reflecting an increasing range of public interests as education and culture expanded, and as peace with France prevailed. Acknowledgement of the event as a sign of British success continued. In a debate in parliament reported by the *Morning Chronicle* on 30 April 1823, Agincourt and Crécy were invoked alongside Minden and Waterloo to emphasize that Britain always came out on top. But financial problems in the wake of the Napoleonic Wars also prompted a poem in the same paper a week later:

> To Agincourt we tune our lays
> To noble deeds of other days
> But all the chords unruly get
> We fain would sing of Waterloo
> But spite of all that we can do
> They sound to nothing but debt.

Agincourt seemed to be everywhere. In 1821 a new crown (the Imperial State Crown) was deposited in the Jewel House. Many newspapers ran articles on its ruby, allegedly worn by the Black Prince at Poitiers and Henry at Agincourt. The burial place at Christ's Hospital (previously Greyfriars) of the duke of Bourbon, a prisoner of the battle who was never ransomed but died in England, was also noted. The discovery of the skull of Thomas Beaufort, duke of Exeter, in works for St Katherine's Docks in 1825, led to an outpouring of (incorrect) comments on his presence at the battle. When Frederick, duke of York died on 5 January 1827, it was an excuse for papers to produce articles on the duke of York who had died at Agincourt.[24]

Agincourt also had a political use. On 30 October 1819 the Boot and Shoemakers of London held a St Crispin's Day meeting, the saint being their patron. This not only gave an opportunity to applaud the glorious victory at Agincourt but also to express opinions on 'a recent military achievement of a very different description at home', namely the 'atrocity' at Manchester ('Peterloo'), for which they set up a fund for victims.[25] Agincourt was even useful in the campaign for Catholic Emancipation. Those in favour were able to recollect that many of the names of Crécy and Agincourt heroes were also the names of heroes at Waterloo—and Catholics.

The publication of Harris Nicolas's *History of the Battle of Agincourt* in the summer of 1827 influenced newspapers to start listing the anniversary of the battle, on St Crispin's Day, in 'events of the week'. The *Morning Post* of 26 October 1827 included a long article prompted by the anniversary, recalling that the day also marked the accession of George III. 'It may be called the last great battle of chivalric times...We have always looked with a patriotic pride upon the battle...because it is one of a long chain of proofs that the strength of England is in her infantry.'

It is also relevant that after 1815 possibilities of travel to France reopened. The *Morning Post* of 2 October 1833 included a report from a man who had visited the battlefield in 1831. This is the earliest non-military visit to Azincourt I have come across. The writer lamented that 'your cockney traveller' tended to rush from Calais direct to Paris without bothering 'to investigate scenes hallowed in the recollection of national glory and immortalised in one of the most spirit-stirring dramas to which the pen of Shakespeare has given birth'. But if the traveller had a picture in his mind of blood and carnage, he would find calmness and tranquillity: the sword really had been turned into the ploughshare. 'The field of battle wore the appearance of an immense corn field some miles in extent.' A merry band of peasants sang their way home 'as though the whole crop of the "great battlefield" and one of the most productive harvests in the memory of man, had been their own'. The writer spent much of the day 'listening to the peasants' traditional lore respecting "la grande bataille avec les Anglais"' but was disappointed not to be able to find any arrowheads on the soil.

In the 1830s and 1840s we begin to see increasing emphasis on the archers. The *Odd Fellows* magazine on 20 February 1841 noted that 'the chief dependence of the English was placed upon the archers who struck terror by their savage appearance'. Many, or so the author thought, had stripped themselves naked, thereby taking comments on the archers' loose clothing, first seen in Monstrelet's *Chronique* and transmitted through the sixteenth-century histories, to their logical extremes. The source cited was the popular *British History, Chronologically Arranged* of John Wade (1839) and shows how anecdotes livened up the past for an ever-increasing number of readers. The same account also claimed that the French had attempted to rescue their prisoners and that was why Henry had ordered the 'instant massacre'. A Victorian logic and desire for exactitude was being applied here, even to suggesting that 'the error was not discovered till 14,000 of them had been cruelly butchered'.

One reason for the increased interest in Agincourt archers was the development of archery as a sport from the 1840s, as revealed in publications such as George Hagar Hansard's *The Book of Archery* (1841). Hansard visited the battlefield since he refers to a peasant bringing him the head of an arrow: 'there can be no doubt it belonged to that "iron sleet of arrowy shower"'.[26] The Grand National Archery

Meetings began in York in 1844. A competition in Leeds in June 1850 'reminded us of Agincourt and Chevy Chase', the commentator claiming that it was odd that such events of noble archery had been forgotten.[27] Archery also blossomed as one of the first competitive sports for women.

The 1840s and 1850s witnessed major social change. Economic prosperity made the upper working classes increasingly affluent. They were a target audience for the Great Exhibition of 1851. Amongst the many exhibits, Agincourt was not forgotten. 'What a sight to a thinking man to see the flags which flaunted against one another at Agincourt and Waterloo now ranged in friendly salute alongside ... we cannot sufficiently appreciate the great influence which is surely yet steadily going on', wrote one visitor to the editor of the *Leeds Mercury* on 21 June 1851. A meeting in Preston on 4 May 1850, reported by the *Preston Guardian*, had set up a fund so that the 'working man' should be able to visit the Exhibition to see the triumphs of the English in peace and in war. As the speaker put it, the English should be proud of 'the simple share of the laurel wreath gained by proving ourselves to be the first nation of the world for industry, skill, talent and integrity, than if the triple coronet of Agincourt, Trafalgar and Waterloo encircled his brow alone'.

The mood of the moment is well indicated in a meeting of the British Archaeological Association at Manchester in August of 1850 which eulogized 'the first found traces of [Lancashire men] as a distinct race in the battles of Crécy, Poitiers, Agincourt and Flodden Field', since it was on such occasions that the Lancashire bowmen 'much distinguished themselves'. In the same month the Lord Mayor of London visited Southampton and was shown where the armies for Crécy and Agincourt had gathered.[28] There was much to be proud of. In 1850 Joseph Hunter produced a short study of the Agincourt army based on original records:

> I begin this series of critical and historical tracts with a word
> [i.e. Agincourt] which never fails, whenever it is pronounced, to fill

the minds of Englishmen with ideas of the prowess and splendid achievements of their ancestors, to remind them of what they are capable in a great struggle...and thus to sustain their spirits in time of danger and to establish and secure their national independence.[29]

The 1840s and 1850s are highly significant to the perception of the English archer as the true victor of Agincourt. Such an emphasis was epitomized in Charles Dickens's *The Child's History of England* (1853): 'on the English side, among the little force, there was a good proportion of men who were not gentlemen by any means, but who were good stout archers for all that'. Such Englishmen were able to defeat 'the proud and wicked French nobility who dragged their country to destruction'. Behind this remark lay pride in the peaceful establishment of British democracy in contrast with the birth pangs it had suffered in France. It was also believed that the English had done well in the past, including at Agincourt, because their soldiers were 'extemporised' out of civilians, as a report in the *Liverpool Mercury* of 30 January 1852 put it. The notion was encouraged by the threat of invasion from France in the light of political upheavals in the late 1840s and in the early 1850s the aggressive foreign policy of Napoleon III, stimulating revival of interest in local defence, aimed at providing a militia against attack.[30]

During the Crimean War (1853–6) France and Britain were allies, rendering the tone of allusions to Agincourt less bombastic than in the past. As a speech in parliament on 19 February 1853 put it, Agincourt, Crécy, and Poitiers had not been wars between England and France but between kings of those countries. Now the people wanted peace. In a guide to the military characteristics of each of the Allied armies, the French were praised for their quickness whilst the British were seen as the most intrepid and bravest in Europe, with Agincourt cited as proof.[31] Even the French felt able to reconsider Agincourt. In 1855 Liskenne published his *Crécy, Poitiers, Azincourt, Waterloo*. Ten years later René de Belleval produced the first extended study of the battle in French.[32]

The coincidence in 1854 of the Battle of Balaclava, which included the Charge of the Light Brigade, with the anniversary of the battle elicited the expected responses. The *Bury and Norwich Post* reflected that the St Crispin's Day speech would have fitted the bill well, just as the wish for more men 'is echoed in our own country'. According to the *Cheshire Observer*, the Battle of Inkerman on 5 November 1854, 'for the first in rank to the last, was a prodigy of valour scarcely inferior to the miracle of Agincourt'. Note again the emphasis on the lower ranks. This also coloured *The Times* correspondent's report from the Crimea in February 1855 on the British army: 'let her know them as the descendants of the starved rabble who fought at Agincourt and Cressy'.[33]

In 1859, however, there were again fears that Napoleon III was planning to invade Britain, prompting newspapers to claim that the contemporary Frenchman 'is the self same being as at the period when Agincourt was fought. Our boastful neighbours treated their antagonists as an undisciplined rabble easily swept away by the armed chivalry of France until ignominious defeat proved the contrary.' There was a wish that the British rifleman might be as brave as their medieval predecessors, since 'the archers of the middle ages were beyond all comparison the most formidable troops of Europe and their training was entirely individual'.[34] This marked the peak of the volunteer movement. In November 1859 a national rifle association was formed, but the medals awarded at the first meeting on 2 July 1860 bore the image of a medieval archer and rifleman together with the motto 'sic perpetuum' (thus for always). There were even some who thought longbows would still be useful for local defence.[35] Even in the 1870s, the rifleman was seen as the true descendant of the archers who fought at Agincourt and of the 600 who had ridden to death and fame at Balaclava.[36]

The emphasis on the archers, alongside Henry V, is also seen in one of the most popular history books of the period, Charles Knight's *History of England* (1856–62), which was abridged into a school history in the late 1860s. Knight visited the battlefield in 1856. In his autobiography he introduces the visit by mentioning first his viewing of the battlefield at Shrewsbury, the place where Henry V as prince had his first experience of battle in 1403 against Hotspur:[37]

> Young Harry has to fight even a more doubtful battle than that of Shrewsbury. I followed him over the ground of Agincourt—saw him marching with his few and exhausted men up the little hill from Blangy to behold the French filling a very wide field, 'as if with an innumerable host of locusts' [a quotation from the *Gesta* thanks to Nicolas's book]—and marked how favourable was the ground for a daring attack, when the hundred and fifty thousand of his enemies were couped up between two woods. I have seen the inclosed potato ground where the flower of the chivalry of France was buried and have heard in the little neighbouring inn a discussion about projects for raising a monument to their memory on the fatal plain. A survey, rapid even as that I was able to take of Agincourt, gives a precision to our notion of great battlefields, which cannot be derived from plans and verbal explanations.

It was in the context of fears of French invasion that George Musgrave published a lengthy account of his visit to Crécy and Azincourt in 1861:[38]

> It was in a ramrod-like descent of pelting rain that I set out, invested in Tweed and Courage, to make a cross country excursion in search of the plains of Azincour or Agincourt—the scene of one of the most memorable events in the annals of martial glory of England, and the yet living monument of the prowess which Time has proved to be hereditary: and kings and people, even our enemies, forgetting all rivalry and hostile antagonism, have agreed to acknowledge and honour . . . The gratification derivable from accurate details of this battle of Agincourt is now only to be felt on the spot where it was fought.

Musgrave found it difficult to 'fix upon the very localities referred to in the numerous accounts of the action'. 'That such perplexity and difficulty of identification should interfere with positive decision on the subject ought not to be a matter of surprise. The whole face of the country has, of course, materially changed.' Trees had been scrubbed out in the early sixteenth century for arable cultivation, hollows filled, and houses demolished. Therefore all was 'confusion and uncertainty, doubt and disappointment'. He could not detect the confined space in which the French had been so constricted.

Musgrave's guide was a common labourer who the previous day had taken an English general and his sons around the field. But, as Musgrave commented cynically, 'he would have selected any site if he thought the gentleman was of the opinion that that was the actual locality where all the fighting had occurred'. The guide pointed out a hollow way in the rear of the French position close to one of the mills near the main road 'down which, he said, everybody knew the blood had run like a stream into the causeway'. Another local came up to Musgrave as he sketched the site and told him that 'The English camped over there', pointing towards Blangy. Musgrave's patriotic pride got the better of him. 'I suppose he had picked up this informa-tion from some of our countrymen able to enlighten him on the matter. The French, as may be imagined, very rarely visit the place.' Indeed, he assumed the locals would have spent all their time trying to destroy any landmark or feature which would help anyone—especially the English—in recognizing the routes which the French took in their flight!

The remainder of Musgrave's account follows what he had read in Nicolas's *History of the Battle of Agincourt* even to the point of copying the latter's diagram of the battle. Musgrave's Britishness is also revealed by his comment that the French 'are ever ready to fall into conversation . . . but it would have been bad taste to introduce, in such circles as I entered, the subject of Azincour'. Yet the changing times are revealed in his view that the French were essentially a brave nation. The main problem had been disunity caused by over-powerful magnates 'against Freedom and Liberty', a comment reminiscent of Dickens's *Child's History of England*.

How many British visitors there were to Azincourt remains uncer-tain. Thomas Cook began to organize overseas tours in 1855. In 1886 a tour to Azincourt and Crécy was advertised by him, 'for the benefit of gentlemen connected with colleges and large public schools' but open to 'any gentlemen who feels a real interest in inspecting the scenes of British prowess and in fighting over again the great battles recorded in English history'. The tour guide is not named but is described as 'a gentleman who combines a thorough knowledge of the language and locality with real antiquarian zeal and the ability to impart information in a clear and intelligent manner'.[39] That no similar tour was offered in 1887 may be a comment on the take-up in the previous year but we know that there was a visit paid to Azincourt and Crécy in that year by an artist, John Absolon. This resulted in an article in *The Graphic* with two drawings of the field: one a large flat expanse covered in corn stooks, the other an area of woodland 'where the archers were placed'.[40] These visits provide insights into Victorian attitudes to the past and emphasize how the Battle of Agincourt formed part of a sense of national superiority.

Agincourt as an element in the glorious British past never disappeared. In a civic banquet in Southampton in 1899 Henry V's 6,000 men-at-arms and 24,000 archers [sic] were applauded for their 'glorious fight at Agincourt'.[41] The archers remained centre stage. When new historical figures were placed into the Rotunda Museum, Woolwich Common, in 1890 to demonstrate the use of armour from the reign of Edward I to Oliver Cromwell, the longbowman of Agincourt alone represented the fourteenth and fifteenth centuries.[42] In his *The Great Battles of the British Army* (1890), Charles Rathbone emphasized that Henry V had 'the finest army England had ever sent into France'. His account of the battle combined narrative sources with Drayton and Shakespeare as well as revealing the influence of contemporary military thought: crucial to English success at Agincourt, as in the late nineteenth century, was the devotion to duty of the officers as well as the 'stubborn valour' of the rank and file. Rathbone also saw the bowmen as the ancestors of the invincible infantry of Marlborough and Wellington.

That Agincourt had a firm place in the long list of British military achievements is witnessed by its inclusion in the Army Pageant held at

Fulham Palace in 1910 to raise funds for military charities.[43] (The event followed shortly after the death of Edward VII but a black-edged sheet placed within the copy of the programme expressed the new king's wish that 'the Army Pageant should be in no way postponed owing to the recent National calamity'.) The Master of the Pageant was F. R. Benson, the well-known Shakespearean director. It comes as no surprise, therefore, that he should quote from *Henry V* in the very first sentence of his introduction to the event or that he relied mainly on Shakespearean speeches and characters for the Agincourt scene. To this he added five 'Welsh chiefs', including Davy Gam, whose inclusion no doubt helped to make Agincourt a British rather than simply English victory.

The pageant saw what was probably the first ever re-enactment of the battle. Agincourt was used to demonstrate the effectiveness of 'line against column'.[44] The French entered in three groups, one of which remained mounted. The English commanders rode in, but dismounted, sending their horses to the rear, and drawing up the army in three main bodies. Gam returned from his scouting to make his famous speech 'enough to be killed, enough to be taken and enough to run away', which had its origins in Walter Raleigh's *History of the World* of 1614. The wish for more men was followed by a shortened version of the St Crispin's Day speech. York was given command of the vanguard. The archers were deployed in front of the main bodies of troops, filling in gaps between them as well as forming up on the flanks. Each archer had a pointed stake. Sir Thomas Erpingham threw his baton in the air and the line moved forward. Whether archers actually loosed their arrows at the pageant and entered the fray with axes, sword, and hammers 'to shiver the French to fragments' is unconfirmed, but these descriptions are in the programme. Henry was saved from a French attack by the Welsh chiefs. The whole scene is a fascinating mix of historical accuracy, literary allusions, and creative inspiration.

The pageant's image of Agincourt was very much that projected in school histories of the late nineteenth and twentieth centuries, where the leadership of Henry and the bravery of his 'happy few' were given central place. This was encouraged by the view of educationalists that 'the history reader should simply consist of graphically told and picturesquely illustrated biographies and stories drawn from the history of England and of the world'.[45] The archer fared well in this. He continued to be prominent in schools after the Second World War when there was a conscious desire not to limit history to kings and queens. R. J. Unstead's *Looking at History* (1953) emphasized the skill of the English archers as well as the effectiveness of the stakes against the French cavalry but fell into the Shakespearean trap of claiming that, because of Agincourt, Henry became king of nearly all France. It is hardly surprising, therefore, that many today think Agincourt was Henry's only campaign and success, and enough to bring him a crown.

The First World War

Almost as soon as the First World War started, a link with Agincourt was created. On 29 September 1914 Arthur Machen, a journalist on the *Evening News*, published in his newspaper a short story, 'The Bowmen'. In this imagined account of the retreat from Mons in late August, British soldiers saw St George and the ghostly archers of Agincourt fighting for them.[46] What is fascinating is the response the article triggered, with some coming forward to substantiate it and others seeking to discredit Machen as a liar.

The episode indicates not only the yearning for a spiritual element in what was already a frightening war but also the inspiration and comfort gained by recalling a glorious medieval past. In *The Times* leader on the anniversary itself on 25 October 1915, an invocation of Agincourt, as well as Crécy, Poitiers, Trafalgar, Waterloo, the Marne, and Ypres, led to the conclusion that 'the English sense of duty is the secret of our discipline and our success'.[47] Nor did this end in 1918. A recruitment poster for the Hampshire Regiment in 1928 listed the battle honours, including those of 1914–18, with figures of an Agincourt archer and a modern-day Tommy shaking hands over the regimental badge.[48] In 1963 Robert Hardy's reconstruction of Agincourt for the BBC, *The Picardy Affair*, juxtaposed a roll-call of the battle dead with 1918 gravestones, coming to rest on one with the inscription 'Sometime we'll understand'.[49]

A link to the medieval past was also notable in the memorialization of the dead of the First World War. Plans for a post-war Catholic memorial chapel at St Mary's Lowe House in St Helen's, Lancashire, were announced in 1918.[50] The proposal invoked the creation of chantries in the time of the 'old days of faith in this country' which served the dual purpose of monuments and places where the souls of the dead were prayed for. Two precedents were cited. The first was the endowment (although misdated to the reign of Henry V) of the chapel of All Souls College, Oxford to pray for those who died in the French wars. The second was a local example. 'After the battle of Agincourt A.D. 1415 Sir Thomas Gerard of Bryn built the little chapel of which the Tower still remains, known as Windleshaw Abbey, where Mass should be offered daily for the souls of his ancestors.'[51] Historically this is dubious. No man of this name can be traced on the campaign and the Sir Thomas who founded the chantry was born in 1431.

What is important is that a link with Agincourt was drawn in the first place. The memorial chapel at St Helen's, completed in 1923, includes many representations of soldier saints including St George and St Louis (Louis IX of France). St George was a common image in First World War memorials as was the medieval knight. This elevated those who had fallen into the pantheon of past heroes.

The burial of the Unknown Warrior in Westminster Abbey on 11 November 1920 also evoked a recollection of Agincourt. The *Daily Telegraph* imagined Henry V, himself buried in the abbey, hailing the Warrior (via Shakespeare)

> as one of his grim and indomitable company to whom the honour he promised them on the morning of his great fight has at last been rendered, 'For he to-day that sheds his blood with me, shall be my brother.' As a brother of Kings he was given a place in our Abbey yesterday.[52]

The Unknown Warrior had been buried in specially provided French earth but in a quintessentially English location. *The Times* of 11 November saw it as wholly appropriate that the Warrior should rest 'in French soil, the gift of French hands, beneath the chapel where hang the helmet and sword of the conqueror of Agincourt'. That so many of his companions now slept in that same soil across the Channel 'has washed away, we hope for ever, the memories of an old enmity from the bosoms of the two peoples, and has cemented between them an amity that will know no end'.

Such a sentiment occasioned plans for an Anglo-French remembrance at the battlefield on the 500th anniversary of the battle, 25 October 1915. The British had been present at the annual Joan of Arc celebrations at Rouen earlier in the year. As a reciprocal gesture, the officers of the 3ème Battalion of Chasseurs-à-pied stationed at the Château de Tramecourt invited British officers in the area

> to join them on the scene of the battle and commemorate the day in unison. The nobly inspired invitation was responded to in the chivalrous spirit which prompted its sending.

The event was reported in the *Illustrated London News* of 11 December 1915 along with photographs.[53] The French lined up in front of the Château de Tramecourt and saluted the arrival of the British (see Fig. 12). The lieutenant colonel of the Chasseurs (M. Pineau) related in detail the leading incidents of the battle, typed plans of which had been provided for British and French officers. He pointed out the different parts of the battlefield, the party moving from place to place and the rank and file following. In stirring and eloquent words he paid a soldier's tribute to the brave combatants on both sides. A second photograph displays the scene, with Pineau using his shooting stick to indicate the various sites. As the reporter concluded:

> There could surely be no more convincing or finer testimony to the reality of brotherhood-in-arms now so fortunately established between the soldiers of France and Britain and the closeness of the tie between the

Le 5e Centenaire de la Bataille d'Azincourt fêté par les Chasseurs à pied
Remise de Décorations devant les Officiers Anglais

Fig. 12. The 500th anniversary of Agincourt occurred during the First World War. The French invited British troops to the field. In this photograph from the *Illustrated London News* we see soldiers from both armies in front of the Château de Tramecourt.

nations than this joint celebration of an ancient battle-day of honourable memory to both.

The event was also reported in the French magazine *L'Illustration* of 27 November 1915 using the same photographs.[54] This report also tells us that it rained on 25 October. In fact, that contributes to another Agincourt legend. Military records of the 3ème Battalion for 25 October note the anniversary and explain that the commander wanted to 'retrace the events of the battle before his whole battalion but had to postpone it to the next day'. The record for the following day provides an account of the event with the British troops. Therefore, despite the newspaper reports, the battlefield commemoration in 1915 actually took place on 26 October not 25th!

The French newspaper report also spoke of reconciliation, of hand-shakes without rancour. The French and British were, after all, two brave and loyal races. This was very much the line taken by a leader in *The Times* on 25 October 1915. Whilst Henry V's success was applauded (and Shakespeare's version of events all the more so), mutual Anglo-French respect was now established and crucial to the war effort:

> Our French friends and Allies understand our pride in Agincourt as we understand their pride in the feats of Joan of Arc. These memories on both sides serve but to stiffen our resolve in the fray that is upon us to prove ourselves worthy of the blood of which we come.

During their visit to 'The Battlefield of France' between 3 and 14 July 1917 King George V, Queen Mary, and Edward, Prince of Wales stayed overnight at the Château de Tramecourt where they were joined by the king and queen of the Belgians. We can only assume that they saw the battlefield of Azincourt. No mention was made of it in newspapers or in the film made of the royal visit under the sponsorship of the War Office Cinema Committee. The film simply shows the royal parties entering and leaving the doors of the château.[55] George V was at the Château de Tramecourt again in August 1918 where he was photographed inspecting Fijian troops.[56]

A definite visitor to the battlefield in 1917 was Charles ffoulkes, curator of the Royal Armouries. This occurred during a visit to GHQ France linked to his work on a planned National War Museum. In his autobiography he recalled,

> On one occasion when I lunched at the Visitors' Château (I think that was the official designation) at Azincourt some historically minded office reminded us that the day was the 25th October, the anniversary of the Battle of Agincourt fought 502 years ago. It was suggested that we should go up to the site of the battle and that we should all go in tin hats. At the side of the road the French had set up many years ago a monument with an inscription commemorating the gallant English and French who had fallen in the battle. As we stood there some French poilus straggled past and saluted and so again the wheel of history turned full circle.[57]

Agincourt was invoked in other military contexts during the First World War. The *Illustrated London News* for 18 November 1916 featured a drawing of troops from the Coldstream Guards in action during the September phase of the Battle of the Somme, along with a text invoking the spirit of the Battle of Agincourt.[58]

There is further evidence of how the 500th anniversary stimulated interest. At the Public Record Office a list of documents relating to Agincourt was drawn up in order to mount a small exhibition in October 1915.[59] Today we might choose to show the muster of the Welsh archers given the popular fame of this group. In 1915 it was the archers from Lancashire which had the honour, but even in the PRO the words of Shakespeare rang loud. Next to the document description of E101/45/14, 'permission by the king for certain named persons to depart freely', we find: 'Rather proclaim it Westmoreland through my host | That he who hath no stomach to this fight | Let him depart, his passport shall be made | And crowns for convoy put into his purse.' This is totally ahistorical. The document concerns the licence for men to be invalided home from Harfleur. It was Shakespeare's invention that Henry allowed men to leave on the eve of battle. He also invented the presence of the earl of Westmorland at the battle. The latter was one of the few peers ordered to remain in England to defend the northern marches.[60]

The 500th anniversary was also noted in Australasia. *The Mercury*, published in Hobart on 23 October 1915, recalled that 'our own men, once more treading the very ground that Henry trod, will seem to hear his voice urging them to valiant deeds'. Even our French allies, 'always chivalrous in their appreciation of merit', might also recall the story with the same interest but perhaps without the same pride that it occasions for the English. In New Zealand the *Otago Daily Times* of 26 October 1915 was pleased to link Agincourt's 500th to the 100th anniversary of Waterloo as well as to remind readers that 25 October was also the date of the Battle of Balaclava. Events of the last fourteen months (i.e. since the outbreak of war) had brought home to all that fearless courage, dauntless endurance, and other qualities which had characterized our race in times of old and which still burned bright. 'The men of today were born into a goodly heritage.' Agincourt had been an infantry battle. The current war made it clear that infantry were still of paramount importance. Artillery only had a value in enabling infantry to advance. The *New Zealand Herald* also carried an article on 23 October 1915 emphasizing how the men of Agincourt were of a similar stamp to the soldiers of the present war, in terms not only of fearlessness but also courtesy to the enemy: 'it helps us all to grasp how the men of British birth form one family in every age'.

Another military perspective was put forward by Sir Herbert Maxwell in the *Cornhill Magazine*. He admitted that the invasion of France in 1415 had been an act of aggression but argued that the conduct of Henry V and his army was so much less destructive than the war the Germans were now waging.[61] After providing a standard account, including emphasis on the role of the archers and the bravery of Henry, Maxwell concluded that 'it was a fruitless and costly enterprise but one that contributed not a little to establish the prestige of British Infantry, which is being so nobly sustained by King George's troops on the same old ground at the present time'. Maxwell, as many others, sought to unite past and present.

W. Rhys Roberts, Professor of Classics at the University of Leeds, gave talks on 25 October 1915 on 'Patriotic Poetry, Greek and English', first to the Literary and Historical Society of his own university and then to the boys of St Peter's School, York.[62] The subsequent publication of his talk began with a Latin dedication to the knights of the past and present who died for their country as well as for the liberty of mankind as a whole. This was not the only link of past and present. Roberts's talk was stimulated by a recent message of George V to his people and by German threats to Greece.

As a Welshman speaking on the anniversary of Agincourt Roberts also invoked 'the ancient and patriotic Welsh element in British unity' as well as looking forward to 'a great confederation in which the USA may one day be leagued with other free English-speaking peoples'. There was more Greek poetry in his talk than English. For the latter there was only Shakespeare. But this was enough to stress the main theme. 'In England we make too little, rather than too much, of anniversaries. All true patriotism should be firmly rooted in history.' After all, had not Chaucer died on 25 October 1400, and had not the Charge of the Light Brigade occurred on the same day in 1854, 'which Tennyson commemorated in the metre of Drayton's Battle of Agincourt'. Even if Roberts's main message was that 'Ancient Greece and modern Yorkshire here join hands', he used the anniversary of Agincourt to voice optimism for the future, an important point in the context of the war in 1915. 'Some nineteen centuries passed between Salamis and Agincourt; some nineteen between the birth of Christ and today. What of the next nineteen centuries?' What indeed?

6

'Agincourt PLC'

Traditions, Myths, and Creations

Ay, we have some English blood in our veins, though peasants and the sons of peasants. But there was one of us who drew a bow at Azincourt, and I have heard greater things, but I believe they are old wives' tales.

I could not help telling you that my fathers fought at Azincourt though I was only the overlooker at Mr. Trafford's mill.

In Disraeli's *Sybil* (1845) Agincourt symbolizes family antiquity and respectability as well as national pride.[1] The Brown family of *Tom Brown's Schooldays* (1857) were also stalwart sons who did yeomen's work 'with the yew bow and cloth-yard shaft at Cressy and Agincourt' as well as service in later wars. The Agincourt factor worked for the upper classes too. In Evelyn Waugh's *Brideshead Revisited* (1945), the Marchmains ascribed their elevation to the battle: 'knights then, barons since Agincourt'.[2]

Tennyson used the battle in similar vein in his narrative poem *The Princess* (1847), by having Sir Walter Vivian recall his ancestors and show visitors items associated with them. 'And this, he said, was Hugh's at Agincourt, and that was Sir Ralph's at Asculon.' The family had kept a chronicle all about them. In the same year as *The Princess* was published, the freethinking Norfolk farmer William Skinner Phillipo was tried and imprisoned for eating his own pheasants outside the gaming season. He commemorated this by an inscription on his barn, and on the front entrance of his house, Severals Grange, Wood

Norton, he inscribed both 'Agincourt' and 'Liberty and Fraternity'.[3] Phillipo claimed descent from Henry V's standard bearer at the Battle of Agincourt and from Matthias de Phillipeaux at the Battle of Hastings.

These examples stand for the many families, real or imagined, keen to claim the presence of an ancestor at the battle. The Welsh have also taken pride from the idea that they were particularly important at Agincourt as archers. More generally, the name 'Agincourt' has come to mean something well beyond the events of 25 October 1415, inspiring works of literature, art, and music. Objects associated with the battle are claimed to exist, and it is popularly believed to have generated a new rude gesture. Agincourt is the stuff that legends are made of—literally. How has this come to be so?

Agincourt Ancestors and the Search for Gentility

The story here takes us back to the age of Shakespeare when Robert Glover, Somerset herald from 1571 to his death in 1588, made three copies of what has become known as the 'Agincourt Roll' (Fig. 13).[4] These appear to have been made in the 1570s or early 1580s. Glover's work as a clerk in the Tower of London, where many royal records were kept, enabled him to copy a document which has since disappeared—a roll which Sir Robert Babthorp, controller of Henry V's household, delivered to the Exchequer on 19 November 1416 as part of the post-campaign accounting process.[5]

The roll listed some of those with the king at the Battle of Agincourt. Glover copied out only the names of retinue leaders and men-at-arms. For the archers he simply totalled the numbers. But why should he be interested in Agincourt at all? It was because of increased interest in family pedigrees and rights to coats of arms. The College of Arms, incorporated by Richard III in 1484, developed from the 1530s onwards procedures for validating pedigrees and rights to arms through heraldic visitations. It was in this context that the presence of an ancestor at Agincourt might be claimed. For instance, in the

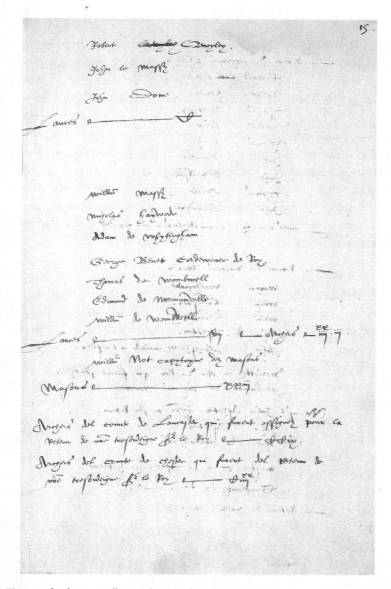

Fig. 13. This list in Bodleian Library Ashmolean MS 825 was compiled by Robert Glover who was Somerset herald from 1571 to 1588. It is one of three versions of the so-called Agincourt Roll noting those present at the battle. Although the list derives directly or indirectly from a now lost roll of 1416, heralds were only interested in the names of the men-at-arms and excluded the names of archers even though these were in the original roll.

Visitation of Cheshire in 1580 carried out by Glover himself, the Savage of Clifton family tree includes 'Sir John Savage made knight by K H 5 at the batell of Agincourt 1415' and 'Sir Piers Legh of Hanley slain at the battle of Agincourt'.[6] The Visitation of Essex in 1612 has in the Crochrode family entry 'Thomas Crochrode gentleman, son and heir, who went with the Erle of Oxford to Agencourte'; an early seventeenth-century text concerning visitations in Surrey claims Sir Anthony Dod was knighted at the battle.[7] Agincourt was not the only battle mentioned, however. In the Cheshire Visitation, presence at Blore Heath (1459) is mentioned three times and Wakefield (1460) twice. One of the Savage descendants, also a Sir John, was noted as slain at the siege of Boulogne in the time of Henry VIII.

On the evidence of surviving visitations, it is difficult to suggest that families were keener to identify ancestors with Agincourt than with any other battle, but Glover may have been especially keen to copy the Agincourt names because of his knowledge of another document in royal records. This was an order made by Henry V on 2 July 1417 just as troops were gathering for another invasion of Normandy.[8] The king had heard that men going on campaign were assuming coats of arms to which they had no right. He ordered that no one was to be permitted to have arms unless by ancestral right or by the grant of someone who had power to grant them. On the day of the muster, men were to give proof of their right to hold their arms, on penalty of being excluded from the expedition, losing their wages, and having their coats stripped off and broken.

Henry made an exception 'for those who bore arms with us at the battle of Agincourt'. The order exempted Agincourt veterans from the need to provide proof of their right to arms, presumably because they had gone through a similar checking process in 1415. The king's order did not give an automatic right to Agincourt veterans to have coats of arms. That is a false interpretation which later commentators have made, encouraged by a misreading of a passage in Henry's pre-battle speech in the chronicle of the Frenchman Jean Juvénal des Ursins of the 1430s or 1440s:[9]

> he granted that all of his company who were not noble he would ennoble, giving them letters, and that he willed that from thenceforward they would enjoy the same privileges as the nobles of England. And so that they might be recognised he gave them licence to carry a collar, made up of the letters of his order.

We do not know the source of des Ursins's information, if there was any. He may simply have made it up. His text shows confusion about social status in England. Ennoblement was not the same thing as the right to a coat of arms. Knights and gentry in England were not noble as they were in France but they often had a coat of arms. Des Ursins was calling to mind French definitions. In France 'nobles, those living nobly and those following the wars', as the expression went, were exempt from taxation.

Men-at-arms in the English army were often listed in muster rolls, including those for 1415, under the heading 'armigeri'. This term means 'the bearer of arms', i.e. a coat of arms, and is commonly translated into English as 'esquire'. Yet not every man-at-arms had a coat of arms. Knowledge of how heraldic coats were granted is scanty, although Henry's order of 1417 indicates that he sought greater control over the process.[10] In his reign we see important developments in the organization of the royal heralds, including the creation of their common seal and of a Garter King of Arms from at least September 1417. The first Garter was William Bruges who served on the 1415 expedition as Guyenne herald and who, after the surrender of Harfleur, carried Henry's summons to the dauphin.[11]

The Agincourt Roll came to public knowledge after its printing by Harris Nicolas in his *History of the Battle of Agincourt* in 1827. However, Glover's blanket omission of the names of the archers prompted the false belief that we did not know their names at all. In fact, the names of over 5,000 archers have now been retrieved from the embarkation musters as well as other lists submitted to the Exchequer when the campaign accounts were terminated.[12] What these other materials show is that the Agincourt Roll is not a complete list of even the men-at-arms who were at the battle. None the less, it adds to our knowledge of how Henry and his officials tried to deal with the complex post-campaign accounting process.

The Agincourt Roll has achieved quasi-mythical status. On some websites there is a claim that the roll was secret and that only certain families held it. In reality, these family-held versions were copied from Harris Nicolas but over the generations that fact was lost sight of. Commentators have not understood that the roll was simply one element in a complex accounting process, aimed at preventing fraud on the part of the captains. They have claimed that it was an 'honour roll'—that Henry had the names of those who were with him at the battle recorded in order to honour them. This is an anachronistic interpretation influenced by the move, from the late nineteenth century onwards, to memorialize indi-vidual soldiers by listing them on war memorials. There were no collect-ive monuments or memorializing for the Agincourt troops. There was no sense of a band of brothers. That is an invention by Shakespeare.

Families have claimed that their ancestors distinguished themselves at the battle and, in some cases, that a special coat of arms was accorded as a result. Such claims are difficult to substantiate, although there is only space to discuss key examples here. Most claims seem to belong to the late sixteenth or early seventeenth centuries, a period when upwardly mobile families were keen to prove their antiquity and gentility. But this was not unique to Agincourt. A legend that the Pelham family had been involved in the capture of John II at the Battle of Poitiers was fabricated around 1620. By that time the surviving Pelham line was an illegitimate descent, but through the assistance of Somerset herald, they made a new quartering of their arms.[13]

An example of an Agincourt misreading concerns John Codrington. The claim is that he had his coat of arms confirmed by Clarenceux herald in July 1441 because of his role as standard bearer to Henry V at the Battle of Agincourt.[14] In fact, the grant does not mention the battle at all but simply acknowledges Codrington's service to Henry V in generic terms: 'in Battaile, Watch and Warde under the said our Soveraigne Lord's banner'.

(Incidentally, this reads more like a sixteenth- than fifteenth-century wording.) Codrington was on the 1415 campaign. A John Codyngton (we should not worry about the slightly different spelling) is listed on the Agincourt Roll. A John Codyngton was also noted in the post-campaign account of Thomas, Lord Camoys as present at the battle.[15] But there is no proof whatsoever that he bore any of the king's standards.

The Wodehouse family who became earls of Kimberley in 1866 (giving their name to the town in South Africa), claim that their ancestor, John Wodehouse, had been granted a crest by Henry V for his special service at the battle: 'on a wreath, an arm erect, holding a club in the hand, and this motto on a scroll, frappe forte, i.e. strike strong, and at the bottom Agincourt' (see Fig. 14b). It is also claimed that, as a result of the battle, his coat of arms had drops of blood added to its chevron.[16] Wodehouse was definitely closely connected with Henry, having been his chamberlain and chancellor when he was prince. At his accession he was appointed chancellor of the duchy of Lancaster and received robes for the coronation as an esquire of the chamber. He loaned £100 for the expedition but seems to have remained in England. He does not appear in any of the financial records for the expedition and it is very unlikely that he was at Agincourt at all.

In the early seventeenth century a fictitious pedigree was created which gave Wodehouse a distinguished Norfolk ancestry.[17] In addition, Michael Drayton invented a special role for Wodehouse as he invented much else in his *Battaile of Agincourt* (1627). We first find Wodehouse in stanza 203 urging the English to regroup after a counter-attack by the duke of Orléans. Later he is associated with Davy Gam in an attack on a fort in which the French had taken refuge (stanzas 264–8). Gam is killed but Wodehouse survives. This story was a complete invention, and 'frappe fort' no more than Drayton's poetry, but it led to the special crest and motto being accorded by the College of Arms. Crests and mottoes were heraldic inventions from the early seventeenth century onwards and were not part of heraldic practice at the time of Agincourt. Precisely when the Worshipful Company of Bowyers gained the motto of 'Crecy, Poitiers, Agincourt' is not known but the addition of a bowyer and Agincourt archer as supporters dates to 1996.[18]

The Waller family claim that Richard Waller was granted an augmentation to his arms for capturing the duke of Orléans at Agincourt and subsequently accommodating him at his house at Groombridge in Kent, in the form of an escutcheon 'charged with the arms of France

Wodehouse

Fig. 14. Claims that ancestors had played a significant part in the battle generated visual expression in seventeenth-century coats of arms. The Waller family added a French escutcheon to their walnut tree on the spurious grounds that Richard Waller had captured the duke of Orléans. The Wodehouse family claimed that their original coat of an ermine chevron and three ermine cinquefoils on black was modified after the battle to have a chevron gilded and scattered with drops of blood.

Waller

Fig. 14. Continued

with a label of three points argent' (i.e. the arms of Orléans) (see Fig. 14a).[19] This was added to the arms between the visitations of 1592 and 1619. By the latter date the tale included the notion that the keeping of the duke of Orléans had been so beneficial to Waller that he was able to rebuild his house at Groombridge and contribute to the repairs of Speldhurst church 'where the duke's arms now remain in stone over the porch'.[20]

Whenever it was granted, it was also based on a confusion. Waller did not capture the duke of Orléans but was responsible for the custody of his younger brother, Jean, count of Angoulême, who had been given as hostage to the duke of Clarence following the 1412 campaign and who was not released until 1445.[21] However, Waller did serve in 1415 as a man-at-arms in the retinue of William Bowys within the troops under Thomas, duke of Clarence.[22] He served in France on later occasions. Any role he played in the capture of the duke of Orléans remains unsubstantiated.

It is also claimed that Bertin Entwisel was made a knight (i.e. dubbed) at Agincourt and given a special crest and motto for his conspicuous bravery, consisting of a hand grasping a fleur-de-lys and 'Par ce signe. Agincourt'.[23] It is not certain that Bertin was on the campaign, unless he was the Bertin de France who brought two archers. He certainly had a distinguished career in later French wars. He cannot have been knighted at Agincourt, however, since he is still referred to in royal records as an esquire in the early 1420s.[24] As in the case of Waller, the heraldic augmentations belong to a later century.

There are several other claims of the creation of knights at Agincourt. A family cartulary for the Woodford family claims the dubbing of Sir Robert Woodford: 'and on the friday in the fest of Saynt Cryspyn and Cryspynyan erly in the morning he [Henry V] dubbyd Robert Woodford knight and many others at that sege being present. And anon after that same Friday he faught manfully ayens a C thousand of Frencheman at Agyngcourt and had the victory of hem.'[25] I have not been able to find a man of this name in the records. The mention of the French as numbering 100,000 indicates the influence of the *Brut* tradition. As we can see, there is also confusion between the siege of Harfleur and battle.

It was not uncommon for dubbings to take place before a battle. Monstrelet, Waurin, and Le Fèvre say that 500 French were dubbed before Agincourt. Basset's Chronicle gives the names of eleven Englishmen dubbed at Pont-Saint-Maxence, adding 'several others'. The post-campaign account of Sir Thomas Erpingham notes that Thomas Geney and John Calthorpe were knighted at the landing at the Chef de Caux, although both were then invalided home from Harfleur.[26] The *Gesta* includes amongst the English dead 'two newly dubbed knights'. No source, however, mentions Henry creating knights before or after the battle. Yet it is likely that he did: there are certainly some men bearing the title 'knight' in 1416 who did not hold it when recruited for the campaign of the previous year. These include Sir Robert Babthorp, responsible for handing the Agincourt Roll to the Exchequer.[27] Henry rewarded some of his Agincourt companions with the Order of the Garter. Lord Camoys, who had commanded the rearguard, was amongst a number of Agincourt commanders who were admitted in 1416. Over the five years after the battle, thirteen new Garter Knights were Agincourt veterans.[28]

In addition to the examples noted earlier, other families claim that ancestors distinguished themselves at the battle. None can be substantiated from contemporary sources. If there were deeds of valour they are not recorded and there was certainly much later invention, stimulated by the attitudes to Agincourt with which I began this chapter. The most obvious is the story of Sir Piers de Legh. Allegedly his mastiff bitch stood over him to protect him when he fell, but survived to return home and start the strain of Lyme Hall mastiffs. The origins of this myth are not known. The first mention is in a family history of the early twentieth century.[29] Sir Piers died at the siege of Meaux in 1422 not at the battle, although the latter was asserted in a heraldic visitation in 1580. A cairn in Lyme Park claims to be 'traditionally the burial place of Piers Legh after the battle of Agincourt'.[30]

Family traditions were encouraged by the heraldic visitations and by county histories between the seventeenth and early nineteenth centuries. These replicated earlier errors, such as the presence of Thomas Beaufort, duke of Exeter, as commander of the rearguard at the battle.[31] John Anstis, Garter King of Arms from 1718, invented the notion that Sir John Fastolf (not at the battle) took the duke of Alençon prisoner there (rather difficult since the duke was killed at Agincourt) and 'that duke agreed as ransom to build a castle [at Caistor] similar to his own in France, in consequence of which agreement this castle was erected at this expense'.[32]

Any potential link of a person or place to Agincourt is today interpreted as a mark of esteem as it has been from the late sixteenth century onwards. Many people have written to me either claiming that their ancestors fought at the battle or else wanting to find out whether they did. No other military engagement until the First World War has generated such personal interest or emotional investment.

The Welsh

In 1995 Baroness White of Rhymney (1909–99) took *The Times* to task for a leading article which spoke of Agincourt as an inspiration to Englishmen, arguing that this was unconvincing for Welsh ears since the victory was 'primarily due to the 5,000 longbowmen, mainly from Gwent'.[33] It is a common misconception that the Welsh predominated in Henry's army. Despite research in the mid-2000s on the surviving muster rolls, which led to details of 7,500 soldiers being put on line, writers continue to make unsubstantiated claims on Welsh participation.[34]

Administrative records show that only 500 archers, along with a handful of men-at-arms to lead them, were raised from Wales (see Fig. 4). The same number was raised from Lancashire and 650 from Cheshire.[35] The Welsh troops came from the two southern counties of the Principality, Cardigan and Carmarthen, and the Lancastrian lordships of Brecon, Hay, and Kidwelly. There was no recruitment in North Wales because there remained doubts about loyalty in the wake of Glyndŵr's rebellion. (Owain had never been captured but is thought to have died sometime in 1415.)[36] Some of the Welsh archers recruited in 1415 did so in return for pardons for supporting Glyndwr earlier. To the 500 can be added Welshmen who substituted for those invalided home in the retinue of the earl of Arundel, and others serving under captains from Wales or the marches. These included Davy Gam of Penywaun, Brecon, of whom more anon, and Sir Roland Lenthale of Hampton Court, Herefordshire (another man whose family later used the motto Agincourt and claimed a battlefield dubbing despite the fact that Roland was a knight already at the point of indenting).[37]

We know the names of over 7,500 troops on the campaign. A maximum of 10 per cent were Welsh. Adam Chapman's research on the Welsh soldier shows that Welsh participation in royal armies was higher in the fourteenth century than the fifteenth.[38] In no chronicle or sixteenth-century history are Welsh archers mentioned in connection with the battle. Significantly, Agincourt does not feature in Welsh praise poetry of the period, even though such poetry does commonly interest itself with the war in France. Welsh poets wrote in honour of individuals in return for patronage and payment. It is clear there was no Welsh patron involved in the battle who might stimulate such writing.

That Davy Gam died at the battle is noted in five chronicles, of which two note his nationality: Basset calls him 'Davy Gam esquire, Welshman', Adam Usk 'David Gam of Brecon'.[39] He is included in the list of dead in Hall and Holinshed but without any mention of nationality. The same is true in Shakespeare's *Henry V* where the dead are named (Act 4 Scene 8, line 96). Gam is not a character in the play, but there is a Welshman, Fluellen. In an exchange with the king in Act 4 Scene 7 Fluellen refers to the good service of Welshmen 'in a garden where leeks did grow' which is the origin of the tradition of wearing leeks on St David's Day. Shakespeare's intention may have been to link this to the Black Prince's victory at Poitiers which Fluellen has mentioned in previous lines but critics consider that it more likely concerns a legend about a battle against the Saxons in 540 CE. The exchange allows Henry to admit that he himself is Welsh, but there is no sense in the play that the Welsh have made a special contribution to his victory at Agincourt. Shakespeare's Fluellen follows the late sixteenth-century stereotype of the verbose and bombastic Welshman within a comedic four nations' situation. It is a later invention that Shakespeare modelled Fluellen on Gam.

It remains unclear why Gam was singled out by chroniclers in the list of dead. If it was for some notable act at the battle, there is no record of it. In the early seventeenth century a special role was invented for Gam. Sir Walter Raleigh's *History of the World* (1614) has Gam sent to spy out the French, returning with a report 'that of the *Frenchmen*, there were enough to bee killed; enough to bee taken prisoners; and enough to run away'. Drayton put this into poetic form in his *Battaile of*

Agincourt (1627). 'My Liege I'll tell you if I may be bold, | We will diuide this Army into three: | One part we'll kill, the second prisoners stay, | And for the third, we'll leave to runne away' (stanza 149). Drayton adds further activity for Gam. In stanzas 242–3 he is involved in a dispute with Christopher Morisby over which of them captured Philip of Nevers. Gam, 'whose Welch blood could hardly brooke this blot' (an invocation of the swaggering Welshman as in Shakespeare), hit out at Morisby with his axe until Lord Beaumont intervened to prevent him. Gam is subsequently involved with Sir John Wodehouse in an assault upon a fort. There is competition between them for battle honours but in this action Gam is killed (stanzas 264–8).

When in 1697 Wynne expanded David Powel's *History of Cambria* of 1584, he developed Drayton's stories, adding that when the king was in danger during the battle, Gam came to his defence: both Gam and his son-in-law were mortally wounded in this action. When the king heard this, he knighted them both but they died soon afterwards.[40] Powel's book had not included the Battle of Agincourt at all. Thomas Goodwin used Wynne's edition when writing his *History of the Reign of Henry the Fifth* published in 1704. Thereafter, thanks to Drayton, Wynne, and Goodwin, the invented stories about Gam were widely distributed, encouraging Harris Nicolas in 1827 to assume that one of the *Gesta*'s 'two recently dubbed knights' in the list of dead had to be Gam.[41] A pocket diary for 1842 even portrayed the supposed scene. There is no evidence for his knighting. He is named in the chronicle lists of dead as an esquire. Even Wynne did not claim he was knighted posthumously (which was not a medieval practice anyway) but the tale became popular.[42]

Whilst Drayton created activities for Gam, he did not privilege the Welsh as a whole. Writing of the troops as they made their way to muster at Southampton, he speaks of the Welsh as follows (stanza 74): 'who no lesse honour ow'd | To their own king nor yet less valiant were | In one strong regiment had themselves bestowed'. But Drayton was equally flattering about companies from the various counties of England. To those from Lancashire, for instance, he allocated a banner which

emphasized their significance as archers: 'not as the least I weene |
Thorough three Crownes, three Arrowes smear'd with blood'.

Where and when the idea originated of the importance of the Welsh
at Agincourt remains a mystery. A clue may be found in the
Flintshire Observer of 3 June 1915, where the mention of the prowess
of the Royal Welch and of the Welsh Fusiliers in the current war
invokes the Welsh as heroes of 'Cressy, Poitiers, Agincourt, Blenheim and Ramilles'. These military links cross the centuries, as we
saw in Chapter 5, are a common theme. In 1916 it was suggested
that the special devotions ordered by the archbishop of Canterbury
in January 1416 for St David, St Chad, and St Winifred were 'especially to commemorate the glorious part shown by the Welsh
during the battle'.[43] We know that Henry V visited the shrine of
St Winifred at Holywell (Clwyd) in early 1416 but this was no
more than a personal devotion. Besides, St Chad was distinctively
a Midlands saint.[44]

The Welsh archer at Agincourt has become a significant element of
popular culture and of Welsh identity in the modern age, generating
further stories in its wake. Cadw, the Welsh government's historic
environment service, has decorated Tretower Court, the home
of Roger Vaughan, as it might have been in 1470 with wall hangings
which include a depiction of Agincourt. Vaughan was Gam's son-
in-law. His presence at the battle is unproven and he certainly did
not die there. Neither he nor Watcyn Llwyd were knighted on the
field posthumously despite popular claims. Llwyd was invalided
home from Harfleur.[45] A notion has also developed that 'The
Tudor dynasty was actually founded through the liaison of a
young Welsh squire at Agincourt with the widowed Katherine'.[46]
Owen Tudor certainly married Henry V's widow and their son
Edmund was the father of Henry VII, but there is no evidence that
Owen was at Agincourt. His military service in France began in
1421. The story seems to derive from a poem written in 1603 by
Hugh Holland and dedicated to James I as heir of both Owen and
Catherine.[47]

The V-Sign

A common assertion today is that Agincourt saw the invention of the V-sign, a rude hand gesture involving two fingers.[48] In filming the 'Longbow' episode in the *Decisive Weapons* TV series (1996) the producers filmed contributors making the sign. Afterwards my young son was told by his friends that his Mummy had been seen swearing on television!

The story goes that the French threatened to cut off the index and third finger of any archer they captured, the assumption being that they were so strong and the English so weak that there would be many suffering a mutilation that would make them incapable of ever using a longbow again. After the battle the archers allegedly made the V-sign to the French in order to show they still had their fingers, using the gesture as a mark of disdain for French pretension.

In two fifteenth-century chronicles there is reference to possible mutilation.[49] According to Thomas Walsingham, 'the French published that they wished no-one to be spared except certain named lords and the king himself. They announced that the rest would be killed or have their limbs horribly mutilated. Because of this our men were much excited to rage and took heart, encouraging one another against the event.' The second reference is within Henry's supposed battle speech in the chronicles of Jean Le Fèvre and Jean de Waurin: 'In addition, he told them that the French had boasted that if any English archers were captured they would cut off three fingers of their right hand so that neither man or horse would ever again by killed by their arrow shot.'

No chronicle or sixteenth-century history says that English archers made any gesture to the French after the battle in order to show they still had their fingers. There is no evidence that, when captured in any scenario, archers had their fingers cut off by the enemy (despite Bernard Cornwell's graphic scenes in *Azincourt*). Mutilation was used as a military punishment in the period, however, as revealed in ordinances issued for Richard II's army when it invaded Scotland in

1385, which were reissued by Henry V in 1415 and which remained the basic disciplinary controls to the early sixteenth century.[50] The punishment for foot archers who cried 'to horse' without good cause or who went out foraging without permission was to lose their right ear. If servants or pages started quarrels in the host, they might have their left ear cut off.

The V-sign may have a long history but it has so far eluded identification. It is not found in treatises of the sixteenth century on hand gestures.[51] That the sign was in popular use in the early twentieth century is shown in a film of 1901 when an employee of a works at Rotherham used it to indicate his displeasure at being filmed. When an alleged connection was first drawn with Agincourt is unknown but it is certainly a modern urban myth.

Agincourt Objects and Legends

Discounting administrative records and early chronicles, there is no existing physical object in existence which has a proven link with the battle. The desire of later centuries to have memorabilia has had an effect on the creation both of myths and forgeries.

In the Victoria and Albert Museum (V&A) there is a spur set into a tree root which is claimed to have come from the battlefield (Fig. 15).[52] A similar object is in the Burrell Collection in Glasgow although it does not claim an Agincourt link.[53] Both are genuine late medieval spurs but have been set into tree roots to give the impression they were lost on the field and only recovered after a long period. Analysis of the V&A example indicated the timber had not grown around the spur naturally but had been softened with water in order to place the spur within it. In addition it was spruce, a type of tree not found in the Pas-de-Calais in the period of the battle. That two examples survive is indicative of a deliberate fraud in the late nineteenth or twentieth century. Another example was sold at auction in 1962. Such created antiquity and association was a common means of boosting the value of otherwise commonplace objects.

Fig. 15. This rowel spur set in a tree root, now in the Victoria and Albert Museum, is alleged to have been discovered on the battlefield at Agincourt but it is a forgery of the late nineteenth or early twentieth century.

There is a similar problem with a set of objects in the V&A—a pommel, quillons, and by-knife from a sword.[54] These items, as well as a rosary of coral and gold, were said to have belonged to John Wodehouse who, as we have seen earlier in this chapter, had legends created about him by Drayton. In fact the objects were made in England around 1610. The cross-hilt was deliberately made in a medieval style to fit the legend. Another forgery is a single leaf of an illuminated manuscript claiming to be a scene of the battle, which has often been used to illustrate books on the Hundred Years War (Fig. 16). Although the parchment is of medieval date, the illumination was painted in the early twentieth century.[55] On websites the picture is also misinterpreted as a tapestry.

The problem surrounding the Stonyhurst Froissart is rather different. It is a genuine copy of part of Froissart's *Chroniques* produced under the direction of the book dealer Pierre Liffol in Paris *c.*1413–14. The claim is that it was captured from its French owner at the battle and brought to England. Sir John Arundell of Lanherne in Cornwall was probably on the campaign. The manuscript bears the signature of a later Sir John Arundell, most likely the man who died in 1545. A cadet branch of the family was created Baron Arundell of Wardour in 1605, and it was through a descendant that the manuscript came to Stonyhurst College

Fig. 16. This representation of the Battle of Agincourt (Victoria and Albert Museum E. 1169–1921) has found its way into several modern studies but is a forgery painted around 1900 using parchment from the medieval period.

in 1837. It is unlikely that a manuscript of this quality and large size (folio, several inches thick) would have been taken on campaign by its French owner. What we have is another example of the desire to link a special object with a special event without justification or proof.[56]

Another Agincourt legend revolves around the large ruby set in the Imperial State Crown.[57] This stone was in the royal collection by 1685 and may go back earlier, being one of the items sold during the Commonwealth but repurchased after the Restoration of Charles II. By the end of the eighteenth century several legends had grown up around the stone, first that it had been given to the Black Prince by Pedro the Cruel, king of Castile, after the Battle of Nájera in 1367, although some also claimed that the Black Prince had worn it at the Battle of Poitiers in 1356. An exotic element was added with the story that Pedro murdered the king of Granada to acquire his jewels. The final tale was that Henry V wore the ruby in his crowned helmet at Agincourt. It was all made to fit with Shakespeare. 'Henry's "sudden and hotte alarmes in France" were symbolised by this flaming beacon which he bore as a badge' and it was this ruby 'which turned the sword of the duke of Alencon'.[58] All of this was invention.

Even the funeral achievements of Henry V in Westminster Abbey are not all they are claimed to be (Fig. 17).[59] In 1682 Henry Keepe commented: 'the saddle which this heroic Prince used in the wars in France with his shield and other warlike furniture is to be seen'.[60] In fact the saddle was not the king's but was made for one of the four horses used in his funeral ceremonial and was not hung with the funeral achievements until the late seventeenth century. The sword dates to the late fifteenth century and was discovered in the abbey storerooms in 1869. There is no proof that it was linked to Henry's tomb. Websites specializing in replicas none the less claim that 'it could be the very sword Henry V carried at Agincourt'. The remaining pieces (helmet and shield) were probably hung above the king's tomb following his funeral on 6 November 1422. The helmet dates to the late fourteenth century. Although it may have been used at the funeral, a

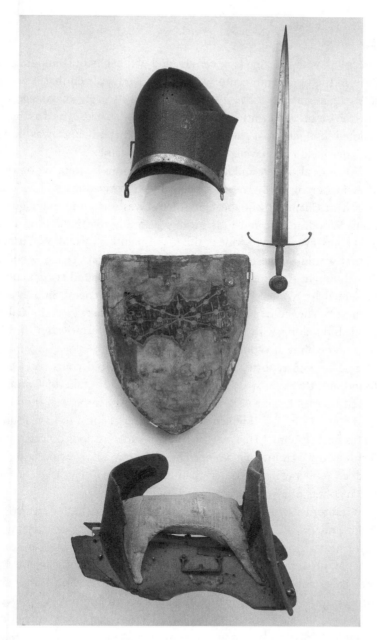

Fig. 17. The funeral achievements of Henry V in Westminster Abbey. Not all of the pieces, however, can be shown to have a definite link with the king's funeral.

direct link with the king is uncertain, and with Agincourt impossible. Even in the nineteenth century, Charles Knight realized that it was a tilting helmet and not the type worn in battle. The signs of damage are not the result of an attack on the king at the battle, as has been claimed, but rather of the method by which the helmet was hung up. The shield may have belonged to Henry's father.

Problems also surround the finds of excavations by John Woodford at Azincourt in 1818. The context of these excavations will be discussed in Chapter 7 but the finds themselves raise important questions. Woodford wrote to his brother claiming that he dug up two gold coins, even drawing one of them.[61] A painting by J. M. W. Turner in 1823 within a collection called 'Fairfaxiana' portrays Henry V and a French knight standing either side of 'a gold coin found at Agincourt presented by Walter Fairfax esquire by Major General Sir Edward Barnes'.[62] The coin is still in existence at Fairfax's seat in Otley (Yorkshire) along with the Turner drawing. The relationship of this coin to the finds of Woodford remains unclear. The *Caledonian Mercury* of 25 May 1818 reported that more than sixty gold coins had been found and that one was in the possession of the duke of Gordon. When Charles Knight visited the battlefield in 1856 he was shown a gold coin of Charles VI which a local labourer claimed to have found 'in his field labour'.[63] This may be true but such precious objects were just the kind of thing that a nineteenth-century visitor would hope to find at Agincourt and, other than the coin in Otley, the current whereabouts of all the others is unknown.

Woodford also described finds of metal objects (including an arrowhead) and rings. The report in the *Caledonian Mercury* even claimed that 'one brass ring was found filled with clay and a finger bone sticking in it', and that the rings were pledges given to the French knights by their ladies as they departed for the wars. None of Woodford's finds are now extant. All were apparently brought back to England. A reviewer of Harris Nicolas's *History of the Battle of Agincourt* (1827) mentions handling a ring with a little blue flower and other objects. In 1846 Woodford showed 'a plain gold ring with a cabalistic inscription' to a meeting of the Archaeological Institute in London.[64] In a letter to his brother in 1818 he had spoken of an intention to have rings made in imitation of one of his finds, which had white enamelled flowers and red lettering. In a letter he wrote on 30 September 1874 Woodford speaks of facsimiles of four golden rings in the possession of the duke of Richmond and Gordon at Goodwood.[65] A privately printed catalogue of 1907 referred to a gold ring in a case at Goodwood made following one found at Azincourt but the subsequent existence of even the facsimile rings cannot be traced.[66]

Woodford's letter of 1874 claimed that the originals of the rings were destroyed in a fire at the Pantechnicon on 13 February 1874.[67] The Pantechnicon, in Belgrave Square, was a huge furniture and goods storage facility which also housed a bazaar and exhibition rooms. The assumption has been that Woodford stored all his finds there although his letter of 1874 mentions only the rings. A further mystery surrounds whether Woodford had ever publicly displayed his Agincourt finds at the Pantechnicon or elsewhere. No British newspaper mentions it. The claim that Woodford established a 'Musée d'Azincourt' in England is found only in a funding appeal to establish a commemorative chapel in the parish church of Azincourt. This appeal was composed by the Commission des antiquités départementales du Pas-de-Calais in 1856 and was extremely critical of 'L'Etranger' ('the stranger'—whom we can take to mean Woodford) who had carried off objects to London and interfered with human remains at the site.[68] Woodford visited the battlefield again in 1852. When a memoir of his life was written in 1880 it was claimed he had also discovered a very large drinking horn with an inscribed brass collar, which sounds a very unlikely object to be a genuine archaeological find. A lady in Keswick in 1902 apparently had the drinking horn and some coins excavated by Woodford but no one has been able to find where these are now.[69]

It is not surprising that tourist locations should seek Agincourt connections. Publicity for a walk around Bossington in the Test Valley (Hants.) claims that there is a field known locally as 'Agincourt' and that 'Henry V, en route with his army for Southampton and the battle of Agincourt, encamped here unable to cross the Channel because of unfavourable winds'.[70] A leaflet for Sandwich (Kent) advertises the Butts 'used in medieval times as an archery practice field. Believed to be the site where Henry V's archers practised before sailing for their famous victory at Agincourt 1415.' In fact the army departed from the Solent not the Channel Ports. The National Trust website provides notes on the history of the pear trees at Dirham Park. 'Warden pears formed part of the provisions of the troops at Agincourt where Worcestershire bowmen carried banners depicting a pear tree laden with fruit.' That is a fascinating development on Drayton's invention of the banner of the Worcestershire contingent which had the motif of pears. But Drayton had said nothing about the soldiers eating the pears. On the question of diet, a story also developed that the English troops were fed beef on the eve of Agincourt. This found its way into *Tom Brown's Schooldays* (1857): Agincourt was a healthy, manly battle suitable to inspire the young of Victorian Britain.

The Created Agincourt

Literature

The inspiration of Agincourt on literary creativity in England did not end with Drayton. In 1819 another long poem was written, *The Lay of Agincourt*, presented as if a genuine ballad of the period.[71] The reviewer in the *Leeds Mercury* on 31 July certainly thought it gave 'an accurate description of that celebrated battle'. Its 'author' was a wandering minstrel who came to Ewood Hall near Halifax. The owner of the hall, Lord Clifford, identified him as the Master Bard Llewellin, recalling that he had heard him at Windsor in the presence of the late king (i.e. Henry V), his nobles and beauties, where he 'tore our spirits with the lay of Agincourt's embattled day'. Offered an opportunity to reprise his poem, the Bard claimed to speak from bitter

experience since the French had captured him, but he had known
how to retaliate:

> I bore their taunts with fit disdain
> And sang then Poictiers' battle strain
> And Edward's feats on Cressy's plain
> Till sham'd they left the place
>
> (stanza 44)

Shakespeare is a major influence on the poem both in Henry's wan-
derings around the camp and his pre-battle speech. The French spend
the night carousing: 'Already in their feasting eye | They see the red-
cross prostrate lie.' New stories are introduced. The sire de Dampierre
had given his gauntlet to Lord Willoughby at the surrender of Harfleur: they meet again at the battle. Davy Gam and two other Welsh
came to defend the king. The Bard invokes the aid of St David. The
choice of a Welsh bard as narrator may have contributed to the idea
of major Welsh involvement in the battle. That said, there is also
emphasis on English success. The contrived poem omits the killing
of the prisoners completely.

Over the nineteenth and twentieth centuries many novels for adults
and children have taken Agincourt as their theme. G. P. R. James's
Agincourt (1844) was not deemed amongst the best of his works,
according to *The Spectator* of 23 November of that year, but it set the
tone for a romantic as well as heroic approach. Like several subsequent works it followed the fortunes of English participants as they
joined the army and journeyed to France, mixing fictional and real
characters and ensuring there was love interest. A similar approach
colours Katherine Phipps's *The Sword of De Bardwell: A Tale of Agincourt*
(1881). G. A. Henty's *At Agincourt: A Tale of the White Hoods of Paris* (1897)
was in the swashbuckling mode of his other adventure stories. Over
his eighty or so books, Henty sought to recall British war successes
from the Norman Conquest onwards, aimed at inculcating manliness
in the teenage boy. His hero of Agincourt, Guy Aylmer, was aged 16.
Henty's works were very popular, selling 25 million copies by 1914.[72]

The teenage archer hero—usually Welsh—has been a common feature in twenty-first-century works.[73]

Bernard Cornwell's *Azincourt* (2008) also follows the fortunes of an archer, although this time an Englishman, Nicholas Hook. Cornwell took the name and those of other archers from the campaign lists presented in my *Agincourt: A New History*, but the French girlfriend is invented. Modern taste is reflected by the greater role assigned to women in this previously 'boy's own' world. Martha Rofheart's *Cry God for Harry* (1972) has some chapters narrated by women. *The Agincourt Bride* of Joanna Hickson (2012) ('Her beauty fuelled a war. Her courage captured a king') also has a female narrator and views the battle through news brought to Princess Catherine. In Laurel O'Donnell's *The Angel and the Prince* (2014), the heroine voices concerns about the forthcoming battle but takes things into her own hands by dressing as a knight to fight. Perhaps because of the dominance of Shakespeare's *Henry V*, there has been no attempt as yet to produce a film which does not use his play, but there has been talk of Cornwell's novel reaching the screen. To date, no *Dr Who* episode has been situated at the battle but the Doctor was there: in 'Talons of Wen Chiang' (1976, part 5) he tells his companion, 'It's the wrong time my dear, you'd have loved Agincourt'. To fill the gap, a story has been written. The Doctor's granddaughter Susan is disguised as Simon, a page: it is her task to distract Henry V from the rockets the Doctor is launching to make the rain fall.[74] We now know the reason for the English victory!

Art

The first known free-standing painting of Agincourt was one of three works commissioned in 1729–31 from William Kent by Queen Caroline, wife of George II.[75] They were intended to be hung as a quasi-triptych, the largest, portraying the battle, in the centre flanked by the smaller paintings of Henry meeting Charles VI's queen, Isabeau, and Henry's marriage to Catherine. This juxtaposition emphasized female mediation. Caroline was also keen to emphasize British identity as part of Hanoverian political strategy. For her library at St James's

Palace she commissioned from the sculptor Rysbrack in 1737 terracotta busts of English rulers, including Henry V and Catherine. She may also have prompted the purchase from Lord Cornwallis of sixteenth-century portraits of kings of England, Henry V included.[76]

The three Henry V paintings were hung in the queen's dressing room at St James's Palace. Horace Walpole saw them there in 1758, twenty years after her death. Kent's battle painting places Henry V centre stage in gold armour in close combat presumably with the duke of Alençon (Fig. 18). Although the scene portrays the melee, three archers are seen with arrows drawn to their ears.

Other eighteenth-century portrayals of Agincourt also focused on Henry V and were inspired by historical narratives or else Shakespeare (Figs. 19 and 20). A print of 1783, based on a painting by John Mortimer (1740–79), well known for his depictions of scenes from British history, reveals an effort to make Henry and the battle fit with classical

Fig. 18. This is one of three paintings of the life of Henry V produced by William Kent for Queen Caroline, wife of George II, around 1729. The largest scene, the battle, was flanked by smaller paintings of Henry meeting the French queen and marrying Catherine de Valois.

HENRY 5.th defeats the FRENCH at AGINCOURT.

J. Wale del. A. Parr sculp.
Publish'd March 7. 1746. by J. Astley.

Fig. 19. This book illustration from *A New History of England by Question and Answer*, published in 1746, shows how Agincourt was portrayed in order to emphasize the personal greatness of Henry V as king. Note the fleuret which has been hacked off from Henry's crown, a popular story which has its roots in the early narratives.

The Battle of *AGINCOURT* named by
King HENRY the FIFTH.

Fig. 20. This print from around 1750 recalls the scene in Shakespeare's *Henry V* where the king, having asked the French herald, orders the battle to be named after the nearby castle. Note here the image of the castle on a hilltop, which may be derived from fifteenth-century illuminations, and also the attempt at verisimilitude through stripped bodies.

Fig. 21. This print of 1783, inspired by Rapin de Thoyras's *Histoire d'Angleterre* (1727–36), is dedicated to the duke of Rutland. It portrays the battle using dynamic classical forms. Note the archers behind the stakes on the far left, below the imagined hilltop castle of Agincourt.

norms (Fig. 21). Such prints tend to show several phases of the battle simultaneously. The 1783 illustration, taking its lead from the influential history of Rapin de Thoyras, shows archers massed behind stakes as well as the melee.

Agincourt did not dominate. In the reign of George III, Edward III was the favoured subject because of his founding of the Order of the Garter: a series of paintings commissioned from Benjamin West for Windsor Castle ignored Agincourt but included Crécy scenes. No paintings of Agincourt are linked to Queen Victoria and Prince Albert despite their keenness for historical scenes: for their *bal costumé* of May 1842 the theme was again Edward III and the Garter, with the royal couple dressed as the king and his queen.[77] Agincourt also missed out in the redecoration of the new Houses of Parliament. A Royal Commission of Fine Art chaired by Prince Albert in 1847 sought large paintings on British history but *The Battle of Agincourt* submitted by Eyre Crowe (1824–1910) was not selected. A hostile reviewer explained why:[78]

> Mr Eyre Crowe may possibly have thought confusion a necessary element towards the realization of such a scene. He has accordingly produced so much of what it involved ... aided by no arrangement of light and dark to bring out some forms or subdue others—that the eye cannot rest on any point. The picture is so minute in archaeological details as to appeal more to the antiquary than to lovers of Art.

Melling's *Battle of Agincourt*, exhibited in 1842, depicted Henry V defending his wounded brother, Gloucester. As the reviewer in *The Spectator* of 21 May noted, 'this was a victory that is famed in our annals': although the artist had captured the spirit of the scene, the execution was deficient not only technically but also in fit of character and arrangement of groups. Agincourt was difficult to live up to but a special effort was made in 1805 by Sir Robert Ker Porter (1777–1842) who claimed descent from the Sir William Porter who fought at the battle. Ker Porter was known for his large-scale panoramas of battle scenes, including in 1801 a canvas over 40 metres (131 feet) long of the victory against the French at Alexandria fought in March of that year. He produced a similarly large representation of the Battle of Seringapatam, the British victory against Tipu Sultan in 1799.

In 1805 Ker Porter painted an Agincourt occupying 261 square metres (2,807 square feet) of canvas and 30.5 metres (100 feet) long. It was displayed at The Lyceum in the Strand with a printed explanation of the battle to guide visitors, who paid 1s. for entrance (Fig. 22).[79] Whilst the focus was again on the king protecting his brother as well as responding to the attack of Alençon, the size of the painting allowed for much imagination. Ker Porter even included a peaceful cottage with its smoking chimney and a woman in male attire who had followed her French husband and was now bent over his body in grief. The painting was shown in New York in 1809. In 1819 Ker Porter presented it to the City of London who placed it in the Egyptian Hall

Fig. 22. Robert Ker Porter was already well known for his large paintings of great military events when he painted in 1805 a great canvas of Agincourt, covering 261 square metres (2,807 square feet). Such an ambitious project generated much public interest, as this advertisement shows.

of Mansion House. During renovations it was taken down and not seen for several years until found in the cellars of the Guildhall in 1834, when it was mistakenly thought to be an ancient work placed there for safekeeping during the Great Fire of London. The City intended to redisplay it but it had been damaged by dampness and by 1880 had been cut into three sections. At that point, a committee was appointed to explore where the painting could be hung but its subsequent fate is unknown.[80]

It was not the first painting of the battle to have been given to the City. Josiah Boydell (who was also responsible for setting up the Boydell Shakespeare Gallery and illustrating several play scenes) had presented his *Battle of Agincourt* in 1794. The painting, which no longer survives, was described by his uncle John, who was Lord Mayor in 1790, as demonstrating 'the presence of a mind, dexterity, firmness and precaution' of the common English soldier, contrary to the confusion and vain confidence of the French.[81]

Nineteenth-century representations continued to feature the same themes as in the previous century. Shakespeare remained a strong influence, encouraging a continuing emphasis on the king himself, as the paintings of Sir John Gilbert (1817–97) demonstrate. To celebrate the anniversary of Agincourt in October 1863 Gilbert produced an etching for the *Illustrated London News* entitled *The Battle of Agincourt* based on his watercolour of the previous year. An accompanying article explained how the artist had conceived the subject by selecting a passage from *Henry V* (Act 4 Scene 7), the king's exchange with the French herald after the battle. An oil painting *The Morning of the Battle of Agincourt*, showing the prayerfulness of the English army

Fig. 23. Sir John Gilbert was renowned for historical paintings as well as for his 511 illustrations in *The Works of Shakespeare* (1857). The moment portrayed here in his *The morning of the Battle of Agincourt* of 1884 (Guildhall Art Gallery) is the prayerfulness of the English army before battle commenced.

before the battle, was painted in 1884 and is in the Guildhall Art Gallery (Fig. 23). Another oil painting, *King Henry V at the Battle of Agincourt*, in the Atkinson Art Gallery, Southport, shows the king commanding an imaginary cavalry charge.[82]

In the 1840s chessmen were produced in the armour of Agincourt, and a statue of the duke of York at the battle was displayed in Westminster Hall.[83] Statues of Henry V featured in several locations, including the Shire Hall at Monmouth in 1792 and the Houses of Parliament in the 1860s. In the twentieth century there have been so many representations of the battle, both figurative and imaginative, that it is impossible to review them here but they demonstrate the never-failing inspiration which the battle provides. *Agincourt* by Neville Gabie (b.1959), part of his series 'Playing Away', portrays it as a football pitch with scarecrow-like figures: 'Pitch. Flat with a thick covering of grass. But the surface is uneven, soft and muddy underfoot. Located in Northern France...' (Fig. 24).[84]

Music

As a battle, Agincourt is unique in inspiring in its immediate wake a piece of vocal music, 'Deo Gracias Anglia', known as 'the Agincourt Carol' (Fig. 6). It may be the 'Song with the old music made at the battle of Agincourt' mentioned by Thomas Hearne in 1727, and that advertised in the *Public Advertiser* of July 1757, but the first full transcription of the Agincourt Carol was in Charles Burney's *General History of Music* in 1776. Burney described it as 'a venerable relic of our nation's prowess and glory... from which we are perhaps entitled to more honour than from the poetry and Music with which they were then celebrated'.[85] The carol has undergone various arrangements in later years. Percy Whitlock composed a fanfare on it in 1940, its subject matter deemed appropriate for wartime, and William Walton put the tune to good use in his film score for Olivier's *Henry V* (1944).

From the mid-nineteenth century onwards, a number of composers have taken inspiration from Agincourt. Victorian taste for heroic ballads is seen in James Smythe's 'Frappe Forte Song' of 1865 (that title recalling the arms of the Wodehouse family) which begins

AGINCOURT

Pitch. Flat, with a thick covering of grass. But the surface is uneven, soft and muddy underfoot. Located in northern France, winter weather can be very cold. More typically though, it's wet and often foggy.

Goalposts are metal and standard size 8^FT × 24^FT.

Fig. 24. In 1998–9 Neville Gabie produced 'Playing Away', a series of 24 photographs first exhibited at the Tate Liverpool and now in the Tate collection. The majority were of improvised fields in South Africa. The artist drew parallels between the battlefield and the modern football field as a place of racial competition. This photograph was taken at Azincourt.

'On Agincourt's old rampart', and William Wallace's song 'Agincourt' of 1892. At a dinner for the Guards on 26 August 1856, reported in the *Morning Chronicle*, a song by Mr G. Linley invoked the link between past and present: brave were the mailed English knights at Agincourt, but just as much valour recently (i.e in the Crimea) had been displayed by brave British hearts. In 1897 Edward Davey Rendall set Drayton's 'Ballad of Agincourt' to music for baritone and chorus. That male voices were deemed the most appropriate for Agincourt is seen in Myles Birket's *Agincourt: A Cantata for Male Voices* of 1908, and Rutland Boughton's *Agincourt: A Dramatic Scene for Male Voices* of 1926. But the female voice was not forgotten. The *Morning Chronicle* of 1856 also reported on Mme Novello's rendition of 'The Captive of Agincourt', with words by Charles d'Orléans hearing of the death of his wife Bonne.

The military context has inspired marches, including Stanley Cooper's 'Agincourt—grande marche militaire' of 1892 and John Philip Sousa's 'March to Agincourt' of 1907 to celebrate the fiftieth anniversary of the founding of Agincourt in Iowa. Another anniversary, the Silver Jubilee of King George V in 1935, prompted a BBC commission of the concert overture 'Agincourt' from Walter Leigh (1905–42). The recalling of the glories of 1415 in connection with these memorable events demonstrates yet again the power of the Agincourt story.

In 1955 George Dyson wrote a cantata *Agincourt* for mixed choir and orchestra, drawing on speeches from Shakespeare as well as the Agincourt Carol. Dyson (1883–1964) had developed a specialism in grenades during his First World War service, even publishing a book on the training and organization of grenadiers in 1915. It was the heady mixture of Agincourt and the First World War which inspired the pop group 'Agincourt' (who had already released a track called 'Agincourt' in 1994 three years after their formation) to release in 2011 an album *Angel of Mons* inspired by the Machen story. As their publicity states, 'From such humble origins the legend was born. In a similar way, in years to come "Angel of Mons" may too be looked upon as a legendary release from a hard-working, well-deserving and really great bunch of guys.'[86] The 'Agincourt' playlist can be continued with a sonata for two cellos in 1995 by the French composer Olivier Greif (1950–2000) and a short fiery rhythmic piece for string orchestra by the Cincinnati-based Doug Spata (b.1975). There has even been *Agincourt: The Musical*, book and lyrics by Nathan Joseph (d.2005), as well as an opera by George Lloyd (d.1998), commissioned for the Festival of Britain in 1951—*John Socman*, named after a supposed Wiltshire soldier at the battle.[87]

What's in a Name?

Agincourt Care Home, Agincourt Solicitors, Agincourt Financial, Agincourt Insurance Brokers, Agincourt Designs, Agincourt Roofing, Agincourt School Nursery, Agincourt Solutions. 'Agincourt' is obviously seen to be a business asset, epitomizing a positive approach bound to generate success. Agincourt in London Road, Camberley is the longest-running rock club in the UK, the name deriving from its venue, the Agincourt Hall, built in the early twentieth century. No doubt Google could reveal many more 'Agincourts' across the world, whether businesses, buildings, or street names.

The Napoleonic Wars started the trend. A search of newspapers reveals that in 1805 a horse called Agincourt was running at Newmarket.[88] In 1817 (although 1830 is also a possibility) the marketplace in Monmouth was renamed Agincourt Square in honour of Henry V's birth in Monmouth castle.[89] The really significant moment was the naming of a ship of the line as HMS *Agincourt* in 1796. (An HMS *Cressy* had to wait until 1810.)[90] In 1817 a new HMS *Agincourt* was built for the fleet. In its report on the launch, the *Caledonian Mercury* mused that 'the very name carries with it such a degree of interest and importance in every British recollection as to demand no inferior accomplishments'. The ship remained in service until 1884 although renamed HMS *Vigo* in 1865. In that year the first iron-clad HMS *Agincourt* was commissioned. She remained in service until 1904 although twice renamed, and was not broken up until 1960.[91]

In 1914, in the naval arms race before the First World War, an HMS *Agincourt* was commissioned but never built. Instead, at the outbreak of hostilities, the Royal Navy requisitioned a ship initially constructed in Britain for the government of Brazil but which had been purchased in December 1913 by the Sultan of Turkey. Her renaming as HMS *Agincourt* was announced on the very day war began and was seen as a triumph for Churchill as First Lord of the Admiralty: 'he has acted decisively and fearlessly in a great national emergency', commented the *Daily Telegraph*.[92] The ship had the largest number of heavy guns and gun turrets of any dreadnought battleship. (As a pun on her name, she was popularly known as 'the Gin Palace'.) She was sold in 1922 and scrapped two years later. The last HMS *Agincourt* was a destroyer launched in January 1945 which was decommissioned in 1972.

The ship name prompted the use of 'Agincourt' for a locomotive.[93] To celebrate Queen Victoria's Diamond Jubilee in 1897 the London and North Western Railway Company built a number of 'Jubilee Class' locomotives to which the names of Royal Navy ships were given. One of the first was 'Black Prince' of June 1897. 'Agincourt' was built in 1900 and remained in service until June 1930. A second 'Agincourt', again one of a number of ship names chosen for a class of trains, was a British Rail Class 50 Diesel of 1978 which remained in service until 1988.

A diesel shunter, 'The Empress of Agincourt', began life in Montreal in 1957 and ran until 1995. It also had a less respectful name—the 'Agincourt Tramp'. The engine is now in the Elgin County Railway Museum in St Thomas, Ontario.[94] Its name was occasioned by the place name Agincourt, now a suburb of Toronto. The story of the naming of the settlement may be apocryphal. In June 1858 a John Hill had a post office approved for his general store but needed financial support. A friend in Quebec agreed to help so long as a French name was used. Allegedly the name 'Agincourt' satisfied his French-Canadian friend whilst not offending his English and Scottish neighbours.[95] The settlement developed strongly once a railway station was built in 1871.

There is an older Agincourt in Fennimore County, Iowa which began life as a 1-mile-square plot registered at Muskrat City Courthouse on 25 October 1853. The choice of date was obviously significant. The city was incorporated on the anniversary in 1857. At its fifty-year celebrations in 1907 a public fountain was erected and opened to the strains of the specially commissioned Sousa 'March to Agincourt'. A public library was built in 1915. Crispin Creek forms the southern boundary of the original township site, and State Highway 7 is named Agincourt Avenue.

The name 'Agincourt' had particular appeal in pioneer societies since it epitomized a heroic spirit under challenging circumstances. Agincourt, in the Mpumalanga province of South Africa (until 1995 East Transvaal) was developed in the 1880s. A group of four reefs at the outer edge of the Great Barrier Reef off Queensland is called Agincourt reef. The Australians have a particular penchant for Agincourt, beginning in the late nineteenth century with the Agincourt Hotel, George Street, Sydney, and Agincourt Villas in Annandale, and moving on to Agincourt Crescent in Valentine, New South Wales and the Agincourt Beachfront Apartments in Queensland.[96] This is about as far as one can get from a muddy field in wet October in northern France.

7

'Rival Experts Prepare To Do Battle over Agincourt'

In 2008 British newspapers reported on a conference of French academics at the Centre historique médiéval at Azincourt to mark the 593rd anniversary of the battle. They claimed that the centre's director had described the English as 'war criminals' because of the killing of the prisoners. This report was as misleading as some of the accounts and histories of the battle. There was no academic conference and the director protested that he 'never once used the phrase war crime'. In his opinion it was yet another piece of British myth-making on St Crispin's Day.[1]

A historian is only as good as his or her sources but historical sources themselves have to be demonstrably reliable. Sixteenth-century authors showed some awareness of this by listing the works they had consulted and occasionally even commenting on differences between them. But they were limited by having only chronicle sources to draw on, and by their desire to write narrative rather than analysis. The real leap forward in the study of Agincourt came when a wider range of sources was used and when a truly critical edge was applied to them. We see tentative steps in the first biography of Henry V published in 1704 by Thomas Goodwin, even though his approach remained narrative and laudatory. This was hardly surprising given the context of the War of the Spanish Succession and the focus on a hero king. Goodwin drew on unpublished administrative records of the crown, then housed in the Tower of London, and on the documents collected by Sir Robert Cotton which were first catalogued in 1696.[2] In this Goodwin had assistance from Thomas Rymer who had been commissioned by the government to search out and publish materials on diplomatic relations from the Middle Ages to the present.

Historians are still in Rymer's debt. The volume for the reign of Henry V, first published in 1709, includes many key documents for the 1415 campaign including army indentures.[3] Further benefits came from the publication in the 1770s of the records of parliament and in the 1830s of the privy council. The editor of the latter was Harris Nicolas. Nicolas had served as a naval officer during the Napoleonic Wars but then trained for the Bar, specializing in peerage cases. His career as a historian was dogged by a tendency to fall out with the antiquarian establishment, and by an inability to manage his finances.[4] Nor could he distance himself completely from the time in which he wrote. The preface to the first edition of his *History of the Battle of Agincourt* (London, 1827) was dedicated to George IV, Prince Regent during the recent wars with France, 'under whose auspices the splendour even of that victory [i.e. Agincourt] has been rivalled, if not eclipsed'.

In Nicolas's view, historians had done as much as might be expected to illustrate Agincourt. A reading of his book shows the influence of Sharon Turner's *History of England in the Middle Ages* of 1815, which provided the best narrative to date although using chronicle sources alone. But, Nicolas argued, this was not the same as 'the herculean task of examining and relating every material transaction in the annals of this century'. This was the only way 'to arrive at just conclusions, to reconcile conflicting testimony, or from the mass, sometimes of prejudiced, often of ignorant chroniclers, to compose a true and consistent statement'. Nicolas's study, which was reordered and expanded into a second edition in 1832 and reprinted in 1833, is extremely important for its inclusion of non-narrative material. Nicolas had been stimulated into writing the book by his discovery of the Agincourt Roll, which he printed from the version in the British Museum (now Library), Harley 782. Whilst he assumed wrongly that the roll had been compiled deliberately by Henry 'to preserve their

names from oblivion', he was sceptical of family claims that special
arms and mottoes derived from the battle and commented critically
on the dangerous influence of Shakespeare's speeches. He also
included a list of those who entered into indentures for the campaign,
drawn from another post-medieval text.[5] It is important to realize that
Nicolas did not use original governmental records but copies made by
heralds and antiquarians. His lists need to be used carefully, but we
cannot deny the impact his work had on knowledge and awareness of
the battle.

Nicolas also provided the first plan of possible deployments at the
battle (Fig. 27) as well as maps derived from the Cassini maps published between 1756 and 1815, based on surveys completed by 1789.
Nicolas's most important contribution was a translation into English
of the *Gesta Henrici Quinti*.[6] Using this alongside other chronicles he
wrote a narrative of the campaign 'deduced from such contemporary
statements as were consistent with each other and with truth'. For the
battle itself, he relied mainly on the Burgundian writers whose military
detail was the richest. Nicolas emphasized that the battle began with
'the English archers shooting their arrows as soon as they were within
reach of the enemy and much execution was done among them before
the combatants closed'. The French cavalry failed to override the
archers, causing disarray in the French vanguard. Henry took immediate advantage of this by 'causing his men to advance upon them with
the greatest celerity, at which moment the flanks of both armies
immerged into the woods on each side'. The French vanguard caused
some damage to the English but the entry of the English archers into
the melee led to a 'dreadful slaughter'.

A sympathy for the French characterizes Nicolas's work. 'If an
author be permitted to anticipate that his work will be attended by
any particular result, the hope may be expressed that this account of
the Battle of Agincourt will tend to remove the absurd impression that
the victory must be contemplated with humiliating feelings in France.'
This impacts upon his narrative. Nicolas emphasizes that the French
were victims of 'the unfortunate situation', especially the soft ground

and restricted space, as much as of the valour of their enemies. He makes much of the last-effort 'gallant charge' by the counts of Marle and Fauquembergues. Although he comments that the French rearguard fled when they saw what was happening to the front divisions, he has part of that rearguard collecting 'as if they intended to renew the conflict and Henry being informed that they had actually attacked his rear and plundered his baggage'. Therefore Nicolas has French bravery and achievement as the cause of Henry's order to kill the prisoners. 'Imperative necessity consequently dictated what no other circumstances could possibly palliate.'

The killing of the prisoners concerned Nicolas to a degree not seen in earlier writings. Drawing on the Burgundian narratives, he emphasized the reluctance of the English to obey the king's command. Nicolas wanted to explain this as the result of 'an honourable trait in the character of the conquerors … from feelings of honor and humanity', but had to admit 'unfortunately' that it was an unwillingness to lose the benefit of ransoms. He speaks of the killing as 'this shocking massacre', his choice of wording being taken up in other nineteenth-century accounts of the battle. 'This measure has scarcely a parallel in modern warfare and nothing but the most urgent motives of self-preservation can prevent its being deemed an act of barbarous atrocity … it is not too much to consider that Henry had recourse to it with repugnance.' Nicolas was not alone in this tone. Sharon Turner had also exonerated Henry by claiming his exertions 'may be admitted as his apology for a precipitate act of inhumanity into which the general excitation and alarm of his wearied, tho' conquering countrymen, combined to urge him'. Turner emphasized that French historians also saw it as 'a mistake not intentional cruelty'. This line was followed by Endell Tyler in his biography of Henry in 1838.[7]

For Nicolas, the French were brave and patriotic and should take lustre from Agincourt:

The defeat was the result of a concatenation of unfortunate circumstances, and left no stain on its military fame, beyond error in judgment on the part of its leaders ... Brilliant as is the event in the English annals, it is no otherwise humiliating to the French than from consideration that it arose from want of military skill in their commanders. He, therefore, who attempts to deduce from the battle proof of superior prowess on the part of the conquerors, or founds on it a reflection on the courage of the vanquished betrays consummate ignorance on the real merits of the case.

Nicolas considered Henry's decision to march north to Calais to be foolish, since surely he knew his enemies would intercept him. For him this deprived Henry of praise as a wise or prudent general, a surprising remark given the glory which the battle brought the king. Henry is less centre stage despite the use of the *Gesta*. Nicolas considered that the victory should be chiefly attributed to the 'gallantry and steadiness' of the archers. His conclusion also emphasizes the contribution of Henry's army:

> By Englishmen that victory is justly contemplated as one of the most splendid events in the annals of their country. Though the recent achievements of our armies tend to throw former triumphs in the shade, the glory of Agincourt is imperishable; and base indeed must be the man whose valour is not strengthened when he remembers the prowess of his ancestor on that glorious day.

Nicolas had not been able to use surviving fifteenth-century records because they were in a chaotic state. This elicited a characteristically caustic remark that the public records were 'in their present condition perfectly useless and as little heeded as if, instead of illustrating the history of this country, they were the papers of an insolvent tradesman'.[8] In the early nineteenth century there were efforts to redeem this situation, culminating in the establishment of the Public Record Office in 1837—although its search rooms did not open until 1866. As assistant keeper, Joseph Hunter (1783–1861), became interested in the records of the Queen's Remembrancer and began to assemble these into what later became PRO E 101 (Exchequer Accounts Various). These included muster rolls as well as accounts returned to the Exchequer by captains in later years, which were sometimes accompanied by retinue lists indicating the fate of soldiers during the campaign.

In 1850 Hunter produced a short book, *Agincourt: A Contribution towards an Authentic List of the Commanders of the English Host in King Henry the Fifth's Expedition to France in the Third Year of his Reign.* This summarized his findings to date, at a time when the records were still quite disordered. His book catered for the continuing interest in those who had served on the campaign. Hunter was able to be more precise than Nicolas on retinue size and on individual soldiers. Although his work was not widely known it stimulated William Durrant Cooper to use the public records for a study of 'Sussex Men at Agincourt' in 1863, stimulated by fears that Napoleon III would invade Britain and by the boost to the military volunteer movement.[9] Cooper was pleased to find many family names in common between 1415 and the 1860s, observing how even after four and a half centuries these same families were prepared 'to defend their own hearths and homes as were their predecessors to uphold the military renown of their sovereign before the walls of Harfleur and on the banks of the Ternoise'. Hunter's work also influenced James Hamilton Wylie (1844–1914) who, in his study of the Agincourt Roll in 1911, considered this sixteenth-century copy alongside the fifteenth-century Exchequer materials.[10]

Hunter made an even greater contribution to the study of Agincourt through his archival organizing which eventually led to the publication in 1912 of a catalogue of the contents of E 101, to which indentures were later added.[11] Other Exchequer materials were also grouped into easily understood and consultable classes, especially the Issue Rolls which recorded royal expenditure (E 403) and the Warrants for Issue which ordered such expenditure (E 404). Such work facilitated Wylie's major study of the reign of Henry V.[12] The first volume, taking the story to the departure from Southampton in August 1415, was completed within Wylie's lifetime. At his death in 1914, the second volume, covering the period from Henry's landing at the Chef de Caux to the end of 1416, was in manuscript and was published in 1919.

Wylie's book contains so much information that it is difficult to summarize its interpretation of the battle. As Juliet Barker wisely remarked, 'it is for his footnotes, rather than his chaotic text, that the book is valuable'.[13] Wylie used a very wide range of archival and printed materials—more than any previous study—but did so uncritically. The main weakness is that he did not discriminate between contemporary and later sources, or between evidence and assertion. The myriad contents of his book have been exploited by many historians. They assisted Alfred Burne's *Agincourt War* of 1956. Burne also visited the battlefield and applied the eye of a First World War artillery man to the site, which made it possible for him to be scathing about Wylie's approach.[14]

> Wylie was not a soldier, and if he visited the ground he did not attempt to draw a battle plan. One gets the feeling that he was so immersed in detail that he had not himself a clear idea of the actual course of events, still less of the lessons to be drawn from this famous battle.

Wylie was fully aware of the problems of Agincourt and emphasized the mythologizing. 'There is not a single detail of the battle that does not get transformed or turned completely upside down somehow or somewhere except the fact that the French lost and the English won.' He was critical of the fact that plans of the battle tended simply to be copied from one book to another and to be based on invented 'pretty squares, oblongs and triangles'.[15] This was a criticism of Nicolas. Wylie even claimed Nicolas to be French since his great-grandfather was a Huguenot. And had not Jules Michelet, author of a major *Histoire de France* (1833–65), also praised Nicolas for his impartiality?

Wylie reveals changing views towards armies and warfare in the late nineteenth and early twentieth centuries. We see the impact of the relative peace of Victorian Britain and of his civilian calling as HM Inspector of Schools. He had a fondness for the 'quick-eyed clever longbowmen... who could hit the prick or the oyster shell in the centre of the butt with the nicety of a Thames Fisherman garfangling an eel, while in nimble readiness in the field they stood unrivalled in the western world'. As for the killing of the prisoners, he was critical of Henry: 'it was doubtless to this hideous order that a large part of the enormous butchery of Agincourt is chiefly due for when the massacre had once begun it was impossible to discriminate or stop it'. By the time of Wylie's book, French historians had also adopted a more critical line: 'un acte d'inhumanité, une cruauté sans excuse', proclaimed Duval-Pineu, contrasting Henry's action with that of the great French hero Du Guesclin who had released his prisoners at the Battle of Cocherel in 1364 (although Wylie was not sure this was true!).[16]

Wylie was the first English-speaking historian to draw extensively on French publications although not on archives from that country. Particularly valuable was René de Belleval's *Azincourt* of 1865, which had as its main aim a listing of French who participated in the battle. Belleval (1837–1900) saw this as a way of commemorating those who had fallen for France. His research linked to a project to build a chapel of remembrance at Azincourt on whose walls the names would be inscribed. To this end, he used chronicle sources, especially the list of 273 dead in Monstrelet's *Chronique*, as well as Père Anselme's major genealogical collection and unpublished archives in the Collection Clairambault housed in the Bibliothèque imperiale de France (now the Bibliothèque nationale). The latter included musters of French troops as well as receipts which gave the sizes of companies.

Belleval also provided a narrative, noting the lack of unity in the French army: 'it had too many diverse elements to be able to have confidence in it'. There are oddities in his version of events. A Sir William Marshall commands the English archers, who were drawn up in a double line in front of the army, with 500 sent to the village of Azincourt against Hector de Saveuse who had occupied it. This derived from Mazas's unreliable but colourful *Vie des grands capitaines français du Moyen Âge*, published in 1828–9. Belleval also condemned the killing of the prisoners as an indelible stain on Henry's reputation: he saw it as triggered by a near simultaneous attack on the baggage by a French detachment and the advance of the French 3rd

Division. Oddly he placed this group at Canlers to the north-east of Ruisseauville, even though his map of the battle places the engagement closer to Maisoncelle. He later has Henry send Lord Roos to Canlers to tell the remaining French (whom Belleval believes to be the *milices des communes*) that they were free to leave, a story also derived from Mazas.

Agincourt Research

Thanks to Nicolas and Belleval, Agincourt was in a unique position. The public could know more about it than any other battle, especially about the captains of both sides. This model encouraged other studies, such as the collection of materials on Crécy and the siege of Calais produced by George Wrottesley in 1897.[17] The late twentieth century has also seen important contributions. Gerald Bacquet published a collection of key texts for Agincourt in 1977 and Clifford Rogers for Edward III's campaigns in 2000.[18] For Agincourt I compiled a collection of sources, translating these into English where necessary and explaining the nature of narratives, administrative records, and interpretations of the battle.[19]

Just as the initial leap forward came with use of non-narrative sources by Nicolas and Hunter, so understanding of Agincourt and of late medieval warfare in general has been boosted by the study of administrative records of France, England, and Burgundy.[20] Take, for instance, Boffa's work on the troops of Anthony, duke of Brabant who died at the battle.[21] Combining financial records with chronicles, Boffa showed that the duke was first informed of the progress of the English army on 21 October. Immediately he alerted the barons and officials of his duchy to raise troops and gather at Cambrai awaiting orders. He was so determined to be at the battle that he set out with a smaller force, intending his main army to follow. Leaving Lens for Pernes at 4 a.m. on Friday 25 October, he received letters en route from his brother, Philip, count of Nevers saying that the battle would be fought that day before dinner. After hearing mass, he rushed to the field, arriving late. He had travelled 186 kilometres (116 miles) in forty-eight hours. Boffa traced the transportation of the duke's body from the battlefield to burial at Tervueren on 3 November. The financial records show that 219 horses were used for the expedition although they do not distinguish between riding and cart horses. Three towns in Brabant can be shown to have provided troops, Antwerp, Leuven, and Brussels, although there is only an exact figure for the first: 57 archers. It is doubtful that they reached the battle in time. Overall, Boffa suggests that the Brabant troops present were much smaller than had been hoped: 37 are known by name, 17 of whom met their end at Agincourt alongside their duke.

Such detailed study of non-narrative records makes it possible to reconstruct the armies at Agincourt, although there are several French musters and *quittances* yet to be analysed. Belleval's list of dead and captured can be expanded by using a wider range of sources, including inheritance disputes in legal records. Olivier Bouzy has contributed an important study of the dead based on the core information of Monstrelet. Although concluding that the list may have been edited to emphasize the Burgundian contribution, the geographical origins it suggests have been used by Fabrice Lachaud and Christophe Gilliot to indicate the predominance of Picardy and other northern territories.[22] Remy Ambühl has used French and English records to trace prisoners and ransoms.[23] To date, via the compilation of a database based on all types of sources, around 500 dead and 321 prisoners can be identified.

Thanks to the work of Ambühl, considerable advances have been made in our understanding of the ransoming process. The crown had an interest as it was entitled to a share of war gains. The owners of the prisoners (called their masters) entered into bonds to pay the crown's share. Surviving bonds reveal that 99 archers had interests in 69 prisoners. For some the ransom was worth as much as an archer's wages for the whole campaign. The most valuable prisoners were in the hands of 9 knights and 12 men-at-arms. Knights were often masters of several prisoners, averaging 5 prisoners as against 0.8 per man-at-arms and 0.7 per archer. The bonds also show that there was a market for prisoners. In forty of the seventy-seven bonds, the masters were based in Calais. In other words, soldiers had sold on their prisoner to a merchant or soldier at Calais. Richard Whittington, the famous London merchant, had purchased a French prisoner called Hugues Coniers (alas we do not know from whom) and had sold him on to an Italian merchant for £296.

The bonds reflect non-payment of the crown's share, and it is likely that many ransoms were never collected at all, even where French prisoners had permission to return home to seek funds. Henry V kept the six most important prisoners himself, promising compensation to their captors. In four cases the financial documentation reveals who had captured the prisoner: the duke of Bourbon (Ralph Fowne, esquire); the count of Eu (Sir John Grey); the count of Vendôme (Sir John Cornwall), Marshal Boucicaut (William Wolf, esquire). No captor is known for the duke of Orléans and Artur de Richemont. In the case of lesser prisoners it was not uncommon for two men to have made the capture: the sire de Corps was taken by two men-at-arms, William Callowe in the retinue of Sir Robert Babthorpe and William Kempton serving under Sir William Phelip.

I have examined all of the surviving English financial documentation and muster rolls.[24] This reveals that at least 320 men indented to provide troops and also gives the names of c.8,000 soldiers on the campaign. Extending this approach to cover the period from 1369 to 1453, military careers are revealed and the 1415 expedition put into context.[25] For instance, at least three men serving Richard FitzAlan, earl of Arundel at sea in 1388 served his successor, Earl Thomas, in 1415. John Sutton, later Lord Dudley, began his career on the 1415 campaign at the age of 14 in the retinue of Humphrey, duke of Gloucester. He served on several expeditions to France in the 1420s but was appointed lieutenant of Ireland in 1428. We find him again in the relief of Calais in 1436. Although he focused his energies on the court and politics in the 1440s, he fought in the king's army at the First Battle of St Albans (1455) and at Blore Heath (1459), where he was wounded. He was constable of the Tower of London from 1470 to 1483, dying at the ripe old age of 87. Whilst the scale of the 1415 expedition makes it likely that for some it was their only experience of war, for others it was part of a long professional military career.

Insights can be gained by looking at the financial records of the nobility and gentry. For instance, the account of the receiver-general of John Mowbray, Earl Marshal (1392–1432), shows how the mechanics of payment worked.[26] Mowbray received money from the crown for 50 men-at-arms and 150 archers but was responsible for paying his men. Several were members of his personal and household staff, such as his steward, the master of his horse, baker, armourer, heralds, and minstrels. At least 15 of his men-at-arms served again under him in the expedition of 1417. The earl's purchases for the campaign included a new 'cote armour' as well as an iron seat for his latrine. He borrowed money from the earl of Arundel and others to support his costs, especially the wages for the second quarter where the crown had given jewels as security but no cash. Barker points to others who had to mortgage and pawn in order to go on the campaign. The royal household provided a large number of small retinues since even domestic staff were expected to serve and provide an archer or two. The supervisor of the royal kitchens, William Balne, took a prisoner at Agincourt worth £10.[27]

With so much information available, we might ask why Agincourt remains so contentious. One reason is that popular interpretations are so ingrained that any attempt to challenge them is newsworthy. A major area of contention is numbers, even amongst professional historians. In 2005 Juliet Barker and I both produced books on Agincourt. She noted that 'our conclusions are broadly similar', but did not consider the financial records complete enough to support my views on the army sizes.[28] Ian Mortimer was broadly supportive of my recalculations but suggested 'room for error, allowing for more Frenchmen and slightly fewer Englishmen', say 15,000 against 8,000. Clifford Rogers believes that more may have died or been invalided home from Harfleur.[29]

French historians generally accept my suggestions for lower figures (*c*.12,000) for the French but British and American historians hold out for the older larger numbers.[30] Until more detailed work is done on the French army this debate will continue. It has a long pedigree. Wylie was apoplectic at the suggestion by Delbrück in 1907 that the English army (at 9,000) outnumbered the French (4,000–6,000). In 1946 Ferdinand Lot suggested the French did not exceed the number of the English and could have been lower, perhaps 6,000, based on the width of the battlefield which he placed at 700 metres (765 yards). In his view, if the French were four times as large as the English, they would have been strong enough to push back their opponent.[31] Honig claims that all chronicles say that the French fielded superior numbers.[32] This is not true. The chronicles of the Berry Herald and Artur de Richemont both place the French at 10,000 and the English at 16,500–17,500 and 11,000–12,000 respectively. Both were written in the 1450s and reflect new-found French confidence after the expulsion of the English from Normandy and Gascony between 1449 and 1453.

A further area of debate is the translation of narrative sources into actual actions on the ground. The title of this chapter derived from a much-publicized debate in 1995 between Robert Hardy and Matthew Bennett on the position of the English archers.[33] Were the archers solely on the flanks (the Bennett view, as also that of Jim Bradbury) or were there some in front of the army (the view of Hardy, of Alfred Burne, and of Christopher Allmand, although placing the majority on the flanks)?[34] The wording of chronicles, especially Latin works using classical terminology, makes this difficult to resolve. There was already a debate in the late nineteenth century. Ramsey, in his influential *Lancaster and York* of 1892, placed the archers entirely on the flanks. The battle plan in his book shows the influence of nineteenth-century military organization, especially with regard to the supposed positioning of the French guns which he placed in front of the cavalry on the right flank.[35] In Kingsford's *Henry V* of 1901 (written for the 'Heroes of the Nations' series), the archers were on the flanks of each of the three English battles, and hence in six groups.[36]

There is a wide range of chronicle narratives to choose from, although John Keegan, in his highly stimulating *Face of Battle*, considered the events of the battle to be 'gratifyingly straightforward to relate'.[37] For him the crucial element was that the French advance was forced to a halt. Under such circumstances the French men-at-arms ceased to constitute a threat to the English and were easy pickings for the archers. Detailed knowledge of positions or numbers may therefore be less significant than outcome. Historians can be overanxious on sources. We can learn from military specialists. Burne's 'inherent military probability'—the likely scenario, based on the accumulation of military knowledge—has been criticized but still offers insights.[38]

Narrative accounts can prove problematic when assessing the intentions of commanders. Clifford Rogers has concluded that Henry's decision to march to Calais was 'because he hoped the result would be a general engagement which he needed for strategic reasons and which, despite facing heavy numerical odds, he could reasonably expect to win'.[39] This is essentially an argument from silence. The chronicles do not explicitly say Henry wished to avoid battle, but nor do they say that he sought it. Rogers is not alone in treating chronicles of many varied dates as of equal value and veracity. Yet it is fair to say that financial records, useful as they are for the armies, are less helpful in reconstructing the battle although we can draw something from them. For instance, the relatively high numbers of dead in the retinue of Edward, duke of York, suggests that these men were with him in the vanguard which suffered the greatest French attack. But were his archers and men-at-arms fighting together? Or were archers from different retinues grouped together? Or both?

There has been debate on whether arrows could pierce plate armour. Despite testing, opinion is still divided.[40] One problem is the lack of surviving armour from the period since its thickness is deemed to be a factor in whether arrows could pierce it or not. Other issues concern the draw-weight of bows as well as the impact of distance. In 2011 research was carried out on the effects of armour on movement.[41] A complete late fifteenth-century steel plate armour weighed between 30 and 50 kilograms (66 and 110 pounds): the mechanical work needed to swing the limbs could be costly in terms of energy. To test this, four fight-interpreters from the Royal Armouries, accustomed to wearing armour, were required to walk and run on a treadmill whilst carrying a sword which they supported by both hands. Measurements were taken of metabolic rate and breathing. The metabolic cost of movement in armour was 2.1 to 2.3 times higher than unloaded walking and 1.9 times higher than unloaded running. Therefore the maximum speed of a man in armour was only 1.7 metres (5.6 feet) per second. For a man aged 55 this diminished to 1.4 metres (4.6 feet) per second. Wearing armour also required greater respiratory effort.

The conclusion was that the 'cost' of moving in armour was a limitation on soldiers' performance. A direct link was made with Agincourt: the heavily armoured French men-at-arms had to walk across muddy terrain and would therefore be exhausted by the time they reached the English. The study was eagerly taken up by the press as the reason why the French lost the battle.[42] Three replica armours were used (English, 1480; Milanese, mid- to late fifteenth century; German, late fifteenth century) but the report did not mention different conclusions based on the type of armour. In 1415 English and French men-at-arms wore the same kind of armour. The English also moved forwards and would have expended energy in the melee. Therefore, the impact on the body of wearing armour would affect both sides equally. An important contrast with modern warfare emerged in the study, however. Although today's infantry units carry about the same weight as fifteenth-century armoured men, the load is largely on the trunk and has much less effect on movement of the legs and arms.

Another useful line of enquiry has considered the effects of arrows on forward movement. How might the French have been funnelled into a narrow space? The TV programme *Agincourt's Dark Secrets* (2003) used research on crowd behaviour to answer this.[43] Dr G. Keith Stills, a crowd control analyst, used video evidence from a well-attended concert as well as computer modelling, showing how crowds tend to move inwards, bumping into each other. This is a promising avenue of enquiry since narratives comment on how the French were so close packed they could not raise their weapons. In 2004 Richard Clements and Roger Hughes applied mathematical modelling on the motion of crowds, providing insights into how the French advance became unstable. Groups of French men-at-arms pushed into the English lines but could easily become surrounded and either be taken prisoner or killed, especially if the English line held firm which it seems to have done. 'There was a natural tendency of troops to cluster around their leader especially in any confused situation such as battle.' This would also explain the piling-up of bodies into a number of mounds, as several narratives relate.[44]

Research on the effect of armour weight also took account of the effect of the mud. For *Agincourt's Dark Secrets* there was input from a soil scientist, Professor Andrew Palmer. Soil from the field was analysed. Since accounts suggest that it had rained during the night before the battle, a crucial element was its water-retaining characteristic. Palmer showed that the suction was considerable, slowing down movement and making it difficult for anyone who fell down to get up quickly, especially in full armour. Visiting the battlefield in a wet winter, it is easy to see that water often stands on the surface rather than draining easily. Deep ruts caused by tractor movements are notable. Some accounts tell of the French exercising their horses on the eve of battle and causing the ground to churn up. Therefore weather and soil conditions are highly relevant. But why did the English not suffer from the same problems? Was there variation in the nature of the soil in different parts of the field? This needs further study and discussion of the knowledge medieval commanders had of terrain conditions. Was it purely accidental that the French were forced across wetter, muddier land or was it the result of careful English planning and positioning? Did the English make a short move forwards in order to goad the French into crossing the most difficult terrain? Such questions take us to the problem of where precisely the battle was fought.

The Battlefield

In recent years I have been involved in a project on Bosworth (1485) where the major challenge was actually locating the battlefield.[45] The battle was known in its immediate aftermath by a variety of names, some no longer in use as place names. It was only with archaeology that the site was identified with certainty, thanks to the discovery of cannon balls and other objects by field walking and metal detecting. Battlefield archaeology is a relatively new discipline but it offers the possibility of enhancing our understanding of Agincourt.

Agincourt appears unproblematic in terms of location, being considered to lie between Azincourt to the west and Tramecourt to the east. Unlike Bosworth there is high consistency in naming: early texts from both sides of the Channel call it 'the field of Agincourt'.[46] In English chronicles the only settlement name given is Agincourt. French chronicles provide additional settlement names but these only came to English knowledge in the sixteenth century, as did the idea that Henry named the battle after the castle at Agincourt, when Edward Hall drew on printed editions of Monstrelet.

On the eve of battle, the Burgundian chroniclers, Monstrelet, Waurin, and Le Fèvre, place the English at Maisoncelle (to the south of the accepted battlefield) and the French at Ruisseauville (to the north of the field). Waurin and Le Fèvre have the French ordering their battles between two small woods, one close to Azincourt, the other to Tramecourt. They also claim that Henry sent a group of archers 'towards Tramecourt to a meadow close to where the vanguard of the French were positioned'. It is only in these Burgundian texts that Tramecourt is mentioned. The *Chronique anonyme* places the battle near Azincourt and Ruisseauville, as does Thomas Basin, whilst the Bourgeois of Paris puts it at 'a place called Azincourt near

Ruisseauville'. In his reminiscence Guillebert de Lannoy calls it 'the battle of Ruisseauville', a name also found in a charter of 1416. A financial account calls it the 'voyage de Blangy'.[47] Pierre Fenin has the French spend the eve of battle at Ruisseauville and Agincourt and the English at Maisoncelle, but he places the battle between Azincourt and Maisoncelle.

Even with the certainty of a battle at, or near, modern-day Azincourt, the precise site is not evident from the chronicles: they give little topographical detail, and where they do, it is too generic to pinpoint locations. For instance, the *Gesta* claims the French withdrew to a field at the far side of a wood, which was close at hand between the English and the French and which had the road to Calais passing through it. More research on road networks would be useful since armies generally moved along roads, as we discovered in the Bosworth project. Christophe Gilliot has pointed out that the road from Blangy to Maisoncelle took a different route in 1415 than today, and has been able to suggest a location where Henry spent the night of 24 October. This is to the west of Maisoncelle on the D107E close to an area which is marked on the modern map as 'Le Chemin des Anglais'. As in the Bosworth project, an attempt to date field and other names could be instructive.

The Latin lives of Henry V speak of Henry choosing a position protected on the flanks by hedges and bushes. Jean Juvénal des Ursins also has the English draw up between two areas of woodland. But the extent of tree cover has fluctuated over the centuries. Photographs from 1915 show much less woodland than today. Another way forward would therefore be analysis of vegetational change. The Burgundian chronicles as well as Thomas Walsingham comment that the ground was sown with grain, which is what we would expect for the time of year. By late October there would be visible shoots of winter wheat, as we see when visiting the field nowadays around the anniversary of the battle. The *Chronique de Ruisseauville*, written with local knowledge fifteen years after the battle, contains an interesting observation: the English were lodged on the unploughed land which was firm ground but the French were in the grain fields. Could this explain why the French were more disrupted by the mud?

The width of the front is potentially important. Vegetius' *De re militari*, a late Roman text still popular in the later Middle Ages, gave a standard spacing for infantry of 3 feet (0.9 metres). The traditional site of the battle suggests a frontage of around 2,625 feet (800 metres). This is about the same as we identified at Bosworth. Applying Vegetius literally, a frontage of that width, with soldiers six deep and exclusively on foot, would require 5,250 troops, but the number is reduced if more individual space is allowed. With a cavalry force of 1,000 taking up more space, only 3,600 foot troops would be needed.[48] More of this kind of modelling could be applied to Agincourt. Thought certainly needs to be given to how the very high numbers of French suggested by some historians could be accommodated in terms of space. But there remains the issue of where precisely the battle was fought.

The first known map of the area is the Cassini map of the late eighteenth century (Fig. 25) which marks the battlefield to the west of the village of Azincourt. The currently accepted site, however, lies to the east of Azincourt. The belief that the battle was fought between Azincourt and Tramecourt already existed in the early nineteenth century. In the aftermath of Waterloo, a British Army of Observation was placed in the Pas-de-Calais. A presentation of medals to English troops in June 1816 was described as being 'on the plains of Agincourt' but reminiscing in 1827, Dr John Gordon Smith was more explicit: 'the scene of the contest [i.e. the battle] lies between this commune [Azincourt] and the adjoining one of Tramecour'. He added that part of the wood belonging to Tramecourt, where Henry had sent a group of archers, was still visible even if thinned in comparison to 1415.[49]

This interpretation of the location is seen in the 'plan of the ground on which the battle of Agincourt was fought', drawn in 1818 by John Woodford (Fig. 26).[50] This map was never published and it is doubtful that it was seen by Nicolas in preparing his *History of the Battle of Agincourt*; the second edition of 1832 includes a sketch map of the position of the French armies on the morning of 25 October (Fig. 27).

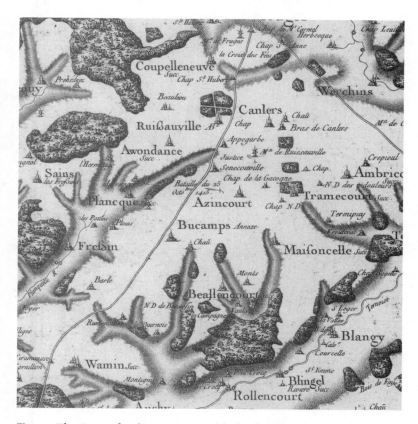

Fig. 25. The Cassini family were responsible for the first full maps of France in the late eighteenth century, using a scale of 1 cm to 864 metres. As can be seen, the battlefield was placed on this map to the west of the village of Azincourt.

Nicolas places Azincourt at the top right of the map and Maisoncelle at the bottom right. Neither Tramecourt nor Ruisseauville are noted. Nicolas was therefore following the Cassini map in placing the battle to the west of Azincourt. He did the same on a larger scale map included in the volume. On Nicolas's map of the route of Henry V, however, the crossed swords for the battle are placed to the north-east of Azincourt roughly in the direction of Ruisseauville, which is closer to the accepted site.

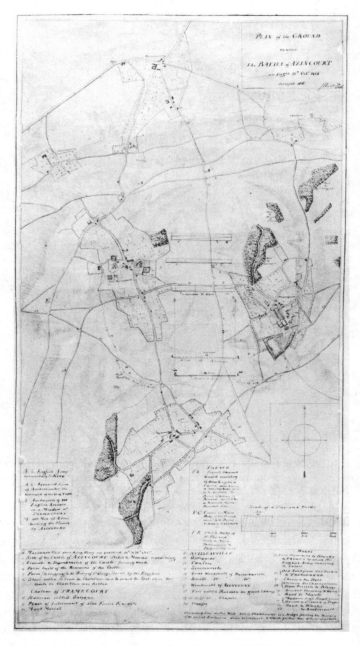

Fig. 26. This is the earliest known plan of the battlefield (British Library Additional MS 16368, map C). It was executed in 1818 by John Woodford when British troops were placed as an Army of Occupation in the area, but is heavily influenced by Woodford's reading of the chronicles. Woodford also carried out some excavations in the area believed to contain the French grave pits.

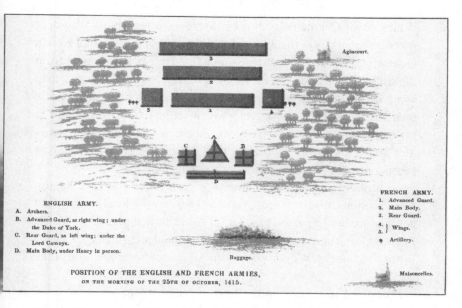

ENGLISH ARMY.
A. Archers.
B. Advanced Guard, as right wing ; under the Duke of York.
C. Rear Guard, as left wing; under the Lord Camoys.
D. Main Body, under Henry in person.

FRENCH ARMY.
1. Advanced Guard.
2. Main Body.
3. Rear Guard.
4. } Wings.
5. }
✠ Artillery.

Baggage.

Agincourt.

Maisoncelles.

POSITION OF THE ENGLISH AND FRENCH ARMIES,
ON THE MORNING OF THE 25TH OF OCTOBER, 1415.

Fig. 27. The second edition of Harris Nicholas's *The Battle of Agincourt* (1832) includes the earliest known attempt to show the deployment of troops in the battle. Note that, following the Cassini map, it places the battle to the west of Agincourt rather than to the east as Woodford's plan had done.

Woodford's map is based on a precise survey of roads and cultivation boundaries. He drew onto it what he believed to be the first and second English positions as well as the French position. He added other elements linked to the battle, including 'the place of interment of 5,800 French knights'. But there is a problem. Whilst the geography might be accurate, Woodford has simply imposed on the map his reading of the battle account in Holinshed, which was essentially based on Monstrelet. In other words, Woodford's was an *imagined* map of the Battle of Agincourt. This point is important for two reasons. First, as we saw, only the Burgundian accounts place the battle between Azincourt and Tramecourt. Secondly, Woodford was the first to carry out excavations at the battlefield. His map does not indicate where he dug but it is assumed that it was at the place he marked as the French burial site.

Lieutenant Colonel Woodford (1785–1879), a veteran of Waterloo, was a commander in the Army of Observation until its withdrawal in October 1818.[51] In April 1817 he purchased land at La Gacogne from the widow Matelin for 500 francs and in the following February began some excavations. Comparing his map with current topography, it seems that his trenches were close to where a *calvaire* was placed in 1870–5 but the precise spot remains uncertain. He reported his activities and finds to his brother in two letters written on 20 and 28 February 1818.[52] The inhabitants protested to the *sous-préfet* about his excavations. As a result an enquiry was ordered.[53] Woodford dug on two occasions, first between 20 and 25 February—a local woman had complained but he had bought her off—and between 11 and 20 March. In mid-May, after disorder during the annual pilgrimage to Saint-Esprit at Saint-Pol, Woodford and his men were withdrawn from the area.[54]

Woodford had gathered the human remains into a box and had plans to bury them in the churchyard at Azincourt. 'I shall put no inscription I think except a mere date. Anything referring to the battle of Azincourt would appear to be the indulgence of national pride in the English Man and perhaps it ought to be a superb mausoleum for the commemoration of such an event as that.' However, Woodford's abrupt departure meant that the trenches had to be filled in by the villagers of Azincourt and the remains buried by the mayor close to the east end of the parish church.

Woodford told his brother that bones—bits of skull and teeth—had been found in a decayed state 1.1 metre (3.5 feet) down. Small bits of iron were also found. 'An arrowhead to my joy at last came up in a very tolerable state—no doubt it was buried there in the body of the man whose death it caused.' Woodford also claimed other finds, including two coins of Charles VI, a ring, and a piece of iron with wood still sticking in it—'either a dagger hilt, or a bit of lance but more like the former'. As we have seen in Chapter 6, the precise nature and subsequent history of these objects are perplexing. Woodford's excavation has become part of the legend of Agincourt. 'I have lived with the departed spirits of lives past,' he wrote. 'I feel as if I was (above) 403 years old and had been at the battle of Azincourt.'

There were rumours of other finds in the nineteenth century but only in 2002 was there an effort to carry out a proper archaeological survey. Based on the success of work at Towton, Tim Sutherland was invited to carry out investigation for the TV programme *Agincourt's Dark Secrets*. Metal detecting of extensive areas between Azincourt and Tramecourt was carried out although limited by growing crops. There were no finds of the sort we would expect for a medieval battle. Although thirty-two coins were found, including a Roman silver denarius, there was not a single medieval coin. Medieval pottery was also lacking and all projectiles were post-medieval. An object thought at first to be an arrowhead was found on closer examination by the Royal Armouries to lack the necessary socket. Worryingly too, it resembled Woodford's drawing of his arrowhead, thereby casting doubt on whether he had found arrowheads at all. It is possible that the nature of the brown rendzina soil, with a wide pH range, has contributed to the lack of survival of metal objects and human remains.[55] But it is also possible that the area between Azincourt and Tramecourt is not the battlefield. In 2002 and 2007 Sutherland also conducted full investigations, including magnetic and resistivity surveys and trial pits, in the place where Woodford is believed to have dug. Nothing was found save an abandoned oil drill and the remains of the wall which had been placed around the *calvaire* at its erection. Whilst medieval pottery has been found in sites near the church in Azincourt, physical evidence that a battle was fought anywhere in the vicinity remains non-existent.

This led Sutherland to question in 2005 whether the accepted location between Azincourt and Tramecourt was erroneous.[56] He seized on a specific wording of the *Gesta* to suggest a different place. 'The French ... took up a position facing us and rather more than half a mile away, filling a very broad field like a countless swarm of locusts, and there was only a valley, and not so wide at that between us and them.' There was an area just to the south of Ruisseauville which matched that description. Sutherland suggested that the French drew up their lines on the northern edge of this valley, using the village of Ruisseauville to protect their rear. The English took position to the southern side of the valley. They goaded the French into attack, first by moving forward to the edge of the valley and subsequently by arrow storms, forcing the French to leave their strong position and come down into the wetter ground of the valley, made soggier by rain on the previous evening. This explains the different ground conditions for the two armies, and also why the French were placed at a disadvantage.

This is a tempting scenario. It still places the English close enough to the village and castle of Azincourt to justify the naming tradition, although the location is further from their supposed camp at Maisoncelle. However, there is a potential problem. The passage in the *Gesta* relates to the arrival of the English on the evening of 24 October not necessarily to the battle itself. After the passage noted, the author goes on to say 'but after the French had watched us for a while, they withdrew to a field at the far side of a wood which was close at hand to our left between us and them where lay our road towards Calais'. Henry was worried that 'they would either circle round the wood to make a surprise attack on him, or would circle round the more distant woodlands in the neighbourhood and so surround us on every side'. He therefore 'moved his lines again so they always faced the enemy'. That night the French occupied hamlets and scrub nearby. The English 'continued to hold our ground' until Henry ordered them to move to a hamlet nearby 'where we had a few houses, gardens and orchards in which to rest'. The author does not give the name of this hamlet. It is commonly assumed to be Maisoncelle, although the presence of the English there is noted only in French sources. All of this suggests substantial troop movements on the eve of battle. As for the battle on 25 October, the *Gesta* says that 'on the next day the French took up position in front of us in that field called the field of Agincourt across which lay our road to Calais'. Later the author comments that the flanks of both the English and French battle lines extended into the woodlands on both sides. It is possible that the position was the same as that noted for 24 October but the narrative is unclear on that point.

As Sutherland notes, his would-be arrowhead was discovered closer to Maisoncelle than Tramecourt and Azincourt. That might argue for a battle site closer to Maisoncelle than Ruisseauville. A spur now in the Centre historique was allegedly found between Maisoncelle and Tramecourt in the early twentieth century. Further archaeology is surely the way forward. At Towton and Bosworth it has enhanced our understanding so much. Yet at Bosworth, as at Agincourt, no graves have yet been found. At Towton whole skeletons have been found as well as disarticulated small bones, the latter suggesting that bodies were moved from their initial burial place at a later date.[57] Such a scenario is documented for the Battle of Poitiers seven months after the battle, when bodies were collected and taken for burial in the city.[58]

Commemoration

At Towton and Battlefield (the site of the Battle of Shrewsbury in 1403) chapels were founded near the site within decades of the event. Although the Agincourt narratives talk of the digging of grave pits, there is no mention of the building of any structures. It was not until 1734 that a chapel was built at La Gacogne, as marked on the Cassini map, but as thanksgiving by the countess of Tramecourt for her son's safe return from war in Italy. In 1794, as a result of the secularization of the French Revolution, it was sold by the mayor to the Matelin family and dismantled. In the next century it was believed that the chapel had a link with the battle. In 1835 Labitte claimed that every twenty-five years a service was held in memory of the French dead, but this seems such a meaningless interval of time as to be unlikely.[59] Belleval commented that peasants viewed the area with suspicion, believing no trees would grow there because of the presence of the Agincourt dead. The exact location of the chapel is yet to be discovered. It is assumed to be close to the grave pits and to the later *calvaire* but Sutherland's excavations failed to reveal its foundations.

The human finds made by Woodford were buried behind the parish church of Azincourt in May 1818 but without any marker. In 1843 the parish priest, Abbé Décobert, began a campaign to erect a chapel as a northern extension to the church in memory of those who fell at the battle.[60] Coats of arms of the most significant dead were to be placed on the walls and other names were to be inscribed on a marble plaque. Two caskets were designed to fit on either side of the altar. It was perhaps intended to exhume the bones buried after Woodford's departure and to find more. Political uncertainties following the 1848 Revolution delayed the project although 'news from France' in the *Daily News* of 8 November 1854 claimed that 'a project was afoot to erect a public monument on the field of Agincourt to the memory of French soldiers who fell in that battle'. The campaign for a chapel was renewed in 1856 and a public subscription launched because central government refused to contribute. Publicity spoke of the 'Chapelle Funéraire d'Azincourt' to commemorate 'une des pages les plus lugubres de notre histoire' ('one of the most lugubrious pages of our history'). It is significant that the publicity lamented the meddling of 'L'Étranger [i.e. Woodford]' in the sacred soil and that he had taken objects off to England.[61]

Despite a number of pledges, the campaign failed and was abandoned. Sometime between 1870 and 1875, in memory of their two sons who had died in the Franco-Prussian War, the vicomte de Tramecourt erected a *calvaire* on the Tramecourt side of the D104 just to the north of the junction with the D71 (Fig. 28). It is still there today. Through well-chosen biblical quotations, the inscription was dedicated to all those who had perished alongside the ancestors of the vicomte and his wife 'dans la fatale journée d'Azincourt'. The cross was at one time surrounded by a wall and high hedge, and was restored and rededicated in 1951.[62] This followed the occupation of the Azincourt area during the Second World War by the Germans, who placed a V-1 flying bomb 'ski-site' at Maisoncelle. The installation was the subject of

Fig. 28. In the aftermath of the Franco-Prussian War of 1870, a *calvaire* was erected by the vicomte de Tramecourt at Azincourt on the site where the French dead were believed to be buried. An inscription at its foot, drawing on biblical quotations, commemorated the valiant warriors who had lost their lives but gained immortality at the battle.

Fig. 29. On 12 May 1963 a simple stone pillar, marked simply 'Azincourt 1415', was erected to the south of the field by local and national initiative. A special event was held for its inauguration.

Allied aerial photography as part of Operation Crossbow in the winter of 1943–4, and was bombed on 1 June 1944 in the run-up to D-Day. The area was liberated in September 1944 by Polish troops who had sailed from Britain in late July.[63]

On 12 May 1963 a new monument commemorating the battle was erected, promoted by 'les chevaliers d'Azincourt', an association established by the parish priest of Fruges, and the national organization 'Le Souvenir français'. It took the form of a stone pillar placed at the very southern end of the field at the junction of the D104 and the D107E (Fig. 29), marked simply 'Azincourt 1415'. A small stone to the right is inscribed 'symbole de courage, fidelité au souvenir, leçon pour toujours'. The memorial was inaugurated in the presence of three generals, clergy, and an audience of 10,000. The march of Henry was re-enacted and there were various speeches as well as British and French hymns. As General Hassler remarked: 'we are here not to celebrate an English victory or a French defeat but to honour those who are buried in the field of the dead. This date of 12 May has been chosen to lighten for us all that is sad in remembering Agincourt, by evoking La Pucelle [Joan of Arc] who fourteen years later, chased the English from France and forged national unity.'[64] An orientation board was placed close to the pillar in 1986 and in 1991 a small stone was placed to the left of the pillar in memory of Le Gallois de Fougières, *prévôt des maréchaux*, who fell at the battle and who is celebrated as the first 'Gendarme' in France to die in battle. He was amongst a number of French dead buried soon after the battle at Auchy-les-Hesdin but was exhumed in 1936 and buried under the monument at Versailles to the Gendarmerie.[65]

In 1978 a small exhibition was opened in the 'salle paroissiale' at Azincourt by the local teacher, Claude Delcusse, and his wife. In 1981 this transferred to the newly built 'salle polyvalente' which also housed a Tourist Information Centre. From 1983 the exhibition began to focus more on the battle than on local history, and a video presentation was added. By 1985 10,000 visitors were received, the figure doubling by 1989. A medieval fete began to be organized every two years. Large cut-outs of archers and knights were placed along the road between Azincourt and Tramecourt marking the likely seat of the battle.

The idea of a Centre historique médiéval dates back to 1993 but was much boosted by the election in 1995 of the mayor of Azincourt, M. Boulet, as president of the Communauté des communes Canche-Ternoise. Important funds from the EU Interreg scheme were gained through an agreement with Southlands Community Comprehensive School in New Romney, Kent (now the Marsh Academy) which had established a base at the Centre Verginiaud at La Gacogne. In 2005 there was Anglo-French cooperation in a protest against plans to build a wind farm close to the battlefield. As the *Daily Telegraph* of 29 December put it, 'British and French unite to win the second battle of Agincourt'.

Construction of the Centre historique médiéval d'Azincourt started in 2000. Within a year the first phase was opened (Fig. 30).

Fig. 30. Designed by Eric Revet and Bertrand Klein, the Centre historique médiéval was officially opened on 1 July 2001. The building was constructed to resemble longbows with arrows ready to be loosed.

An extension in the form of a medieval barn and education area was built in 2005–6.[66] The current exhibition provides background to the battle as well as an audiovisual presentation and replica armour and weapons. Visitors numbers reach 30,000 per annum (of whom 46 per cent are British) and there are regular talks, events, and school visits. Along with plans for a special commemorative event on 25 October 2015 which in part replicates the Anglo-French military event of 1915, discussions have begun on the remodelling of the Centre historique, guided by a Comité scientifique of French and British historians, including myself. Major re-enactments of the battle began with an event on 22 July 2001 organized by the Azincourt Alliance, set up in 2000 by Chris Skinner and others. This event, uniting English and French re-enactors, has happened every year since. 'A big shoot' will be the celebration on 25–6 July 2015.[67] On the anniversary there will be an event recalling 1915 as well as 1415, with a small memorial stone being placed at what is believed to be the heart of the battle on the road between Azincourt and Tramecourt.

Agincourt still strikes a chord in the British psyche but the 600th anniversary has offered an opportunity for Franco-British collaboration and commemoration. On 29 October 2015 a service of commemoration will be held at Westminster Abbey, the date being chosen to replicate events of 600 years earlier.[68] On 29 October 1415 the news of Henry's victory was received in London and the mayor and aldermen made humble procession to the abbey for thanksgiving . The interest of the City of London and its livery companies in the 2015 commemorations has been considerable. The loan of 10,000 marks made by the City to fund Henry's campaign has been enthusiastically remembered.

8

Conclusion

Over the centuries the Battle of Agincourt has become all things to all men (and women). In researching this book I have come across some truly amazing allusions. In a play by Pierre-Yves Millot the battle is seen in a pot of yoghurt—natural of course. On the back cover of the printed edition, 'Shakespeare' provided an excellent review of the play: 'it gave me the idea of writing a play on the battle called Henry V. You can find it in all good libraries.'[1]

Under the headline 'Lunacy and Genius', the *North Otago Times* of 4 January 1902 regaled its readers with the story of a mad gentleman in Carolina who had been an assiduous student of English history while sane. 'He fancies that he was slain at Agincourt and has come to life again.' He insisted that both he and his keeper should wear armour but perhaps the effect was somewhat undermined by the fact he was a smoker: 'ever anon he raises the visor of his helmet to enable him to indulge in a whiff'.

Also good fun are the clever ways journalists have used the word. For Abbie Fielding-Smith in the *New Statesman* in 1996, Antony Beevor's war tomes, *Stalingrad* and *Berlin*, had been 'selling like Elastoplast at Agincourt'. As I started this book with John Lennon, what better than to mention the live broadcast the Beatles made on 25 June 1967 for which Lennon and McCartney wrote, 'All you need is love'. 'This', according to Martin Lewis, 'was their Agincourt.'[2]

In France the battle stands as a warning against pretension. In 2001 the French government warned the country's wine growers that they faced 'a second Agincourt' from New World wine growers unless they changed their arrogant stance and started listening to their customers. The civil servant who wrote the report urged producers to note that 'At Agincourt we were defeated by our own self-certainty and complacency much more than by the English archers'.[3]

The popular image has drifted away from the actual events of 1415. Shakespeare restaged Agincourt in 1599. His image of the battle still predominates today. Drayton rewrote the battle in 1627 as a Homeric epic with invented acts of bravery. Family pride in the late sixteenth and early seventeenth centuries created traditions which are still being built on today. History has become democratized and is no longer simply about kings and queens. From the mid-nineteenth century the Agincourt archer came to the fore and has remained there ever since. Tales of rude gestures and archers with loose bowels generate a warm feeling that people in the past were just like us. A Battle of Agincourt fought by Playmobile figures can be viewed on YouTube. It really is a battle for all time and all people.

National identity and ongoing hostility towards France until the early twentieth century made the battle a symbol of past greatness to be remembered and emulated. Important here too is that an *English* victory became accepted in the eighteenth and nineteenth century as a *British* victory. No one complicates matters by remembering that the Scots were in alliance with the French in 1415. Agincourt was also a symbol of the 'old country', something which appealed particularly to colonial and pioneer societies in the USA, Australasia, and South Africa. In 1915 French and British, now together against a common German foe, were reconciled on the very soil on which the battle was fought. A French commander even guided the British around the field.

Stripping away all of the veneer of later centuries, the invented traditions, the invocation of the name 'Agincourt', what have we left? Agincourt 1415–2015 tells us much about the human psyche, how one event can provide a hook on which personal and national identity can be hung. Facts only need verification once but beliefs need constant reverification and restatement.[4] That is how the myths and legends of Agincourt have persisted and expanded, and will no doubt go on persisting and expanding. They are part of our desire to shape the past to fit our present.

The myths and legends tell us more about now than then. If we strip them away, what is left? In terms of military history, Agincourt is significant for the leadership which Henry gave, the discipline he instilled in his troops, and his skilful exploitation of resources. His archers and his men-at-arms did their duty but their effectiveness was much enhanced by Henry's adroit positioning as well as his total commitment to winning. The lesson of Agincourt is perennial—commanders should never assume an easy victory against a smaller, but well-led, cohesive and skilled, enemy army.

NOTES

Chapter 1

1. www.dailymail.co.uk/news/article-1080764, 27 Oct. 2008.
2. The phrase has stimulated a play of its very own: Michael Frayn's *Alarms and Excursions: More Plays than One* (1998).
3. *Commune*, Azincourt; *canton*, Le Parcq; *arrondissement*, Montreuil-sur-Mer; *département*, Pas-de-Calais; *région*, Nord-Pas-de-Calais.

Chapter 2

1. *Gesta Henrici Quinti: The Deeds of Henry the Fifth*, ed. F. Taylor and J. S. Roskell (Oxford, 1975), 22–3.
2. C. J. Phillpotts, 'The Fate of the Truce of Paris, 1396–1415', *Journal of Medieval History*, 24 (1998), 61–80.
3. TNA E 101/393/11 fos. 79r–116v for the pay accounts.
4. A. Ayton and P. Preston, *The Battle of Crécy, 1346* (Woodbridge, 2005), 189. It used to be claimed that a force of 32,000 besieged Calais in 1346–7. However, research has indicated this figure represents the total number of transportations across the whole siege; the siege army at any one time was 5,000–6,000 strong. C. Lambert, 'Edward III's Siege of Calais: A Reappraisal', *Journal of Medieval History*, 37 (2011), 253.
5. PROME ix. 66. The following section on preparations and on the campaign is based on A. Curry, *Agincourt: A New History*, chs. 2–7; J. Barker, *Agincourt: The King, the Campaign, the Battle* (London, 2005), chs. 4–13; and I. Mortimer, *1415: Henry V's Year of Glory* (London, 2009).
6. *Proceedings and Ordinances of the Privy Council of England*, ed. H. Nicolas (London, 1834), ii. 140–2.
7. A. Curry, 'The Military Ordinances of Henry V: Texts and Contexts', in C. Given-Wilson, A. Kettle, and L. Scales (eds), *War, Government and Aristocracy in the British Isles c 1150–1500* (Woodbridge, 2008), 214–49; A. Curry, 'Disciplinary Ordinances for English and Franco-Scottish Armies in 1385: An International Code?', *Journal of Medieval History*, 37 (2011), 269–94.
8. There is a full discussion on the army in Curry, *Agincourt: A New History*, ch. 3. For an example of an indenture see *Sources*, 436–8.

9. A. Curry, 'The English Army in the Fifteenth Century', in A. Curry and M. Hughes (eds.), *Arms, Armies and Fortifications in the Hundred Years War* (Woodbridge, 1994), 39–68.

10. G. Foard and A. Curry, *Bosworth: A Battlefield Rediscovered* (Oxford, 2013), 40.

11. A. Curry, A. R. Bell, A. King, and D. Simpkin, 'New Regime, New Army? Henry IV's Scottish Expedition of 1400', *English Historical Review*, 125 (2010), 1398. By contrast in 1385 Richard II's army for 40 days' service in Scotland, although larger at 13,764 men, had a ratio of 1:2.

12. J. Stratford, '"Par le special commandement du roy": Jewels and Plate Pledged for the Agincourt Expedition', in G. Dodd (ed.), *Henry V: New Interpretation* (Woodbridge, 2013), 157–70.

13. A. Tuck, 'The Earl of Arundel's Expedition to France, 1411', in G. Dodd and D. Biggs (eds), *The Reign of Henry IV: Rebellion and Survival 1403–1413* (Woodbridge, 2008), 228–39; Curry, *Agincourt: A New History*, 23–30.

14. H. Nicolas, *History of the Battle of Agincourt* (London, 2nd edn, 1832), app., pp. 29–30 and C. Hibbert, *Agincourt* (London, 1964), app. v for this text in English; Curry, *Agincourt: A New History*, 106–9; J. W. Honig, 'Reappraising Late Medieval Strategy: The Example of the 1415 Agincourt Campaign', *War in History*, 19 (2012), 142.

15. A. Curry, 'Lancastrian Normandy: The Jewel in the Crown?', in D. Bates and A. Curry (eds), *England and Normandy in the Middle Ages* (London, 1994), 235–52.

16. *Sources*, 445.

17. M. Bennett, *Agincourt 1415* (London, 1991), 6.

18. *Sources*, 441–2.

19. Honig, 'Reappraising Late Medieval Strategy', 142.

20. Curry, *Agincourt: A New History*, ch. 5.

21. C. J. Rogers, 'Henry V's Military Strategy in 1415', in L. J. A. Villalon and D. J. Kagay (eds), *The Hundred Years War: A Wider Focus* (Leiden, 2005), 399–427.

22. *Sources*, 30.

23. C. J. Phillpotts, 'The French Plan of Battle During the Agincourt Campaign', *English Historical Review*, 99 (1984), 59–66.

24. This summary and discussion is based on Curry, *Agincourt: A New History*, chs. 8 and 9.

25. For the text of the *semonce* issued by Charles VI on 20 September 1415 see *Sources*, 142–3, from its inclusion in the *Chronique* of Enguerran de Monstrelet.

26. I am grateful to Chris Skinner for discussion on this and other points. For full discussion of the archers and archery in the period, see M. Strickland and R. Hardy, *The Great Warbow* (Gloucester, 2005).

27. A. R. Bell, A. Curry, A. King, and D. Simpkin, *The Soldier in Later Medieval England* (Oxford, 2013), ch. 3.

28. TNA E 358/6.
29. *Sources*, 105.
30. M. Prestwich, 'The Battle of Crécy', in A. Ayton and P. Preston, *The Battle of Crécy* (Woodbridge, 2005), 150.
31. M. Bennett, 'The Development of Battle Tactics in the Hundred Years War', in A. Curry and M. Hughes (eds), *Arms, Armies and Fortifications in the Hundred Years War* (Woodbridge, 1994), 15.
32. Ayton and Preston, *Battle of Crécy*, 147.
33. *The Face of Battle: A Study of Agincourt, Waterloo and the Somme* (London, 1976), 85.
34. B. Schnerb, 'La Bataille rangée dans la tactique des armées bourguignonnes au début du 15e siècle: Essai de synthèse', *Annales de Bourgogne*, 61 (1989), 5–32.
35. Curry, *Agincourt: A New History*, app. B.
36. Contamine, *Guerre, état et société: Étude sur les armées des rois de France 1337–1494* (Paris and The Hague, 1972), 223.
37. Contamine, *War in the Middle Ages*, trans. M. C. E. Jones (London, 1984), 133, 169, 171.
38. Curry, *Agincourt: A New History*, 183–7.
39. X. Hélary, *Courtrai: 11 juillet 1302* (Paris, 2012), 129.
40. Curry, *Agincourt: A New History*, app. C.
41. Hélary, *Courtrai*, 132.
42. See below, p. 61.
43. *Sources*, 475.
44. J. G. Monteiro, 'The Battle of Aljubarrota (1385): A Reassessment', *Journal of Medieval Military History*, 7 (2009), 95.
45. *Sources*, 37.
46. *Sources*, 164.
47. *Sources*, 63, 74–5; A. Curry, 'After Agincourt, What Next? Henry V and the Campaign of 1416', *Fifteenth Century England*, 7 (2007), 23–51.
48. 'After Agincourt', 32–40; A. Curry, 'Harfleur under English Rule 1415–1422', in L. J. A. Villalon and D. Kagay (eds), *The Hundred Years War, Part III: Further Considerations* (Leiden, 2013), 259–84.
49. Curry, 'After Agincourt', 36–51.
50. C. J. Rogers, *War Cruel and Sharp: English Strategy under Edward III, 1327–1360* (Woodbridge, 2000), 278–82.

Chapter 3

1. *PROME* ix. 135.
2. *Sources*, 346, trans. from *The Political Works of Alain Chartier*, ed. J. C. Laidlaw (Cambridge, 1974), pp. 198–304, ll. 537–52. See also A. Curry, 'Snatching Defeat from the Jaws of Victory: French Responses to Agincourt', *Proceedings of the Western Society for French History*, 28 (2002), 177–87.

3. Cited in M. G. A. Vale, *Charles VII* (London, 1974), 14.

4. *Sources*, 194.

5. Roy Davids Ltd, *Catalogue VI: Manuscripts and Letters, Portraits, Artefacts and Works of Art* (n.d.). I am grateful to Gregory Cox for this reference. A Venetian chronicle of the 1450s notes twenty-seven dead and captured by name and claims that the battle lasted five hours. Interestingly it also moves straight from the battle to claim Henry was crowned king of France. Giorgio Dolfin, *Cronicha dela nobil cità de Venetia de dela sua provintia et destretto*, ed. A. C. Arico, vol. ii (Venice, 2009), 179–80. I am grateful to Dr John Law for this reference.

6. *Cronica de Don Juan Segundo de Castilla*, ed. C. Rosell (Madrid, 1953), 370.

7. *Scotichronicon by Walter Bower*, ed. D. E. R. Watt, 9 vols (Aberdeen, 1993–8), viii. 85.

8. D. Duarte, *Leal Conselheiro*, ed. João Morais Barbosa (Lisbon, 1982), 81; *Livro dos Conselhos de El-Rei D. Duarte*, ed. J. A. Dias (Lisbon, 1982), 125. I am grateful to Prof João Monteiro for these references.

9. *Sources*, 441–2.

10. H. T. Riley (ed.), *Memorials of London and London Life in the XIIIth, XIVth and XVth Centuries* (London, 1878), 620–2.

11. *PROME* ix. 115.

12. A. Curry, 'After Agincourt, What Next? Henry V and the Campaign of 1416', *Fifteenth Century England*, 7 (2007), 23–51.

13. On 12 August, the day after the king set sail, writs had been issued for a parliament to meet on 21 October but on 29 September the date was moved to 4 November. Edward III had similarly called a parliament after his sacking of Caen during the 1346 campaign (W. M. Ormrod, *Edward III* (London, 2011), 282).

14. *Sources*, 298–300, trans. from *Manières de langage (1396, 1399, 1415)*, ed. A. M. Kristol (Anglo-Norman Text Society, 53. London, 1995), 70.

15. *Sources*, 263–4, trans. from Wiltshire County Record Office, Salisbury Ledger Book A (G23/1/1), fol. 55.

16. Winchester College Muniments 22097, under *expensis et donis*. I am grateful to Dr Custance for this reference.

17. *Sources*, 266–8.

18. *Gesta Henrici Quinti: The Deeds of Henry the Fifth*, ed. F. Taylor and J. S. Roskell (Oxford, 1975), 101. N. Coldstream, 'Pavilion'd in Splendour: Henry V's Agincourt Pageants', *Journal of the British Archaeological Association*, 165 (2012), 153–71.

19. *Gesta*, 113.

20. J. Sumption, *The Hundred Years War*, ii. *Trial by Fire* (London, 1999), 288–90; Coldstream, 'Pavilion'd in Splendour', 163.

21. *Sources*, 268.

22. G. Kipling, *Enter the King: Theatre, Liturgy and Ritual in the Medieval Civic Triumph* (Oxford, 1998), 201–9.

23. H. Deeming, 'The Sources and Origin of the "Agincourt Carol"', *Early Music*, 35 (2007), 30. Two copies survive. The older seems to be the Trinity Roll (Cambridge, Trinity College MS.0.3.55), with a slightly later copy in the Bodleian Library MS 3340 fos. 17v–18r (Arch. Selden B 26).

24. *Sources*, 271–4.

25. *The Register of Henry Chichele, Archbishop of Canterbury, 1414–1431*, ed. E. F. Jacob, 4 vols (London 1943–7), iii. 6, 7, 9–10. The order was not issued in the York province until 1422: *Records of Convocation XIII: York 1313–1461*, ed. G. Bray (Woodbridge, 2006), 375. The duke of York was buried at Fotheringhay on 1 December.

26. *Sources*, 281–6; A. K. McHardy, 'Religion, Court Culture and Propaganda: The Chapel Royal in the Reign of Henry V', in G. Dodd (ed.), *Henry V: New Interpretations* (Woodbridge, 2013), 138–42. Several are to be found in the 'Old Hall' Manuscript: BL, Add. MS 57950.

27. PROME ix. 177–8; C. T. Allmand, *Henry V* (London, 1992), 375.

28. M. Bennett, 'Henry V and the Cheshire Tax Revolt', in Dodd (ed.), *Henry V: New Interpretations*, 171–86.

29. *Sources*, 448–9.

30. *Register of Henry Chichele*, iii. 28–9.

31. PROME ix. 135, 177–8, 207, 231.

32. *Gesta*, 123–5.

33. PROME ix. 249.

34. W. Godfrey with A. Wagner, *Survey of London, Monograph 16: College of Arms Queen Victoria Street* (London, 1963), 229. As this list shows, Henry IV had given George, earl of Dunbar, the Scottish earl of March, the right to call his officer Shrewsbury herald as a reward for services at the battle of 1403. Henry VIII created a Boulogne pursuivant in honour of the capture of the town in 1544 but it lapsed at the return of the town to the French in 1550.

35. McHardy, 'Religion', 142–54.

36. *Gesta*, p. xxiv.

37. For burdens see W. M. Ormrod, 'Henry V and the English Taxpayer' in Dodd (ed.), *Henry V: New Interpretations*, 188.

38. McHardy, 'Religion', 153.

39. I am grateful to Dr Andrea Ruddick for discussion on this.

40. BL, Cotton Julius E. IV. and Sloane MS 1776, the second being a copy of the first.

41. *Sources*, 40–8, trans. from 'Liber Metricus de Henrico Quinto', in *Memorials of the Life of Henry the Fifth, King of England*, ed. C. A. Coles (Rolls Series, London, 1858), 113–24.

42. A. Curry, 'The Battle Speeches of Henry V', *Reading Medieval Studies*, 34 (2008), 77–97.

43. This is revealed by linguistic study. *The St Albans Chronicle: The Chronica Maiora of Thomas Walsingham*, ii. 1394–1422, ed. J. Taylor, W. R. Childs, and L. Watkiss (Oxford, 2011), p. xliv.

44. *The Chronicle of Adam Usk 1377–1421*, ed. C. Given-Wilson (Oxford, 1997).

45. *Sources*, 53, 95–6.

46. *Sources*, 53–75; D. Rundle, 'The Unoriginality of Tito Livio Frulovisi's Vita Henrici Quinti', *English Historical Review*, 123 (2008), 1109–31.

47. *Sources*, 89–96.

48. Lambeth Palace Library, MS 6, fo. 24v.

49. *Chronicles of London*, ed. C. L. Kingsford (London, 1905), 120–2.

50. *Sources*, 451–7. For the petition of an executor, in this case the widow of John Richard of Kilingworth, see TNA SC 8/301/15046, available online.

51. R. Ambühl, *Prisoners of War in the Hundred Years War: Ransom Culture in the Late Middle Ages* (Cambridge, 2013), 77.

52. As in the case of the earl of Huntingdon and the two main prisoners taken at Harfleur: PROME x. 172–3, 209.

53. This is also evident in a sermon given before his final departure for France in 1421 which portrays Henry as the master of the ship of state, who gained the victory at the fierce storm of Agincourt: 'in all perils God has preserved him'. G. R. Owst, *Literature and Pulpit in Medieval England* (rev. edn, London, 1961), 74–5.

54. L. A. Coote, *Prophecy and Public Affairs in Later Medieval England* (Woodbridge, 2000), 186.

55. *Sources*, 77.

56. PROME xii. 92; TNA C49/30/19, transcribed in PROME xii. 207–8.

57. *Sources*, 85–9, trans. from College of Arms MS M9, fols. xxxi–xxxiii.

58. By 1642, if not earlier, however, it was believed that the college had been founded 'for such that were slain in the battle of Agincourt': cited in W. Huddesford, *The Lives of Those Eminent Antiquaries, John Leland, Thomas Hearne and Anthony a Wood* (Oxford, 1772), 353–7.

59. Translated from the Latin inscription: 'Henry the fifth loved him as a friend . . . bravely and strongly at Harfleur John conducted himself well.' N. Pevsner, *The Buildings of England: Worcestershire* (Harmondsworth, 1968), 204–5. The tomb of Thomas Berisforde (d.1473) at Fenny Bentley (Derbyshire) has within its inscription 'Militia excellens, strenuus dux, fortis et audax, Franci, testator curia testis Agen'. The last word has been taken as Agincourt but this is speculative. The tomb was not erected until the early sixteenth century and no man of this campaign has so far turned up in the campaign records. I am grateful to Prof. Brian Kemp for comments.

60. BL, Royal MS 2S XVIII includes a memorandum of the battle (fo. 16v). This MS may have been owned by John Holand, duke of Exeter (d.1447) who had been present at the battle. Its second part, owned by Lady Margaret Beaufort, also lists Bosworth and other key events in her son's life. The

account book of the chamberlain of Canterbury contains a note on Agincourt as well as of many events from the capture of Calais in 1347 onwards: Canterbury Cathedral Archives, CC FA1, fo. 1v.

61. William Worcester, *The Boke of Noblesse*, ed. J. G. Nichols (London, 1860), 17, 28, 32.

62. *Appendix to the Second Report of the Royal Commission on Historical Manuscripts* (London, 1871), 94; C. L. Scofield, *The Life and Reign of Edward IV*, 2 vols (London, 1923), ii. 133.

63. *Sources*, 177–8.

64. Anon., *Le Pastoralet*, ed. J. Blanchard (Paris, 1983); *Sources*, 350–3.

65. O. Bouzy, 'Les Morts d'Azincourt: Leurs liens de famille, d'offices et de parti', in P. Gilli and J. Paviot (eds), *Hommes, cultures et sociétés à la fin du Moyen Âge* (Paris, 2012), 221–55. I am grateful to Dr Bouzy for discussion on the list.

66. Archives nationales, Xia 8603 fo. 2; *Sources*, 335–6.

67. C. E. du Boulay, *Historia Universitatis Pariensis*, 6 vols (Paris, 1665–73), v. 295; J. H. Wylie, *The Reign of Henry the Fifth*, 3 vols (Cambridge, 1914–29), ii. 277–8.

68. Le Religieux de Saint-Denis, *Histoire de Charles VI*, ed. L. Bellaguet, 6 vols (Paris, 1839–52), v. 542–81; *Sources*, 99–110, 336–40.

69. As for the Black Death there was also an astrological explanation for the defeat in the unfavourable conjunction of the planets: J. Boudet, 'Un jugement astrologique sur l'année 1415', in J. Paviot and J Verger (eds), *Guerre, pouvoir et noblesse au Moyen Âge: Mélanges en l'honneur de Philippe Contamine* (Paris, 2000), 111–20.

70. *Sources*, 124.

71. *Sources*, 182–5, trans. from *Chronique d'Artur de Richemont par Guillaume Gruel*, ed. A. Le Vavasseur (Société de l'histoire de France, Paris, 1890), 15–20.

72. *Sources*, 358.

73. *Œuvres de Ghillebert de Lannoy, diplomate et moraliste*, ed. C. Poitvin (Louvain, 1878), 49–50.

74. The complicated relationship is shown in *Sources*, 144–71.

75. It was printed as early as 1500 and is much cited thanks to its translation into English by Thomas Johnes of Hafod in 1809.

76. Archives départementales du Nord, B 1942. I am grateful to Aleksandr Lobanov for a photograph of this entry.

77. Jean Juvénal des Ursins, 'Histoire de Charles VI, roy de France', *Nouvelle collection de mémoires pour server à l'histoire de France*, ed. J.-F. Michaud and J. J. F. Poujoulet (Paris, 1836), ii. 523–4.

78. *Le Débat des hérauts d'armes de France et d'Angleterre, suivi de The Debate between the Heralds of England and France by John Coke*, ed. L. Pannier and P. Meyer (Paris, 1877), 16–17, 19.

79. BN, manuscrit français 5054.

Chapter 4

1. J. Bate and D. Thornton (eds), *Shakespeare: Staging the World* (London, 2012), 274, 107. On the evolution of the battle speech see A. Curry, 'The Battle Speeches of Henry V', *Reading Medieval Studies*, 34 (2008), 77–97.
2. P. Kewes, I. W. Archer, and F. Heal (eds), *The Oxford Handbook of Holinshed's Chronicles* (Oxford, 2013).
3. A. Gransden, *Historical Writing in England*, ii. *c. 1307 to the Early Sixteenth Century* (London, 1982), 223. Caxton's 1482 text is close to the mid-fifteenth-century version of the *Brut* in Cambridge University Library, MS Kk I 112. See *Sources*, 91–6.
4. *Sources*, 220–3.
5. F. Collard, *Un historien au travail à la fin du XVe siècle* (Geneva, 1996). Gaguin had visited England in 1491 at the order of the French king.
6. The text is available on EEBO. See also *Hall's Chronicle containing the History of England*, ed. H. Ellis (London, 1809), 63–73 and *Sources*, 230–43.
7. *Sources*, 230, trans. from *Polydori Vergilii, Anglicae Historia Libri XXVI* (Basle, 1534), 442.
8. H. Wijsman, 'History in Transition: Enguerrand de Monstrelet's *Chronique* in Manuscript and Print (c.1450–c.1600)', in M. Walsby and G. Kemp (eds), *The Book Triumphant* (Leiden, 2012), 199–252. Verard had printed Froissart's *Chroniques* in 1495.
9. C. S. L. Davies, 'Henry VIII and Henry V: The Wars in France', in J. L. Watts (ed.), *The End of the Middle Ages* (Stroud, 1998), 235–62; C. Giry-Deloison, 'The Context of the Field of Cloth of Gold', in *1520: Le Camp du Drap d'or / The Field of Cloth of Gold* (Paris, 2012), 27 ('Henry was fascinated by the legend of Henry V and Agincourt'); Hammer, 'War', in Kewes et al. (eds), *The Oxford Handbook of Holinshed's Chronicles*, 445 ('In many ways Henry VIII yearned to be a second Henry V, just as Henry V himself . . . had sought to emulate the success of his great-grandfather, Edward III'); S. Gunn, 'The French Wars of Henry VIII', in J. Black (ed.), *The Origins of War in Early Modern Europe* (Edinburgh, 1987), 37 ('Henry felt his closest competitor to be Henry V and consciously took him for a model . . . Henry VIII did not let these differences deter him from an almost ritualistic imitation of his namesake'). I am grateful to Drs Davies and Gunn for discussion on this topic.
10. G. Cruickshank, *Henry VIII and the Invasion of France* (Stroud, 1990), 28, from BL, Lansdowne MS 818.
11. *The First English Life of King Henry the Fifth*, ed. C. L. Kingsford (Oxford, 1911): Bodleian Library, Bodley MS 966, written c.1610 for Sir Peter Manwood; BL, Harley MS 35, a text which dates to the later part of reign of James I and which omits the Proem).
12. *First English Life*, ed. Kingsford, p. xxxiv.
13. J. Scarisbrick, *Henry VIII* (London, 1968), 23.

14. *Leland's Itinerary*, ed. L. Toulmin-Smith, 5 vols (London, 1907), i. 5, 138.

15. BL, Cotton Faustina C/II fo. 5, printed in S. Anglo, 'An Early Tudor Programme for Plays and Other Demonstrations against the Pope', *Journal of the Warburg and Courtauld Institutes*, 20 (1957), 178. For the dating see T. Sowerby, *Renaissance and Reform in Tudor England: The Careers of Sir Richard Morrison c. 1513–1556* (Oxford, 2010), 122–30). I am grateful to Prof. George Bernard and Dr David Grummitt for these references.

16. *Le Débat des hérauts d'armes de France et d'Angleterre, suivi de The Debate between the Heralds of England and France by John Coke*, ed. L. Pannier and P. Meyer (Paris, 1877), 85, 95, 96–7.

17. M. Wiggins with C. Richardson, *British Drama 1533–1642: A Catalogue* (Oxford, 2012), vol. ii, no. 773.

18. Wiggins with Richardson, *British Drama*, vol. iii, nos. 912, 1021.

19. He disappears earlier in the Quarto Edition: *King Henry V*, ed. T. W. Craik (The Arden Shakespeare, 3rd ser.; London, 1995), 29.

20. J. Shapiro, *1599: A Year in the Life of William Shakespeare* (London, 2005), 79–83; Bate and Thornton (eds), *Shakespeare: Staging the World*, 107.

21. Bate and Thornton (eds), *Shakespeare: Staging the World*, 116.

22. *King Henry V*, ed. A Gurr (The New Cambridge Shakespeare; Cambridge, 1992), 4–6.

23. J. Baldo, 'Wars of Memory in *Henry V*', *Shakespeare Quarterly*, 47 (1996), 138. The feast was removed from the Catholic liturgical calendar by the Second Vatican Council (1962–5) but is still in the Roman Martyrology as published in 2001. It features as a Black Letter Saint's Day in the Book of Common Prayer of 1662 but is a 'commemoration' in the Anglican *Common Worship* of 2000.

24. *The Yale Collection of the Works of Samuel Johnson*, viii. *Johnson on Shakespeare* (New Haven, 1968), 557 (published in 1765 but written over the twenty years preceding).

25. J. A. Berthelot, *Michael Drayton* (New York, 1967), 84–7.

26. Michael Drayton, *The Battaile of Agincourt*, ed. R. Garnett (London, 1893), 9.

27. STC 11087.

28. C. MacLeod, *The Lost Prince: The Life and Death of Henry Stuart* (London, 2012), 19, 108, 117; S. Orgel and R. Strong, *Inigo Jones: The Theatre of the Stuart Court*, 2 vols (London and Berkeley, 1973), i. 162.

29. I am very grateful to Prof. Ros King and Prof. John McGavin for discussion on the poem.

30. R. Jenkins, 'The Sources of Drayton's *Battaile of Agincourt*', PMLA 41 (1926), 280–93.

31. For Spede's letter to Cotton asking to see the Life, see H. Ellis, *Original Letters of Eminent Literary Men of the Sixteenth, Seventeenth, and Eighteenth Centuries* (Camden Society, 23; London, 1843), 113.

32. The Address is available on EEBO. For newspaper advertisements, see e.g. the *Whitehall Evening-Post or London Intelligencer*, 17–19 Jan. 1749.

33. For a useful guide, see E. Smith (ed.), *Shakespeare in Production: King Henry V* (Cambridge, 2002).

34. Smith (ed.), *King Henry V*, 12.

35. Aaron Hill, *King Henry the Fifth, or, The Conquest of France, By the English: A Tragedy* (London, 1723), 57.

36. T. Goodwin, *The History of the Reign of Henry the Fifth, King of England* (London, 1704), p. iv.

37. *General Advertiser*, 13 Apr. 1744.

38. *London Evening Post*, 30 Dec. 1749.

39. Cited in Smith (ed.), *King Henry V*, 15. See also G. W. Stone, *The London Stage 1660–1800*, part 4. *1747–1776* (Carbondale, Ill., 1960–8).

40. *King Henry V*, ed. Gurr, 44.

41. D. E. Henderson, 'Meditations in a Time of (Displaced) War: Henry V, Money and the Ethics of Performing History', in R. King and P. J. C. M. Franssen (eds), *Shakespeare and War* (London, 2008), 227.

42. Smith (ed.), *King Henry V*, 18.

43. Cited in Smith (ed.), *King Henry V*, 19. *Henry V*, ed. Gurr, 39 cites an alternative version of events: at the production in Manchester in 1804 the actor had made this cry and the reviewer was not sure whether or not it was a deliberate mistake.

44. I. Anstruther, *The Knight and the Umbrella: An Account of the Eglington Tournament 1839* (London, 1963); M. Girouard, *The Return to Camelot: Chivalry and the English Gentleman* (New Haven, 1981), 90–102.

45. *The Times*, 11 June 1893.

46. Smith (ed.), *King Henry V*, 25; *Henry V*, ed. Gurr, 47.

47. Smith (ed.), *King Henry V*, 26.

48. *Shakespeare's Play of King Henry the Fifth Arranged for Representation at the Princess's Theatre, with Historical and Explanatory Notes by C. Kean* (London, 1859) (available online in Project Gutenberg). See also R. W. Schoch, *Shakespeare's Victorian Stage: Performing History in the Theatre of Charles Kean* (Cambridge, 1998).

49. A. Poole, *Shakespeare and the Victorians* (London, 2004), 204–5.

50. R. Foulkes, 'Charles Calvert's *Henry V*', *Shakespeare Survey*, 41 (1989), 23–34.

51. *Shakespeare's Historical Play of Henry V as Produced by Mr George Rignold at Drury Lane Theatre November 1st 1879* (London, 1880).

52. Smith (ed.), *King Henry V*, 34, 41.

53. Smith (ed.), *King Henry V*, 35. The theatre had been completed in 1879.

54. C. Wisner Barrell in the *Shakespeare Fellowship Quarterly* (Oct. 1946).

55. *Henry V*, ed. Gurr, 50.

56. Cited in Smith (ed.), *King Henry V*, 36.

57. H. M. Geduld, *Filmguide to Henry V* (Bloomington, Ind. and London, 1973), 4.

58. I am grateful to Dr Mike Hammond and Bryony Dixon for their thoughts on this film.

59. Smith (ed.), *King Henry V*, 35.

60. *The First Quarto of King Henry the Fifth*, ed. A Gurr (Cambridge, 2000), 4.

61. S. Bucklow and S. Woodcock (eds), *Sir John Gilbert: Art and Imagination in the Victorian Age* (London, 2011), 54, 86.

62. Geduld, *Filmguide to Henry V*, 4–14. The Olivier Archive in the BL contains much relevant material on the film which has been drawn on for this section. I am also grateful to Robert Woosnam-Savage of the Royal Armouries for discussion on the film.

63. C. Barr, '"Much Pleasure and Relaxation in These Hard Times": Churchill and Cinema in the Second World War', *Historical Journal of Film, Radio and Television*, 31 (2011), 561–86.

64. Souvenir card in BL, Add. MS 80475 B. The educational material is to be found in this same file. A special Oscar was invented to give to Olivier for his achievement (and to avoid the potential problem of his sweeping the board for Best Film, Best Actor, and Best Director): P. Ziegler, *Olivier* (London, 2013), 113.

65. BL, Add. MS 80463. The Stothard volume was provided by Roger Furse (BL, Add. MS 80464).

66. Geduld, *Filmguide to Henry V*, 2.

67. B. Hillier, *John Betjeman: New Fame, New Love* (London, 2002), 224.

68. John Huntley, *British Film Music* (London, 1947), 74, quoted in Smith (ed.), *King Henry V*, 51 n. 147. I am grateful to Robert Woosnam-Savage for the information on the Olympic bid.

69. A. Pilkington, *Screening Shakespeare from Richard II to Henry V* (Newark, Del., and London, 1991), 104–5.

70. Cited in Geduld, *Filmguide to Henry V*, 53.

71. I was fortunate enough to see this in Manchester in 1973. Thanks to the good offices of his daughter, Rosamond, and Dr Sinclair Rogers, I have also seen the paintings which he made of the battle.

72. J. W. Young, 'Henry V, the Quai d'Orsay and the Well-Being of the Franco-British Alliance, 1947', *Historical Journal of Film, Radio and Television*, 7 (1987), 319–21.

73. Collection BDIC-MHC.

74. *The Observer*, 8 Oct. 1989, cited in J. N. Loehlin, *Shakespeare in Performance: Henry V* (Manchester, 1997), 130.

75. K. Branagh, *Beginning* (London, 1989), ch. 10.

76. Loehlin, *Shakespeare in Performance*, 115, 120; D. Carnegie, 'So the Falklands. So Agincourt. "Fuck the Frogs": Michael Bogdanov's English Shakespeare Company's Wars of the Roses', in R. King and P. J. C. M. Franssen (eds), *Shakespeare and War* (London, 2008), 213–25.

77. Smith (ed.), *King Henry V*, 75.

78. Loehlin, *Shakespeare in Performance*, 94–5.
79. Henderson, 'Meditations in a Time of (Displaced) War', 230.
80. *Cobbett's Parliamentary History of England*, xxxvi. 29 Oct. 1801–12 Aug. 1803 (London, 1820), 177.
81. Henderson, 'Meditations in a Time of (Displaced) War', 226, 240 n. 1.
82. www.bbc.co.uk/news/entertainment-arts-27858858 [19 Aug. 2014].
83. *The Independent*, 15 Mar. 2014. I am grateful to Peter M. Campbell for this reference.
84. Henderson, 'Meditations in a Time of (Displaced) War', 237–8.
85. www.dctheatrescene.com/2010/03/18/ [15 Aug. 2014].
86. J. Sutherland and C. Watts, *Henry V, War Criminal? And Other Shakespeare Puzzles* (London, 2000), 108–16.
87. *Libération*, 12 July 1999; *Daily Telegraph*, 14 July 1999; and *The Guardian*, 11 July 1999, cited in Smith (ed.), *King Henry V*, 66.
88. www.rsc.org.uk/explore/shakespeare/plays/henry-v/2007.aspx. I am grateful to Prof. Michael Prestwich for bringing this to my attention.

Chapter 5

1. STC (2nd edn) 6054.
2. STC 20403 and 25025. In his *Certain Discourses* of 1590 Sir John Smyth emphasized the importance of archers at Agincourt but commented that, now archers were deployed in hearses and *piquiers*, stakes were no longer needed (STC 22883). The full texts are available on EEBO. I am grateful to Prof. Jackie Eales for alerting me to these materials.
3. BL, Thomason Tracts E.83[28].
4. STC (2nd edn) 17333.
5. EEBO: Wing T2043.
6. Jasper Mayne, *To His Royall Highnesse, the Duke of Yorke on our late sea-fight*. EEBO: Wing M1479.
7. EEBO: Wing M1479; *Mercurius Reformatus or the New Observator*, 3 Apr. 1691.
8. Published as a facsimile edition in 1969 by the Society of Archer Antiquaries and the Grand National Archery Society. For discussion see www.bowyers.com/bowyery_finsburyArchers.php.
9. C. T. Allmand, 'Writing History in the Eighteenth Century: Thomas Goodwin's *The History of the Reign of Henry the Fifth* (1704)', in G. Dodd (ed.), *Henry V: New Interpretations* (Woodbridge, 2013), 273–88.
10. TNA, SP 9/36/7.
11. *The Yale Edition of Horace Walpole's Correspondence*, ed. W. S. Lewis (New Haven, 1937–83), xxxvii. 200 (1 July 1746).
12. *General Advertiser*, 5 Sept. 1751.
13. *Sources*, 374–7.
14. *London Evening Post*, 11–13 Mar. 1755.

15. *The Monitor or the British Freeholder*, 19 Feb. and 1 Oct. 1757.
16. *Universal Chronicle or Weekly Gazette*, 3–10 Feb. 1759.
17. *Lloyds Evening Post and British Chronicle*, 12–14 Nov. 1760.
18. *The British Military Library* (new edn in 2 vols London, 1804), i. 250.
19. *Abridgement of the Postscript to the Third Edition of a Vindication of the Cause of Great Britain on the Situation of the Continent and the Projected Invasion of This Country*, by William Hunter (London, 1803), 14.
20. *Cobbett's Weekly Political Register*, 1 June 1811.
21. *Morning Post*, 24 June 1815.
22. *Morning Post*, 10 Nov. 1810.
23. Cited in J. Endell Tyler, *Henry of Monmouth*, 2 vols (London, 1838), ii. 57. See also *Caledonian Mercury*, 17 June 1816.
24. *Bristol Mercury*, 25 Aug. 1821. *Morning Post*, 12 Apr. 1821, 29 Dec. 1825, and 10 Jan. 1827.
25. *Leeds Mercury*, 30 Oct. 1819.
26. www.archerylibrary.com/books/book_of_archery/chapter10/chapter10.html [21 Aug. 2014].
27. *Bradford Observer*, 27 June 1850.
28. *Preston Guardian*, 24 Aug. 1850; *Daily News*, 27 Aug. 1850.
29. *A Contribution towards an Authentic List of the Commanders of the English Host in King Henry the Fifth's Expedition to France in the Third Year of his Reign* (London, 1850), 1.
30. I. Beckett, *The Amateur Military Tradition 1558–1948* (Manchester, 1991), 144–69.
31. *Morning Post*, 19 Feb. 1853; *The Era*, 6 Aug. 1854.
32. R. de Belleval, *Azincourt* (Paris, 1865).
33. As reported in *Glasgow Herald*, 2 Feb. 1855.
34. *Reynold's Newspaper*, 20 Nov. 1859; *Huddersfield Chronicle*, 4 June 1859.
35. Beckett, *Amateur Military Tradition*, 169.
36. *Huddersfield Chronicle*, 13 June 1878.
37. *Passages of a Working Life during Half a Century*, 3 vols (London, 1864–5), iii. 60–2. For the date of his visit see *The Pictorial Shakespeare*, ed. Charles Knight (London, 1838–41), i. 374.
38. *By-Roads and Battlefields in Picardy: With Incidents and Gatherings by the Way between Ambleteuse and Ham including Agincourt and Crecy* (London, 1861), chs. 14 and 15.
39. *Cook's Excursionist and Tourist Advertiser*, 10 Apr. 1886. I am grateful to Paul Smith of the Thomas Cook Archive for this reference.
40. *The Graphic*, 24 Sept. 1887. Benjamin Robert Haydon may have visited between 1834 and 1840 since his original sketch, 'In the field: Agincourt', survives in BL, RP 7599/1.
41. *Hampshire Advertiser*, 11 Nov. 1899.
42. *The Graphic*, 6 Sept. 1890.
43. *The Book of the Army Pageant*, ed. F. R. Benson and A. Tudor Craig (London, 1910).

44. Crécy was included in the pageant to epitomize 'the use of shot in defence against the shock of horse'.

45. See, amongst many examples, C. R. L. Fletcher and R. Kipling, *The School History of England* (London, 1911); www.history.ac.uk/history-in-education/ [21 Aug. 2014].

46. The story was later published in book form along with other pieces in A. Machen, *The Angel of Mons: The Bowmen and Other Legends of the War* (2nd edn, London, 1915); S. Goebel, *The Great War and Medieval Memory: War, Remembrance and Medievalism in Britain and Germany, 1914–1940* (Cambridge, 2007), 247.

47. *The Times*, 25 Oct. 1915, p. 9; see also *The Times*, 1 Nov. 1915, p. 11.

48. National Army Museum, via the Mary Evans Picture Library item 10795327.

49. *The Times*, 28 Dec. 1963.

50. St Helens Local History and Archives Library, C/LH/1.6, St Mary's Lowe House, 'proposed memorial chapel', 1918, cited in Goebel, *The Great War*, 252.

51. www.windleshawchantry.org.uk gives the foundation date of the chantry as 1435, 'perhaps in gratitude for his surviving the battle of Agincourt'. For the more likely version see *The Victoria County History of Lancaster*, iii. (London, 1907), 371–7.

52. *The Times*, 11 Nov. 1920, 15; *Daily Telegraph*, 12 Nov. 1920, 13, cited in Goebel, *The Great War*, 45.

53. I am grateful to Ahren Lester for this reference. The British HQ was at Montreuil, not far from Azincourt.

54. I am very grateful to Christophe Gilliot for a copy of *L'Illustration*, and for other information on this event drawn from French military records (AN, 26N916/2).

55. http://www.iwm.org.uk/collections/item/object/1060008209. The Tramecourt section is at the end of part 2 and beginning of part 3.

56. Australian War Memorial H09574. I am grateful to Christophe Gilliot for this image.

57. *Arms & The Tower* (London, 1935), 100. Ffoulkes had been appointed curator in 1913 but spent most of his time from 1917 to 1933 at the National (subsequently Imperial) War Museum. On his return to the Royal Armouries in 1933 he added a note of this visit to the 1,917 pages of the Armouries Minute Book (I.188), 44) which is still preserved in the archives of the Royal Armouries. I am grateful to Bridget Clifford for these references. The monument referred to is the *calvaire*.

58. TNA, ZPER 34/149, 604–5.

59. I am grateful to Dr Adrian Ailes for this information.

60. Curry, *Agincourt: A New History*, 62.

61. 'The Campaign of Agincourt: October 25, 1415', *Cornhill Magazine*, 3rd ser. 39 (1915), 524–41.

62. W. Rhys Roberts, *Patriotic Poetry, Greek and English: An Address given on the 500th Anniversary of Agincourt* (London, 1916).

Chapter 6

1. pp. 83 and 174. We know that Disraeli drew on Holinshed for the Peasants' Revolt and therefore may have also read the narrative of Agincourt. A. Taufer, *Holinshed's Chronicles* (New York, 1999), 136.
2. E. Waugh, *Brideshead Revisited* (Penguin edn, Harmondsworth, 1981), 317.
3. English Heritage Grade II listed, list entry number 1049200.
4. Bodleian Library, Ashmolean MS 825, College of Arms, MS1 and BL, Harleian 782. All are now thought to be in Glover's own hand although they have links with other heralds of the period too. I am grateful to Dr Nigel Ramsey for his advice, linked to his forthcoming publication on Glover for the Harleian Society.
5. *Sources*, 407–8, 426–34; J. H. Wylie, 'Notes on the Agincourt Roll', *Transactions of the Royal Historical Society*, 3rd ser., 5 (1911), 105–40.
6. *The Visitation of Cheshire in the Year 1580*, ed. J. P. Rylands (London, 1882), 203, 153. I am grateful to Dr Adrian Ailes for these references.
7. *The Visitations of Essex*, ed. W. C. Metcalfe, 2 vols (London, 1878), i. 184; *The Visitations of Surrey 1530, 1572, 1623*, ed. W. B. Bannerman (London, 1899), 105.
8. *Sources*, 451–2 from T. Rymer, *Foedera, Conventiones, Litterae et Cuiuscunque Generis Acta Publica* (London, 1704–35; 3rd edn, The Hague, 1739–45), IV. ii. 201.
9. *Sources*, 134.
10. Edward, duke of York made a grant of arms at Harfleur on 29 August 1415 to John Bruggeford according to a heraldic visitation of Staffordshire in 1614.
11. A. Ailes, 'Bruges, William (c.1375–1450)', http://www.oxforddnb.com/view/article/50120 [14 Aug. 2014].
12. Curry, *Agincourt: A New History*, app. E; www.medievalsoldier.org.
13. L. Salzman, 'The Early History of the Pelhams', *Sussex Archaeological Collections*, 69 (1927), 70.
14. *Miscellanea Genealogica et Heraldica*, 4th ser., 5 (1911), 206, from Bodleian Library, MS Ashmole 857, 521. This was a transcript made by Elias Ashmole (1617–92) who became Windsor herald in 1660.
15. BL, Harley 782, fo. 86; TNA, E101/47/13 m.1. We find a John Codyngton crossing as a man-at-arms in 1417 and as an archer in 1421, as well as serving in the 1420s and 1430s in the garrison of Caen (TNA, E101/51/2 m.35, E101/50/1 m. 3).
16. C. W. Scott-Giles, *The Romance of Heraldry* (London, 1929; repr. 1967), 106.
17. J. S. Roskell, L. Clark, and C. Rawcliffe (eds), *History of Parliament: The Commons 1386–1422*, 4 vols (Gloucester, 1992), iv. 885–7.
18. www.bowyers.com/aboutUs_coatOfArms.php.

19. F. Huxford, *Honour and Arms: The Story of Some Augmentations of Honour* (London, 1984), 24–5.

20. *The Visitation of the County of Kent, 1619, by John Philipott* (Harleian Society; London, 1863), 320. William Camden's *Britannia* (1586) mentions his keeping of the duke of Orléans but nothing else.

21. Curry, *Agincourt: A New History*, 28.

22. TNA, E 101/45/4 m. 1.

23. B. Grimshaw, *The Entwistle Family* (Accrington, 1924), frontispiece. There is an undated 'Ballad of Sir Bertin Entwistle': 'that sword once felt the craven foe, the hilt was black with gore, and many a mother's heart did rue his might at Agincourt'.

24. BN, manuscrit français 25767/1: man-at-arms in the garrison of Coutances, Mar. 1423. A William Entwistle is found in the Agincourt Roll in the retinue of Henry, Lord Scrope, one of the plotters executed before the expedition set sail.

25. BL, Cotton Claudius A. xiii, fo. 278r.

26. TNA, E 101/47/20.

27. TNA, E 403/643 m. 7.

28. J. Barker, *Agincourt: The King, the Campaign, the Battle* (London, 2005), 366.

29. Lady Newton, *The House of Lyme from Its Foundation to the End of the Eighteenth Century* (London, 1917).

30. English Heritage, NMR 78360.

31. As in D. and S. Lysons, *Magna Britannia*, vi. *Devonshire* (London, 1822), pp. xcv–cviii.

32. F. Grose, *Antiquities of England and Wales*, 7 vols (London, 1783–97), iv. 30.

33. *The Times*, 4 Mar. 1995 in response to the leading article of 25 Feb. headed 'Birth of A Nation: Why the Hundred Years War should be commemorated'.

34. 'The majority of his longbowmen at Agincourt were ... Welshmen': M. Livingstone, 'The Battle of Bryn Glas', in M. Livingston and J. K. Bollard (eds.), *Owain Glyndŵr: A Casebook* (Exeter, 2013), 467; for the claim by Ranulph Fiennes that 80 per cent of Henry's armies were Welsh see *The Times*, 9 Aug. 2014; R. Fiennes, *Agincourt: My Family, The Battle and The Fight for France* (London, 2014).

35. TNA, E 101/46/20.

36. H. T. Evans, *Wales and the Wars of the Roses* (Cambridge, 1915; repr. Stroud, 1995), 11–12.

37. Evans, *Wales and the Wars of the Roses*, 27–8.

38. A. Chapman, 'The King's Welshmen: Welsh Involvement in the Expeditionary Army of 1415', *Journal of Medieval Military History*, 9 (2011), 41–64; id., 'The Welsh Soldier, 1283–1422', unpublished PhD thesis (University of Southampton, 2009); Curry, *Agincourt: A New History*, app. E; www.medievalsoldier.org.

39. *The Chronicle of Adam Usk, 1377–1421*, ed. C. Given-Wilson (Oxford, 1997), 255–9. Usk wrongly claims that Sir John Scudamore (d.1435) died at the battle.

40. *The history of Wales comprehending the lives and succession of the princes of Wales, from Cadwalader the last king, to Llewelyn the last prince of British blood with a short account of the affairs of Wales under the kings of England written originally in British, by Caradoc of Llancarvan; and formerly published in English by Dr. Powel; now newly augmented and improved by W. Wynne* (London, 1697).

41. Nicolas, *History of the Battle of Agincourt* (London, 1827), app., p. 60.

42. BL, 1883, 0714.471.

43. *The Register of Robert Mascall, Bishop of Hereford 1404–1416*, ed. J. H. Parry (Cantilupe Society; Hereford, 1916), p. v.

44. *Chronicle of Adam Usk 1377–1421*, 262–3.

45. TNA, E 101/45/1 m. 7.

46. J. Baldo, 'Wars of Memory in Henry V', *Shakespeare Quarterly*, 47 (1996), 151, n. 68. For Tudor's career, see R. A. Griffiths's biography in the *Oxford Dictionary of National Biography* [http://www.oxforddnb.com/view/article/27797, accessed 31 July 2014].

47. STC (2nd edn) 13592. *Pancharis the first booke: Containing the preparation of the love betweene Owen Tudyr, and the Queene, long since intended to her maiden Maiestie.*

48. The gesture is formed by making a V-shape with the index and third finger of the hand whilst gathering the thumb and remaining fingers together against the palm. The sign is presented by showing the back of the hand.

49. *Sources*, 51, 155.

50. A. Curry, 'Disciplinary Ordinances for English and Franco-Scottish Armies in 1385: An International Code?', *Journal of Medieval History*, 37 (2011), 289–91; ead., 'The Military Ordinances of Henry V: Texts and Contexts', in C. Given-Wilson, A. Kettle, and L. Scales (eds), *War, Government and Aristocracy in the British Isles c 1150–1500* (Woodbridge, 2008), 214–49.

51. J. Bulwer, *Chirologia, or, The naturall language of the hand composed of the speaking notions, and discoursing gestures thereof* (London, 1644); J. Walter, 'Gesturing at Authority: Deciphering the Gestural Code of Early Modern England', *Past and Present*, 203 (2009), 96–127. I am grateful to Prof. Walter for discussion on the matter. In general, see D. Wilton, *World Myths: Debunking Linguistic Urban Legends* (Oxford, 2008) as well as the V-sign page on Wikipedia. I have been unable to substantiate claims that Froissart mentions the sign and am not certain the scene of a glove in the Macclesfield Psalter (1330) fits the bill. According to www.britishshakespearecompany.com Rabelais refers to the sign.

52. V&A, M.484-1927.

53. Burrell Collection, Object 2.27/115. I am grateful to Dr Ralph Moffat, Curator of European Arms and Armour at Glasgow Museums, for information on this object. It was purchased at Sotheby's in 1953.

54. V&A, M.28A&B-1975.

55. V&A, E.1169–1921. It was used for the dust jacket of K. Fowler, *The Age of Plantagenet and Valois* (London, 1967).

56. Stonyhurst College, Arundel Library, MS 1. At the bottom of fo. 160v, written upside down, there is a later inscription 'Je suis a messire Jehan arondell': this is probably the Sir John Arundell of Lanherne who died in 1545. This is in a later hand than the text of the manuscript. I am grateful to Jan Graffius of Stonyhurst College and Prof. Peter Ainsworth for information on this manuscript. For the online facsimile and discussion see http://www.hrionline.ac.uk/onlinefroissart/.

57. A. Keay, *The Crown Jewels* (London, 2011), 92.

58. Scott-Giles, *Romance of Heraldry*, 106.

59. I am grateful to Dr Tobias Capwell of the Wallace Collection for advice on these items.

60. *Monumenta Westmonasteriensa* (London, 1682), cited in Bate and Thornton (eds), *Shakespeare: Staging the World*, 107.

61. Warwickshire County Record Office, Newdegate of Arbury, CR 764/240. I am grateful to Dr Tim Sutherland for the text of these letters.

62. J. Hamilton, *Turner's Britain* (London, 2003), 170–2.

63. Cited in J. H. Wylie, *The Reign of Henry the Fifth*, 3 vols (Cambridge, 1914–29), ii. 226 n. 9.

64. *Naval and Military Magazine*, 2 (1827), 225; W. T. Jones, 'Archaeological Intelligence', *Archaeological Journal*, 4 (1847), 78–9 (with thanks to Dr Tim Sutherland for these references); *Morning Post*, 2 Feb. 1846.

65. F. Crosthwaite, *Brief Memoir of Major-Gen. Sir John Geo. Woodford* (Crosthwaite and Keswick Literary and Scientific Society; Kendal, 1881), app. vi.

66. Wylie, *Reign of Henry the Fifth*, ii. 228 n. 2. I am grateful to Stephen Cooper for information on the catalogue.

67. For this newsworthy fire see *Glasgow Herald*, 14 Feb. 1874. On the Pantechnicon, see J. Flanders, *The Victorian City: Everyday Life in Dickens' London* (London, 2012).

68. *Commission des antiquités départementales du Pas-de-Calais, Chapelle funéraire d'Azincourt, Invitation à souscrire à l'œuvre d'Azincourt pour l'érection d'un monument* (Douai, 1856).

69. Crosthwaite, *Brief Memoir*, 11; Wylie, *Reign of Henry the Fifth*, ii. 229 n. 4. Wylie also speaks of a pair of spurs, two lance heads, and a gisarme supposedly found at Azincourt and placed in the Musée d'Artillerie in Paris (ii. 226 n. 9, citing H. R. Bordier and E. Charton, *Histoire de France*, 2 vols (Paris, 1859–60), i. 501).

70. I am grateful to Prof. Sarah Pearce for alerting me to this walk.

71. *The Lay of Agincourt with Other Poems* (Edinburgh, 1819).

72. H. Carpenter and M. Pritchard (eds), *The Oxford Companion to Children's Literature* (Oxford, 1984), 244–7.

73. For example, Michael Cox's *Agincourt: Jenkin Lloyd, France 1415* (2003), Malcolm Pryce's *A Dragon to Agincourt* (2003), and David Lawrence-Young's *Arrows over Agincourt* (2012).

74. www.drwhoguide.com/whotrip31.htm [21 Aug. 2014].

75. D. Shawe-Taylor (ed.), *The First Georgians: Art and Monarchy 1714–1760* (London, 2014), 283.

76. J. Marschner, *Queen Caroline: Cultural Politics at the Early Eighteenth-Century Court* (London, 2014), 89. Photographs of these were pasted into Windsor Castle Inventory of Busts dated 1875. I am grateful to Colin Ailes for advice on Queen Caroline's patronage.

77. M. Girouard, *The Return to Camelot: Chivalry and the English Gentleman* (New Haven, 1981), 112–15.

78. *The Athenaeum*, 10 July 1847, cited in www.eyrecrowe.com/pictures/1840s/battle-of-agincourt/. The painting does not seem to have survived.

79. See also the report in *Morning Chronicle*, 30 Aug. 1805. A letter written by John Woodford in 1874 also mentions a panoramic view of Agincourt and vicinity by Captain Harding of the Royal Engineers but this has not been traced unless Woodford was referring to the plan of the field, now BL Add. MS 16368 Map C, rather than a visual representation.

80. *Caledonian Mercury*, 16 June 1808; B. Silliman, *A Journal of Travels in England, Holland and Scotland* (London, 1810); T. F. Dibdin, *Reminiscences of a Literary Life* (London, 1836), i. 143–5; *The Times*, 4 Jan. 1834; *Cardigan Observer*, 2 Oct. 1880.

81. *The Star*, 7 Apr. 1794. J. Boydell, *A Description of Several Pictures Presented to the Corporation of the City of London* (London, 1794), 24–7.

82. S. Bucklow and S. Woodcock (eds), *Sir John Gilbert: Art and Imagination in the Victorian Age* (London, 2011), 54, 86. I am grateful to the Swansea Branch of the Historical Association for their kind gift of the print of Gilbert's *The Battle of Agincourt* and its accompanying text.

83. See articles on Charles Augustus Rivers and Benjamin Spence in the online *Biographical Dictionary of Sculptors in Britain 1660–1851*, www.henry-moore.org/hmi/library/biographical-dictionary-of-sculptors-in-britain.

84. Tate Modern, P20203.

85. Burney took this from a transcription in the Pepys Library, Cambridge. I am grateful to Prof. David Owen Norris for this reference. For Hearne's intention 'to print an old song on the battle' see BL, Lansdowne MS 778/36.

86. www.shop-hellsheadbangers.com/Agincourt-angels-of-mons-LP.asp.

87. For plans for 'Agincourt', see *The Times*, 4 Apr. 1973; see Wikipedia for articles on both Joseph and Lloyd.

88. *Morning Post*, 17 Apr. 1805.

89. P. Borsay, 'New Approaches to Social History: Myth, Memory and Place: Monmouth and Bath 1750–1900', *Journal of Social History*, 39 (2006), 867–89; *Guide to the Monmouth Heritage Blue Plaque Trail* (n.d.), 7.

90. J. J. Colledge and B. Warlow, *Ships of the Royal Navy: A Complete Record of All Fighting Ships of the Royal Navy from the 15th Century to the Present* (4th edn, London, 2010); www.wikipedia.org/wiki/HMS_Agincourt [19 Aug. 2014].

91. *The Times*, 27 Sept. 1960. The ship was converted to coal hulk in 1908 and was anchored off Sheerness for 51 years.

92. *Daily Telegraph*, 5 Aug. 1914, 7; R. Hough, *The Great Dreadnought: The Strange Story of HMS Agincourt: The Mightiest Battleship of World War I* (New York, 1967). I am grateful to Prof. Adrian Smith for discussion on this ship.

93. J. Goodman, *LMS Locomotive Names: The Named Locomotives of the London, Midland and Scottish Railway and Its Constituent Companies* (Lincoln, 1994), 14–15; J. Goodman, *L&NWR Locomotive Names: The Named Locomotives of the London and Northwestern Railway and Its Constituent Companies* (Peterborough, 2002), 11, 105, 162; J. Pike, *Locomotive Names: An Illustrated Dictionary* (Stroud, 2000), 2.

94. www.trainweb.org/oldtimetrains/CPR_Trenton/agincourt.htm [19 Aug. 2014].

95. www.neighbourhoodwalks.wordpress.com/2012/05/Agincourt-part-ii-agincourt-south/ [19 Aug. 2014].

96. www.environment.gov.au.

Chapter 7

1. Overview in *The Week*, 24 Nov. 2008.

2. C. T. Allmand, 'Writing History in the Eighteenth Century: Thomas Goodwin's *The History of the Reign of Henry the Fifth* (1704)', in G. Dodd (ed.), *Henry V: New Interpretations* (Woodbridge, 2013), 273–88.

3. Rymer, *Foedera, conventiones, litterae et cuiuscunque generis acta publica* (London, 1704–35; 3rd edn, The Hague, 1739–45), vol. ix. Printed editions of chronicles are also significant in this story, for instance Thomas Hearne's editions of the *Vita Henrici Quinti* (1716) and the *Vita et Gesta Henrici Quinti* (1727). In the nineteenth century the Rolls Series included editions of important texts such as the *Liber Metricus* and Waurin's chronicles.

4. *Sources*, 386–7.

5. Now BL, Sloane 4600, wrongly cited by Nicolas as Sloane 6400. For discussion of the Agincourt Roll see Ch. 6.

6. From the two manuscripts in the then British Museum, Cotton Julius E.iv. and Sloane 1776. Sharon Turner had earlier drawn on the Sloane text in his *History of England*. The Latin text was first printed in *Henrici Quinti, Angliae Regis, Gesta*, ed. B. Williams (London, 1850).

7. Turner, *History of England in the Middle Ages* (London, 1815), ii. 260; J. Endell Tyler, *Henry of Monmouth* (London, 1838), as epitomized in the contents list of volume ii: 'Henry, his enemies themselves being Judges, fully exculpated from every suspicion of cruelty or unchivalrous bearing.'

8. Nicolas, *History of the Battle of Agincourt* (London, 3rd edn, 1833), 106–38; quotes from pp. xiii, 128, 179, 166 note b.

9. *Sussex Archaeological Collections*, 15 (1863), 123–37.

10. 'Notes on the Agincourt Roll', *Transactions of the Royal Historical Society*, 3rd ser. 5 (1911), 105–40.

11. *PRO Lists and Indexes XXXV: List of Various Accounts Formerly Preserved in the Exchequer* (London, 1912).

12. *The Reign of Henry the Fifth*, 3 vols (Cambridge, 1914–29). Vol. iii was completed by William Templeton Waugh from Wylie's notes.

13. J. Barker, *Agincourt: The King, the Campaign, the Battle* (London, 2005), p. xv.

14. 'Lessons from Agincourt', *Army Quarterly*, 62 (1959), 70.

15. *Reign of Henry the Fifth*, ii. 213, 215–16.

16. *Reign of Henry the Fifth*, ii. 174, n. 9.

17. Originally published as G. Wrottesley (ed.), 'Crecy and Calais (1346–1347) from the Public Records', *William Salt Archaeological Collections*, 18 (1897), and as a separate volume in 1898.

18. G. Bacquet, *Azincourt* (Bellegrade, 1977); C. J. Rogers (ed.), *The Wars of Edward III: Sources and Interpretations* (Woodbridge, 2000; repr. 2010).

19. *The Battle of Agincourt: Sources and Interpretations* (Woodbridge, 2000; rev. edn, 2009).

20. The inspiration of Philippe Contamine is significant here: *Guerre, état et société: Étude sur les armées des rois de France 1337–1494* (Paris and The Hague, 1972). Also useful is the work of Bertrand Schnerb on Burgundian armies, especially 'La Bataille rangée dans la tactique des armées bourguignonnes au début du 15e siècle: Essai de synthèse', *Annales de Bourgogne*, 61 (1989), 5–32.

21. S. Boffa, 'Antoine de Bourgogne et le contingent brabançon à la bataille d'Azincourt (1415)', *Revue belge de philologie et d'histoire*, 72 (1994), 255–84. For background on Brabantine armies see Boffa, *Warfare in Medieval Brabant 1356–1406* (Woodbridge, 2004).

22. O. Bouzy, 'Les Morts d'Azincourt: leurs liens de famille, d'offices et de parti', in P. Gilli and J. Paviot (eds), *Hommes, cultures et sociétés à la fin du Moyen Âge* (Paris, 2012), 221–55. F. Lachaud, 'La Structure familiale des Craon du XIe siècle à 1415: Le Concept lignager en question', unpublished thèse de doctorat, Université de Bordeaux-Montaigne (2012), 627.

23. R. Ambühl, 'A Fair Share of the Profits? The Ransoms of Agincourt (1415)', *Nottingham Medieval Studies*, 50 (2006), 129–50; Ambühl, 'Le Sort des prisonniers d'Azincourt (1415)', *Revue du Nord*, 89 (2007), 755–87.

24. For discussion see *Sources*, 408–36.

25. A. Curry, *Agincourt: A New History* (Stroud, 2005); A. R. Bell, A. Curry, A. King, and D. Simpkin, *The Soldier in Later Medieval England* (Oxford, 2013); www.medievalsoldier.org.

26. A. Curry, 'Personal Links and the Nature of the English War Retinue: A Case Study of John Mowbray, Earl Marshal, and the Campaign of 1415', in

E. Anceau, V. Gazeau, and F. J. Ruggiu (eds), *Liens, reseaux et solidarités* (Paris, 2006), 153–67.

27. Barker, *Agincourt*, 135–7.

28. Barker, *Agincourt*, xvi.

29. Mortimer also suggests that the French army looked so much larger because of the higher number of pages compared with the English. I. Mortimer, *1415: Henry V's Year of Glory* (London, 2009), 421–2, 566; C. J. Rogers, 'The Battle of Agincourt', in L. J. A. Villalon and D. J. Kagay (eds), *The Hundred Years War (Part II)* (Leiden, 2008), app. ii (The English numbers).

30. *New York Times*, 25 Oct. 2009; Rogers, 'Battle of Agincourt', 115. Note also the preference of H. Delbrück and F. Lot for lower numbers for the French army: *Sources*, 394–7.

31. H. Delbrück, *Geschichte der Kriegskunst im Rahmen der Politischen Geschichte*, 3 vols (Berlin, 1907). For his section on Agincourt, see the English translation by W. J. Renfroe, *History of the Art of War Within the Framework of Political History* (Lincoln, Nebr., 1990), iii. 463–70; F. Lot, *L'Art militaire et les armées au Moyen Âge en Europe et dans la Proche Orient*, 2 vols (Paris, 1946), ii. 5–15.

32. J. W. Honig, 'Reappraising Late Medieval Strategy: The Example of the 1415 Agincourt Campaign', *War in History*, 19 (2012), 133 n. 41.

33. *The Times*, 25 Feb. 1995. The debate, organized by the Battlefields Trust, was held at the Tower of London. Its outcome led to a further article in *The Times* on 27 Feb. headed 'New battle of Agincourt ends in a convivial truce'.

34. See the different battle plans by Bennett and Hardy in A. Curry and M. Hughes (eds), *Arms, Armies and Fortifications of the Hundred Years War* (Woodbridge, 1994), 18, 175. Burne suggested the archers were divided with the 'army archers' on the wings and 'divisional archers' in the front (*The Agincourt War* (London, 1956), 80). For the debate see *Sources*, 403.

35. J. H. Ramsey, *Lancaster and York* (London, 1892), ii. 214–15. The plan is given after p. 212 and is reproduced in *Sources*, fig. 3. Ramsey's plan was much used in other histories and school textbooks of the late nineteenth and early twentieth century.

36. *Henry V* (London and New York, 1901), 139.

37. *The Face of Battle: A Study of Agincourt, Waterloo and the Somme* (London, 1976), 85.

38. C. Hibbert, *Agincourt* (London, 1964), 178. Hibbert includes a number of appendices drawn from Nicolas.

39. C. J. Rogers, 'Henry V's Military Strategy in 1415', in L. J. A. Villalon and D. J. Kagay (eds), The *Hundred Years War: A Wider Focus* (Leiden, 2005), 422.

40. For a useful review of arrows v. armour, see Rogers, 'The Battle of Agincourt', 109–21.

41. G. N. Askew, F. Formenti, and A. E. Minetti, 'Limitations Imposed by Wearing Armour on Medieval Soldiers' Locomotor Performance', *Proceedings of the Royal Society B*, 279 (2012), 640–4.

42. See various newspaper reports including *Daily Telegraph*, 20 July 2011.

43. Originally broadcast on 23 Nov. 2003. See https://www.youtube.com/watch?v=LVuVtP_xepU&app=desktop [19 Aug. 2014].

44. R. R. Clements and R. L. Hughes, 'Mathematical Modelling of a Mediaeval Battle: The Battle of Agincourt, 1415', *Mathematics and Computers in Simulation*, 64 (2004), 259–69.

45. G. Foard and A. Curry, *Bosworth: A Battlefield Rediscovered* (Oxford, 2013).

46. Wylie's citations of other names (*Reign of Henry the Fifth*, ii. 178–9) offer a good example of his lack of distinction between contemporary and later sources.

47. J.-M. Duvosquel, *Un document d'histoire rurale: Le Dénombrement de la seigneurie de Comines (1470)* (Louvain and Ghent, 1971), 51; B.-A. Pocquet du Haut-Jussé, *La France gouvernée par Jean sans Peur: Les Dépenses du receveur général du royaume* (Paris, 1959), no. 249, p. 119. I am grateful to Prof. Bertrand Schnerb for these references.

48. Foard and Curry, *Bosworth*, 183. For the front at Crécy, estimated at between 1,000 and 1,700 yards (914 and 1,554 metres), see Ayton and Preston, *Battle of Crécy*, 146.

49. *Caledonian Mercury*, 17 June 1816; J. Endell Tyler, *Henry of Monmouth*, 2 vols (London, 1838), ii. 57.

50. BL, Add. MS 16368 Map C.

51. A. Nicholson, 'Woodford, Sir John George (1785–1879)', rev. H. C. G. Matthew, http://www.oxforddnb.com/view/article/29917 [28 Apr. 2014]. F. Crosthwaite, *Brief Memoir of Major-Gen. Sir John Geo. Woodford* (Crosthwaite and Keswick Literary and Scientific Society; Kendal, 1881). On the army, but with no reference to the excavations at Azincourt, see T. D. Veve, *The Duke of Wellington and the British Army of Occupation in France, 1815–1818* (Westport, 1992). I am grateful to Hugh Williams for discussion on Woodford.

52. Warwickshire County Record Office, Newdegate of Arbury, CR 764/240. I am grateful to Dr Tim Sutherland for the text of these letters and for comments on Woodford materials in Keswick Museum and Art Gallery.

53. AN, Carton F. 7. 9903. I am grateful to Christophe Gilliot for this reference.

54. *Morning Chronicle*, 20 Apr. 1818, drawing information from a French newspaper, noted that the researches had been abandoned because of protests.

55. I am grateful to Alan F. Cook for comments here.

56. T. Sutherland, 'The Battle of Agincourt: An Alternative Location', *Journal of Conflict Archaeology*, 1 (2005), 245–63.

57. T. Sutherland and S. Richardson, 'Arrow Point to Mass Graves: Finding the Dead from the Battle of Towton', in D. Scott et al. (eds), *Fields of Conflict: Battlefield Archaeology from the Roman Empire to the Korean War* (Westport, 2007), 160–73.

58. E. Audoin (ed.), 'Recueil des documents concernant la commune et la ville de Poitiers', *Archives historiques de Poitou* (1928), 164–75.

59. Belleval, *Azincourt*, 121; C. Labitte, 'Bataille d'Azincourt', *Revue anglo-française*, 3 (1835), 13–47.
60. H. Boulet and H. Willemand, 'L'Hommage aux chevaliers: Le Project de chapelle de l'abbé Décobert à Azincourt'. I am grateful to Dr Tim Sutherland for a copy of this.
61. *Commission des antiquités départementales du Pas-de-Calais, Chapelle funéraire d'Azincourt, Invitation à souscrire à l'œuvre d'Azincourt pour l'érection d'un monument* (Douai, 1856).
62. *L'Abeille de la Ternoise*, 23 June 1951. I have also seen 1860 put forward as the date of the *calvaire*. Dominique Paladilhe dates it to 25 October 1914 in his *La Bataille d'Azincourt* (Paris, 2001), 11, but this is a misreading of the date at the top of the inscription which definitely says 25 October 1415 not 1914. He does, however, provide the text of the inscription with its quotations from the Book of Kings, Wisdom, and Maccabees.
63. TNA, AIR 37/1392 (I am grateful to Mrs Simpson for these photographs); www.echo62.com [23 Aug. 2014].
64. *L'Abeille de la Ternoise*, 18 May 1963.
65. France3-regions.francetvinfo.fr/nord-pas-de-calais/2014/04/20/sur-les-traces-des-chevaliers-morts-azincourt-le-25-octobre-1415-463107.html; L. N. Patel, 'Le Gallois de Fougières', *Police et gendarmerie*, 48 (2006), 97–8.
66. I am very grateful to the current director of the Centre historique médiéval, Christophe Gilliot, for this information. Many thanks also to Siobhan Stevens, director of the Centre Verginaud, M. and Mme Delcusse, M. Eric Revet, M. and Mme Fenet, and M. Boulet for their hospitality and friendship over the many years I have been working on the battle. I was honoured to be invited to give the annual commemorative lecture on 25 October 2003.
67. www.azincourt2015.info/.
68. www.agincourt600.com.

Chapter 8

1. *Azincourt, deux versions d'une même pièce* (Paris, 2005), 75 and back cover.
2. www.huffingtonpost.com/martin-lewis/the-day-the-beatles-start-b-53620.html.
3. *The Times*, 8 Oct. 2001.
4. Will Self, 'Believing in Beliefs', BBC Radio 4, 10 Aug. 2014.

BIBLIOGRAPHY

Allmand, C. T., *Henry V* (London, 1992).

Allmand, C. T., 'Writing History in the Eighteenth Century: Thomas Goodwin's *The History of the Reign of Henry the Fifth* (1704)', in G. Dodd (ed.), *Henry V: New Interpretations* (Woodbridge, 2013), 273–88.

Ambühl, R., 'A Fair Share of the Profits? The Ransoms of Agincourt (1415)', *Nottingham Medieval Studies*, 50 (2006), 129–50.

Ambühl, R., *Prisoners of War in the Hundred Years War: Ransom Culture in the Late Middle Ages* (Cambridge, 2013).

Ambühl, R., 'Le Sort des prisonniers d'Azincourt (1415)', *Revue du Nord*, 89 (2007), 755–87.

Anglo, S., 'An Early Tudor Programme for Plays and Other Demonstrations against the Pope', *Journal of the Warburg and Courtauld Institutes*, 20 (1957), 176–9.

Anon., *The Lay of Agincourt with Other Poems* (Edinburgh, 1819).

Anon., *Le Pastoralet*, ed. J. Blanchard (Paris, 1983).

Anstruther, I., *The Knight and the Umbrella: An Account of the Eglington Tournament 1839* (London, 1963).

Askew, G. N., Formenti, F., and Minetti, A. E., 'Limitations Imposed by Wearing Armour on Medieval Soldiers' Locomotor Performance', *Proceedings of the Royal Society B*, 279 (2012), 640–4.

Ayton, A., and Preston, P., *The Battle of Crécy, 1346* (Woodbridge, 2005).

Bacquet, G., *Azincourt* (Bellegrade, 1977)

Baldo, J., 'Wars of Memory in Henry V', *Shakespeare Quarterly*, 47 (1996), 132–59.

Barker, J., *Agincourt: The King, the Campaign, the Battle* (London, 2005).

Barr, C., '"Much Pleasure and Relaxation in These Hard Times": Churchill and Cinema in the Second World War', *Historical Journal of Film, Radio and Television*, 31 (2011), 561–86.

Bate, J., and Thornton, D. (eds), *Shakespeare: Staging the World* (London, 2012).

Beckett, I., *The Amateur Military Tradition 1558–1948* (Manchester, 1991).

Bell, A. R., Curry, A., King A., and Simpkin, D., *The Soldier in Later Medieval England* (Oxford, 2013).

Bennett, Matthew, *Agincourt 1415* (London, 1991).

Bennett, Matthew, 'The Development of Battle Tactics in the Hundred Years War', in A. Curry and M. Hughes (eds), *Arms, Armies and Fortifications in the Hundred Years War* (Woodbridge, 1994), 1–20.

Bennett, Michael, 'Henry V and the Cheshire Tax Revolt', in G. Dodd (ed.), *Henry V: New Interpretations* (Woodbridge, 2013), 171–86.

Benson, F. R., and Tudor Craig, A., *The Book of the Army Pageant* (London, 1910).

Berthelot, J. A., *Michael Drayton* (New York, 1967).

Boffa, S., 'Antoine de Bourgogne et le contingent brabançon à la bataille d'Azincourt (1415)', *Revue belge de philologie et d'histoire*, 72 (1994), 255–84.

Bouzy, O., 'Les Morts d'Azincourt: Leurs liens de famille, d'offices et de parti', in P. Gilli and J. Paviot (eds), *Hommes, cultures et sociétés à la fin du Moyen Âge* (Paris, 2012), 221–55.

Branagh, K., *Beginning* (London, 1989).

Bucklow, S., and Woodcock, S. (eds), *Sir John Gilbert: Art and Imagination in the Victorian Age* (London, 2011).

Burne, A. H., *The Agincourt War* (London, 1956).

Burne, A. H., 'Lessons from Agincourt', *Army Quarterly*, 62 (1959), 70–9.

Carnegie, D., 'So the Falklands. So Agincourt. "Fuck the Frogs": Michael Bogdanov's English Shakespeare Company's Wars of the Roses', in R. King and P. J. C. M. Franssen (eds), *Shakespeare and War* (London, 2008).

Chapman, A., 'The King's Welshmen: Welsh Involvement in the Expeditionary Army of 1415', *Journal of Medieval Military History*, 9 (2011), 41–64.

Chartier, Alain, *The Political Works of Alain Chartier*, ed. J. C. Laidlaw (Cambridge, 1974).

The Chronicle of Adam Usk 1377–1421, ed. C. Given-Wilson (Oxford, 1997).

Chronicles of London, ed. C. L. Kingsford (London, 1905).

Chronique d'Antonio Morosini, ed. G. Le Fèvre- Pontalis and L. Dorez, 4 vols (Paris, 1898–1902).

Clements, R. R., and Hughes, R. L., 'Mathematical Modelling of a Mediaeval Battle: The Battle of Agincourt, 1415', *Mathematics and Computers in Simulation*, 64 (2004), 259–69.

Coldstream, N., 'Pavilion'd in Splendour: Henry V's Agincourt Pageants', *Journal of the British Archaeological Association*, 165 (2012), 153–71.

Colledge, J. J., and Warlow, B., *Ships of the Royal Navy: A Complete Record of All Fighting Ships of the Royal Navy from the 15th Century to the Present* (4th edn, London, 2010).

Contamine, P., *Guerre, état et société: Étude sur les armées des rois de France 1337–1494* (Paris and The Hague, 1972).

Contamine, P., *War in the Middle Ages*, trans. M. C. E. Jones (London, 1984).

Cooper, W. D., 'Sussex Men at Agincourt', *Sussex Archaeological Collections*, 15 (1863), 123–37.

Coote, L. A., *Prophecy and Public Affairs in Later Medieval England* (Woodbridge, 2000).

Cornwell, B., *Azincourt* (London, 2008).

Crosthwaite, F., *Brief Memoir of Major-Gen. Sir John Geo. Woodford* (Kendal: Crosthwaite and Keswick Literary and Scientific Society, 1881).

Cruickshank, G., *Henry VIII and the Invasion of France* (Stroud, 1990).

Curry, A., 'After Agincourt, What Next? Henry V and the Campaign of 1416', *Fifteenth Century England*, 7 (2007), 23–51.

Curry, A., *Agincourt 1415: Henry V, Sir Thomas Erpingham and the Triumph of the English Archers* (Stroud, 2000) (reissued in 2008 as *Agincourt 1415: The Archer's Story*).

Curry, A., *Agincourt: A New History* (Stroud, 2005).

Curry, A., *The Battle of Agincourt: Sources and Interpretations* (Woodbridge, 2000; rev. edn, 2009).

Curry, A., 'The Battle Speeches of Henry V', *Reading Medieval Studies*, 34 (2008), 77–97.

Curry, A., 'Disciplinary Ordinances for English and Franco-Scottish Armies in 1385: An International Code?', *Journal of Medieval History*, 37 (2011), 269–94.

Curry, A., 'The English Army in the Fifteenth Century', in A. Curry and M. Hughes (eds), *Arms, Armies and Fortifications in the Hundred Years War* (Woodbridge, 1994), 39–68.

Curry, A., 'Harfleur under English Rule 1415–1422', in L. J. A. Villalon and D. Kagay (eds), *The Hundred Years War, Part III: Further Considerations* (Leiden, 2013), 259–84.

Curry, A., 'Lancastrian Normandy: The Jewel in the Crown?', in D. Bates and A. Curry (eds), *England and Normandy in the Middle Ages* (London, 1994), 235–52.

Curry, A., 'The Military Ordinances of Henry V: Texts and Contexts', in C. Given-Wilson, A. Kettle, and L. Scales (eds), *War, Government and Aristocracy in the British Isles c 1150–1500* (Woodbridge, 2008), 214–49.

Curry, A., 'Personal Links and the Nature of the English War Retinue: A Case Study of John Mowbray, Earl Marshal, and the Campaign of 1415', in E. Anceau, V. Gazeau, and F. J. Ruggiu (eds), *Liens, reseaux et solidarités* (Paris, 2006), 153–67.

Curry, A., 'Snatching Defeat from the Jaws of Victory: French Responses to Agincourt', *Proceedings of the Western Society for French History*, 28 (2002), 177–87.

Curry, A., Bell, A. R., King, A., and Simpkin, D., 'New Regime, New Army? Henry IV's Scottish Expedition of 1400', *English Historical Review*, 125 (2010), 1382–1413.

Davies, C. S. L., 'Henry VIII and Henry V: The Wars in France', in J. L. Watts (ed.), *The End of the Middle Ages* (Stroud, 1998), 235–62.

Le Débat des hérauts d'armes de France et d'Angleterre, suivi de The Debate between the Heralds of England and France by John Coke, ed. L. Pannier and P. Meyer (Paris, 1877).

Deeming, H., 'The Sources and Origin of the "Agincourt Carol"', *Early Music*, 35 (2007), 23–38.

Dickens, C., *The Child's History of England* (London, 1853).

Drayton, M., *The Battaile of Agincourt*, ed. R. Garnett (London, 1893).

Ellis, H., *Original Letters of Eminent Literary Men of the Sixteenth, Seventeenth, and Eighteenth Centuries* (Camden Society, 23; London, 1843).

Evans, H. T., *Wales and the Wars of the Roses* (Cambridge, 1915; repr. Stroud, 1995).

Ewert, K., *The Shakespeare Handbooks: Henry V* (Houndmills, 2006).

Fagan, E. H. de L., 'Some Aspects of the King's Household in the Reign of Henry V', unpublished MA thesis (University of London, 1935).

Famiglietti, R., *Royal Intrigue: Crisis at the Court of Charles VI 1392–1420* (New York, 1986).

The First English Life of King Henry the Fifth, ed. C. L. Kingsford (Oxford, 1911).

Foard, G., and Curry, A., *Bosworth: A Battlefield Rediscovered* (Oxford, 2013).

Geduld, H. M., *Film Guide to Henry V* (Bloomington, Ind. and London, 1973).

Gesta Henrici Quinti: The Deeds of Henry the Fifth, ed. F. Taylor and J. S. Roskell (Oxford, 1975).

Girouard, M., *The Return to Camelot: Chivalry and the English Gentleman* (New Haven, 1981).

Godfrey, W., with Wagner, A., *Survey of London, Monograph 16: College of Arms Queen Victoria Street* (London, 1963).

Goebel, S., *The Great War and Medieval Memory: War, Remembrance and Medievalism in Britain and Germany, 1914–1940* (Cambridge, 2007).

Goodman, J., *L&NWR Locomotive Names: The Named Locomotives of the London and Northwestern Railway and Its Constituent Companies* (Peterborough, 2002).

Goodman, J., *LMS Locomotive Names: The Named Locomotives of the London, Midland and Scottish Railway and Its Constituent Companies* (Lincoln, 1994).

Goodwin, T., *The History of the Reign of Henry the Fifth, King of England* (London, 1704).

Gransden, A., *Historical Writing in England*, ii. *c. 1307 to the Early Sixteenth Century* (London, 1982).

Grimshaw, B., *The Entwistle Family* (Accrington, 1924).

Grose, F., *Antiquities of England* and *Wales*, 7 vols (London, 1783–97).

Gunn, S., 'The French Wars of Henry VIII', in J. Black (ed.), *The Origins of War in Early Modern Europe* (Edinburgh, 1987), 28–51.

Harris, G. L., *Cardinal Beaufort: A Study of Lancastrian Ascendancy and Decline* (Oxford, 1988).

Hélary, X., *Courtrai: 11 juillet 1302* (Paris, 2012).

Henderson, D. E., 'Meditations in a Time of (Displaced) War: Henry V, Money and the Ethics of Performing History', in R. King and P. J. C. M. Franssen (eds), *Shakespeare and War* (London, 2008).

Henrici Quinti, Angliae Regis, Gesta, ed. B. Williams (London, 1850).

Henty, G. A., *At Agincourt: A Tale of the White Hoods of Paris* (London, 1897).

Hibbert, C., *Agincourt* (London, 1964).

Hill, A. *King Henry the Fifth, or, The Conquest of France by the English: A Tragedy* (London, 1723).

Honig, J. W., 'Reappraising Late Medieval Strategy: The Example of the 1415 Agincourt Campaign', *War in History*, 19 (2012), 123–51.

Hough, R., *The Great Dreadnought: The Strange Story of HMS Agincourt: The Mightiest Battleship of World War I* (New York, 1967).

Hunter, J., *Agincourt: A Contribution towards an Authentic List of the Commanders of the English Host in King Henry the Fifth's Expedition to France in the Third Year of His Reign* (London, 1850).

Jacob, E. F., *Henry V and the Invasion of France* (London, 1947).

Jenkins, R., 'The Sources of Drayton's *Battaile of Agincourt*', *PMLA* 41 (1926), 280–93.

Johnson, S., *The Yale Collection of the Works of Samuel Johnson*, viii. *Johnson on Shakespeare* (New Haven, 1968).

Jones, M. K., *Agincourt 1415* (Barnsley, 2005).

Keegan, J., *The Face of Battle: A Study of Agincourt, Waterloo and the Somme* (London, 1976).

Kewes, P., Archer, I. W., and Heal, F. (eds), *The Oxford Handbook of Holinshed's Chronicles* (Oxford, 2013).

Kingsford, C. L., *English Historical Writing in the Fifteenth Century* (Oxford, 1913).

Kingsford, C. L., *Henry V* (London and New York, 1901).

Kipling, G., *Enter the King: Theatre, Liturgy and Ritual in the Medieval Civic Triumph* (Oxford, 1998).

Knight, C., *Passages of a Working Life During Half a Century*, 3 vols (London, 1864–5).

Labitte, C., 'Bataille d'Azincourt', *Revue anglo-française*, 3 (1835), 13–47.

Lambert, C., 'Edward III's Siege of Calais: A Reappraisal', *Journal of Medieval History*, 37 (2011), 245–56.

Lannoy, Ghillebert de, *Œuvres de Ghillebert de Lannoy, diplomate et moraliste*, ed. C. Poitvin (Louvain, 1878).

Leland, J., *Leland's Itinerary*, ed. L. Toulmin-Smith, 5 vols (London, 1907).

Loehlin, J. N., *Shakespeare in Performance: Henry V* (Manchester, 1997).

McHardy, A. K., 'Religion, Court Culture and Propaganda: The Chapel Royal in the Reign of Henry V', in G. Dodd (ed.), *Henry V: New Interpretations* (Woodbridge, 2013), 131–56.

Machen, A., *The Angel of Mons: The Bowmen and Other Legends of the War* (2nd edn, London, 1915).

MacLeod, C., *The Lost Prince: The Life and Death of Henry Stuart* (London, 2012).

Marschner, J., *Queen Caroline: Cultural Politics at the Early Eighteenth-Century Court* (London, 2014).

Maxwell, H., 'The Campaign of Agincourt: October 25, 1415', *Cornhill Magazine*, 3rd ser., 39 (1915), 524–41.

Meron, T., *Henry's Wars and Shakespeare's Laws* (Oxford, 1993).

Milner, J., 'The English Commitment to the 1412 Expedition in France', *Fifteenth Century England*, 11 (2012), 9–24.

Milner, J., 'The English Enterprise in France, 1412–1413', in D. J. Clayton, R. G. Davies, and P. McNiven (eds), *Trade, Devotion and Governance: Papers in Later Medieval History* (Stroud, 1994), 81–101.

Monteiro, J. G., 'The Battle of Aljubarrota (1385): A Reassessment', *Journal of Medieval Military History*, 7 (2009), 75–103.

Mortimer, I., *1415: Henry V's Year of Glory* (London, 2009).

Musgrave, G., *By-Roads and Battlefields in Picardy: With Incidents and Gatherings by the Way between Ambleteuse and Ham including Agincourt and Crecy* (London, 1861).

Nicolas, H., *History of the Battle of Agincourt* (London, 1827; 2nd edn, 1832; 3rd edn, 1833).

Orgel, S., and Strong, R., *Inigo Jones: The Theatre of the Stuart Court*, 2 vols (London and Berkeley, 1973).

Ormrod, W. M., *Edward III* (London, 2011).

Ormrod, W. M., 'Henry V and the English Taxpayer', in G. Dodd (ed.), *Henry V: New Interpretations* (Woodbridge, 2013), 187–216.

Owst, G. R., *Literature and Pulpit in Medieval England* (rev. edn, London, 1961).

Paladilhe, D., *La Bataille d'Azincourt* (Paris, 2001).

The Parliament Rolls of Medieval England 1272–1504, ed. C. Given-Wilson et al., 16 vols (Woodbridge, 2005).

Phillpotts, C. J., 'The Fate of the Truce of Paris, 1396–1415', *Journal of Medieval History*, 24 (1998), 61–80.

Phillpotts, C. J., 'The French Plan of Battle During the Agincourt Campaign', *English Historical Review*, 99 (1984), 59–66.

Pike, J., *Locomotive Names: An Illustrated Dictionary* (Stroud, 2000).

Pilkington, A., *Screening Shakespeare from Richard II to Henry V* (Newark, Del. and London, 1991).

Poole, A., *Shakespeare and the Victorians* (London, 2004).

Powel, D., rev. Wynne, W., *The history of Wales comprehending the lives and succession of the princes of Wales, from Cadwalader the last king, to Llewelyn the last prince of British blood with a short account of the affairs of Wales under the kings of England written originally in British, by Caradoc of Llancarvan; and formerly published in English by Dr. Powel; now newly augmented and improved by W. Wynne* (London, 1697).

Proceedings and Ordinances of the Privy Council of England, ed. H. Nicolas (London, 1834), vol. ii.

Ramsey, J. H., *Lancaster and York*, vol. ii (London, 1892).

The Register of Henry Chichele, Archbishop of Canterbury, 1414–1431, ed. E. F. Jacob, 4 vols (London, 1943–7).

The Register of Robert Mascall, Bishop of Hereford 1404–1416, ed. J. H. Parry (Cantilupe Society; Hereford, 1916).

Le Religieux de Saint-Denis, *Histoire de Charles VI*, ed. L. Bellaguet, 6 vols (Paris, 1839–52).

Riley, H. T. (ed.), *Memorials of London and London Life in the XIIIth, XIVth and XVth Centuries* (London, 1878).

Roberts, W. Rhys, *Patriotic Poetry, Greek and English: An Address given on the 500th Anniversary of Agincourt* (London, 1916).

Rogers, C. J., 'The Battle of Agincourt', in L. J. A. Villalon and D. J. Kagay (eds), *The Hundred Years War (Part II)* (Leiden, 2008), 37–132.

Rogers, C. J., 'Henry V's Military Strategy in 1415', in L. J. A. Villalon and D. J. Kagay (eds), *The Hundred Years War: A Wider Focus* (Leiden, 2005), 399–427.

Rogers, C. J., *War Cruel and Sharp: English Strategy under Edward III, 1327–1360* (Woodbridge, 2000).

Roskell, J. S., Clark, L. S., and Rawcliffe, C. (eds), *History of Parliament: The Commons 1386–1422*, 4 vols (Gloucester, 1992).

Rundle, D., 'The Unoriginality of Tito Livio Frulovisi's Vita Henrici Quinti', *English Historical Review*, 123 (2008), 1109–31.

Rymer, T., *Foedera, Conventiones, Litterae et Cuiuscunque Generis Acta Publica* (London, 1704–35; 3rd edn, The Hague, 1739–45).

The St Albans Chronicle: The Chronica Maiora of Thomas Walsingham, ii. 1394–1422, ed. J. Taylor, W. R. Childs, and L. Watkiss (Oxford, 2011).

Scarisbrick, J., *Henry VIII* (London, 1968).

Schnerb, B., 'La Bataille rangée dans la tactique des armées bourguignonnes au début du 15e siècle: Essai de synthèse', *Annales de Bourgogne*, 61 (1989), 5–32.

Schoch, R. W., *Shakespeare's Victorian Stage: Performing History in the Theatre of Charles Kean* (Cambridge, 1998).

Scott-Giles, C. W., *The Romance of Heraldry* (London, 1929; repr. 1967).

Shakespeare, William, *The First Quarto of King Henry the Fifth*, ed. A. Gurr (Cambridge, 2000).

Shakespeare, William, *King Henry V*, ed. T. W. Craik (The Arden Shakespeare, 3rd ser.; London, 1995).

Shakespeare, William, *King Henry V*, ed. A. Gurr (The New Cambridge Shakespeare; Cambridge, 1992).

Shakespeare, William, *Shakespeare's Play of King Henry the Fifth Arranged for Representation at the Princess's Theatre, with Historical and Explanatory Notes by C. Kean* (London, 1859).

Shapiro, J., *1599: A Year in the Life of William Shakespeare* (London, 2005).

Shawe-Taylor, D., *The First Georgians: Art and Monarchy 1714–1760* (London, 2014).

Smith, E. (ed.), *Shakespeare in Production: King Henry V* (Cambridge, 2002).

Sowerby, T., *Renaissance and Reform in Tudor England: The Careers of Sir Richard Morrison c. 1513–1556* (Oxford, 2010).

Stone, G. W., *The London Stage 1660–1800*, part 4, *1747–1776* (Carbondale, Ill., 1960–8).

Stratford, J., '"Par le special commandement du roy": Jewels and Plate Pledged for the Agincourt Expedition', in G. Dodd (ed.), *Henry V: New Interpretations* (Woodbridge, 2013), 157–70.

Strickland, M., and Hardy, R., *The Great Warbow* (Gloucester, 2005).

Sumption, J., *The Hundred Years War*, ii. *Trial by Fire* (London, 1999).

Sutherland, J., and Watts, C., *Henry V, War Criminal? And Other Shakespeare Puzzles* (Oxford, 2000).

Sutherland, T., 'The Battle of Agincourt: An Alternative Location', *Journal of Conflict Archaeology*, 1 (2005), 245–63.

Taufer, A., *Holinshed's Chronicles* (New York, 1999).

Tuck, A. J., 'The Earl of Arundel's Expedition to France, 1411', in G. Dodd and D. Biggs (eds), *The Reign of Henry IV: Rebellion and Survival 1403–1413* (Woodbridge, 2008), 228–39.

Turner, S., *History of England in the Middle Ages*, vol. ii (London, 1815).

Tyler, J. Endell, *Henry of Monmouth*, 2 vols (London, 1838).

Vale, M. G. A., *Charles VII* (London, 1974).

The Visitation of Cheshire in the Year 1580 , ed. J. P. Rylands (London, 1882).

The Visitations of Essex, ed. W. C. Metcalfe, 2 vols (London, 1878).

Walpole, H., *The Yale Edition of Horace Walpole's Correspondence*, ed. W. S. Lewis (New Haven, 1937–83).

Wiggins M., with Richardson, C., *British Drama 1533–1642: A Catalogue* (Oxford, 2012).

Wijsman, H., 'History in Transition: Enguerrand de Monstrelet's *Chronique* in Manuscript and Print (c.1450–c.1600)', in M. Walsby and G. Kemp (eds), *The Book Triumphant* (Leiden, 2012), 199–252.

Worcester, W., *The Boke of Noblesse*, ed. J. G. Nichols (London, 1860).

Wylie, J. H., 'Notes on the Agincourt Roll', *Transactions of the Royal Historical Society*, 3rd ser., 5 (1911), 105–40.

Wylie, J. H., *The Reign of Henry the Fifth*, 3 vols (Cambridge, 1914–29) (vol. iii completed by W. T. Waugh).

Young, J. W., 'Henry V, the Quai d'Orsay and the Well-Being of the Franco-British Alliance, 1947', *Historical Journal of Film, Radio and Television*, 7 (1987), 319–21.

Ziegler, P., *Olivier* (London, 2013).

PICTURE ACKNOWLEDGEMENTS

1. © John Stillwell/PA Archive/Press Association Images
2. Redrawn with alterations from *Agincourt 1415: Triumph Against the Odds*, by M Bennett (Osprey Publishing, 1991)
3. © Peter Hoskins
4. The National Archives
5. © Trustees of the British Library (Cotton Caligula DV, f. 44r)
6. Bodleian Library, University of Oxford (MS 3340 f. 17v)
7. © Lambeth Palace Library, London/Bridgeman Images
8. © The Art Archive/Bibliothèque Nationale Paris
9. Bibliothèque Nationale de France, Paris
10. © Illustrated London News Ltd/Mary Evans Picture Library
11. Society of London Theatre
12. www.cartes-postales-anciennes.com
13. Bodleian Library, University of Oxford (Ashmolean MS 825 f. 15)
14. (a) From *Honour and Arms: The story of some augmentations of honour*, J.F. Huxford (Regency Press, 1984). © Estate of J F Huxford
    (b)European Heraldry
15. © Victoria & Albert Museum, London
16. Victoria & Albert Museum. Photo © Heritage Images/Glowimages.com
17. Copyright Dean and Chapter of Westminster
18. © Royal Collection Trust, Her Majesty Queen Elizabeth II, 2014/Bridgeman Images
19. © The Trustees of the British Museum
20. © The Trustees of the British Museum
21. © The Trustees of the British Museum
22. © The Trustees of the British Museum
23. © Guildhall Art Gallery, London/Topham Picturepoint
24. Tate Gallery Collection. © Neville Gabie
25. David Rumsey Map Collection, www.davidrumsey.com
26. © Trustees of the British Library (Add. MS 16368 map c)
27. From H. Nicolas, *The Battle of Agincourt*, second edition, 1832
28. © Maurice Savage/Alamy
29. Paul Hermans/Wikimedia Commons
30. © Anne Curry

INDEX